W9-BUB-602

3 4004

155.433 Sim
Simmons, Rachel, 1966-
The curse of the good girl :
raising authentic girls with
courage and confidence

WITHDRAWN

# THE CURSE
# OF THE
# GOOD GIRL

ALSO BY RACHEL SIMMONS

*Odd Girl Out: The Hidden Culture of Aggression in Girls*

*Odd Girl Speaks Out: Girls Write About Bullies, Cliques,
  Popularity, and Jealousy*

# THE CURSE

# OF THE

# GOOD GIRL

· · · · · · · · · · · · · · · · · · · · · · · · · · · · · · · · · · · · · · ·

*Raising Authentic Girls with*
*Courage and Confidence*

R ACHEL  S IMMONS

SALINE DISTRICT LIBRARY
555 N. Maple Road
Saline, MI 48176

THE PENGUIN PRESS    *New York    2009*

AUG – – 2009

THE PENGUIN PRESS

Published by the Penguin Group

Penguin Group (USA) Inc., 375 Hudson Street, New York, New York 10014, U.S.A. • Penguin Group
(Canada), 90 Eglinton Avenue East, Suite 700, Toronto, Ontario, Canada M4P 2Y3 (a division of Pearson Penguin
Canada Inc.) • Penguin Books Ltd, 80 Strand, London WC2R 0RL, England • Penguin Ireland, 25 St. Stephen's
Green, Dublin 2, Ireland (a division of Penguin Books Ltd) • Penguin Books Australia Ltd, 250 Camberwell Road,
Camberwell, Victoria 3124, Australia (a division of Pearson Australia Group Pty Ltd) • Penguin Books India Pvt Ltd,
11 Community Centre, Panchsheel Park, New Delhi – 110 017, India • Penguin Group (NZ), 67 Apollo Drive,
Rosedale, North Shore 0632, New Zealand (a division of Pearson New Zealand Ltd) • Penguin Books
(South Africa) (Pty) Ltd, 24 Sturdee Avenue, Rosebank, Johannesburg 2196, South Africa

Penguin Books Ltd, Registered Offices:
80 Strand, London WC2R 0RL, England

First published in 2009 by The Penguin Press,
a member of Penguin Group (USA) Inc.

Copyright © Rachel Simmons, 2009
All rights reserved

The author has changed the names and identifying details of interview subjects.
The ages of the girls have not been changed.

LIBRARY OF CONGRESS CATALOGING IN PUBLICATION DATA
Simmons, Rachel, date.
   The curse of the good girl : raising authentic girls with courage and confidence / Rachel Simmons.
      p.   cm.
Includes bibliographical references and index.
ISBN 978-1-59420-218-6
1.  Girls—Psychology. 2.   Girls—Conduct of life. I.   Title.
HQ777.S56 2009
155.43'3—dc22      2009003566

Printed in the United States of America
10  9  8  7  6  5  4  3  2  1

Designed by Meighan Cavanaugh

Without limiting the rights under copyright reserved above, no part of this publication may be reproduced, stored in
or introduced into a retrieval system, or transmitted, in any form or by any means (electronic, mechanical, photocopy-
ing, recording or otherwise), without the prior written permission of both the copyright owner and the above publisher
of this book.

The scanning, uploading, and distribution of this book via the Internet or via any other means without the permission
of the publisher is illegal and punishable by law.  Please purchase only authorized electronic editions and do not participate
in or encourage electronic piracy of copyrightable materials. Your support of the author's rights is appreciated.

*For my brother*

*and*

*for the Girls Leadership Institute alumnae:*
  *for teaching me, for trusting me*

# CONTENTS

· · · · · · · · · · · · · · · · · · · · · · · · · · · · ·

# INTRODUCTION

Our culture is teaching girls to embrace a version of selfhood that sharply curtails their power and potential. In particular, the pressure to be "Good"—unerringly nice, polite, modest, and selfless—diminishes girls' authenticity and personal authority.

The Curse of the Good Girl erects a psychological glass ceiling that begins its destructive sprawl in girlhood and extends across the female life span, stunting the growth of skills and habits essential to becoming a strong woman. This book traces the impact of the curse on girls' development, and provides parents with the strategies to break its spell.

Almost ten years ago, I founded the Girls Leadership Institute, a summer enrichment program for middle- and high-school girls. I began asking largely middle-class groups of girls to describe how society expected a Good Girl to look and act. Here is a sample response:

| | | |
|---|---|---|
| Blue eyes | Honorable | Respectful |
| Little girl | Tons of friends | Always busy |
| Quiet | Polite | Organized |
| Perfect | Enthusiastic | Flirtatious |
| Sheltered | Generous | Skinny |
| Good grades | Kind | Speaks well |
| Studies | Boyfriend | Follows the rules |
| No opinions on things | Intelligent | Doesn't get mad |
| Well rounded | Conservative | Healthy |
| Follower | Popular | Average |
| Preppy | Wealthy | Barbie |
| Has to do everything right | Athletic | Confident |
| | Natural hair | Perfect attendance |
| Doesn't show skin | Listens | Façade never cracks |
| High expectations | Honest | People pleaser |

The Good Girl was socially and academically successful, smart and driven, pretty and kind. But she was also an individual who aimed to please (*people pleaser*), toed the line (*no opinions on things*) and didn't take risks (*follows the rules*). She repressed what she really thought (*doesn't get mad*) and did not handle her mistakes with humor (*has to do everything right*).

The Good Girl walked a treacherous line, balancing mixed messages about how far she should go and how strong she should be: she was to be *enthusiastic* while being *quiet; smart* with *no opinions on things; intelligent* but a *follower; popular* but *quiet.* She would be something, but not too much.

We live in the age of the fiercely successful "amazing girl." Girls outnumber boys in college and graduate school. They graduate at higher rates. In high school, girls pursue more leadership roles and extracurricular activities than boys do, and they are significantly more likely to see themselves as leaders.

But if their college applications are stamped with twenty-first-century girl power, girls' psychological résumés lag generations behind. The Curse of the Good Girl erodes girls' ability to know, say, and manage a complete range of feelings. It urges girls to be perfect, giving them a troubled relationship to integrity and failure. It expects girls to be selfless, limiting the expression of their needs. It demands modesty, depriving girls of permission to commit to their strengths and goals. It diminishes assertive body language, quieting voices and weakening handshakes. It reaches across all areas of girls' lives: in their interactions with boys and other girls, at school, at home, and in extracurricular life. The Curse of the Good Girl cuts to the core of authentic selfhood, demanding that girls curb the strongest feelings and desires that form the patchwork of a person.

The curse is the product of a culture that remains confused about gender equality. In *Meeting at the Crossroads,* Lyn Mikel Brown and Carol Gilligan documented a crisis of connection in girls approaching adolescence. Girls withheld their true thoughts and feelings in an attempt to maintain "perfect" relationships. Nearly twenty years later, little has changed. In a 2006 study by Girls, Inc., 74 percent of girls said they were under a lot of pressure to please everyone, a nearly nine-point *increase* from 2000. Nearly half the girls surveyed said that "girls are told not to brag about the things they do well" and that the "smartest girls in my school are not popular." A majority said they were expected to speak softly and not cause trouble.

In a 2008 study by the Girl Scouts, girls aged eight to seventeen worried that leadership positions would make them seem "bossy" and lead to negative attention from peers.[1]

Another study found girls significantly less likely than boys to want to be the boss or in charge of others.[2]

Our culture's mixed feelings about girl power emerge most clearly in girls' descriptions of "Bad Girls":

| | | |
|---|---|---|
| Piercings | Doesn't care about | Steals |
| Dyed hair | her body | Tough attitude |
| Dark hair | Artistic | Punk |
| Jelly bracelets | Doesn't plan long- | Proud |
| Dark clothes | term | Dramatic dress |
| Arguing | Doesn't care what | Loud |
| Rule breaker | people think | Selfish |
| Backtalking | Parties | Speaks her mind |
| Foul mouth | Eye makeup | Obnoxious |
| No respect for self or | Fights | Center of attention |
| others | Cheats | Rebel |
| Loud music | Lies | Slut |

The Bad Girl was the picture of female failure, a reckless rejection of femininity, everything a girl was told not to be. She was the odd girl out with a bad reputation, low to no status, and few friends.

Yet she was also independent and authentic. The Bad Girl was outspoken (*speaks her mind*) and self-possessed (*proud*), a risk taker (*rule breaker*) and critical thinker (*artistic, rebel, doesn't care what people think*). She was comfortable being in charge (*center of attention*). But she was nothing if not an outcast, an example to Good Girls of what happened when you strayed from the program. Being Bad was social suicide: a big, red F in Girl.

So despite the age of girl power, attitudes are slow to change. Go on, we seem to be telling girls, but not too far, and at your own risk. Buckle down, but don't speak up. Debate your peers in class, but be "nice" about it. Be something, but not too much.

Being Good is a richly rewarded pursuit. Good Girls enjoy social largesse, holding center court in cafeterias and dominating leadership positions at school. Yet many of these overachieving girls learn to succeed by sequestering the most genuine parts of their developing selves. Mia was fourteen, overbooked, and underslept: a golfer, avid volunteer, and staff writer for the school newspaper. But, she told me,

> when I'd go to school, a switch went on. Time to be Mia that everyone wants to be friends with . . . like everyone loves me, I don't do bad things, I'm just Miss Perfect. My parents love me. I do all the activities that everyone wants to do. If my teachers ask me to do something, I'll do it. One of those pleasing people.

Good Girl pressure threw a "switch" and split Mia's personality. It was as if, she told me, "I had two identities." To be Good, Mia had to project a false self to the world, acting one way in public and another way in private. She would behave one way to someone's face and another way behind her back; one way in person, another way online.

Psychologist Roni Cohen-Sandler observed a spike in stress levels and psychological crises among girls who, she writes, are

> prone to becoming estranged from their inner lives. . . . [They] are so busy living up to others' expectations that they either don't develop or eventually relinquish their own goals. They are so focused on achieving external emblems of success that they don't get the chance to figure out what really excites them and gives them pleasure. They barely know who they are or who they want to become.[3]

At what price success? Many of the most accomplished girls are disconnecting from the truest parts of themselves, sacrificing essential self-knowledge to the pressure of who they think they ought to be.

The curse is not confined to overachievers or to girls' external pursuits. The pressure to be Good runs deep into the core of the self, circumscribing a girl's ability to know, express, and accept her most challenging feelings.

Told to be "quiet," "perfect," "shy," and "enthusiastic," to have "no opinions on things" and never "get mad," Good Girl pressure places girls on strict emotional diets, telling them that certain feelings are better than others. Just as a girl might say, *I shouldn't eat this because it will make me fat*, girls often tell themselves, *I shouldn't feel this. I'm making too big a deal out of it. I shouldn't say this: it will make me a bitch, a drama queen, an outcast.*

Placed at odds with their most important feelings, many do not develop the skills to speak their minds when they need to, or the skin to endure the claims of someone else. Lacking a full emotional vocabulary or the permission to use it, some girls turn inward, ruminating self-destructively. Others become explosive, able to articulate little more than anger and frustration. The psychological muscles a girl uses to manage difficult feelings begin to atrophy. Emotional intelligence is compromised, stunting healthy self-expression: the more Good girls try to be, the more they must discredit themselves. These toxic lessons in relationship and conflict management follow many girls into adulthood.

To be absolutely kind and selfless is impossible, making Good a finish line girls never get to cross. As a result, girls who aspire to Goodness are ruthlessly hard on themselves. When the standards for selfhood are beyond reach, self-acceptance is futile. Girls become their own worst enemies. The terms of being an acceptable girl are rigged: Good Girls are doomed to fail.

The Curse of the Good Girl thus diminishes girls' resilience, or ability to cope with stress. Being Good is a fundamentally self-limiting experience: the need to be "perfect" and "do everything right" leaves many girls uncomfortable with feedback and failure, making it difficult to push through a challenge. The need to be nice or right at all costs leaves these girls on the sidelines as they avoid the situations that aren't sure things: moments of self-assertion that require healthy risk-taking and which might lead to failure, disappointment, or another person's unhappiness. The Curse of the Good Girl is both a warning not to try and a setup to fail when you do.

The cost of the curse emerges initially as a relational phenomenon. In my first book, *Odd Girl Out: The Hidden Culture of Aggression in Girls,* the curse played a leading role in the drama of girls' aggression. The need to be nice forced girls to hide their true feelings, go behind each other's backs, and explode in uncontrolled anger and cruelty.

All of these girls shared the same psychic DNA: they couldn't speak their minds directly. When I asked why, I heard countless variations on a single answer: "If I tell her how I feel," the girls said, "she won't be my friend anymore. She'll turn everyone against me." Conflict would terminate their relationships. "The truth hurts," an unforgettable fifth-grader told me. "That's why I lie."

But what emerges as a social phenomenon in relationships begins to limit individual strength and potential. At the Girls Leadership Institute, I watched thirteen-year-old Julia play rambunctiously with friends, while in classes her sentences trailed off like a volume dial being turned down. When I asked why, she said, "I feel like if I sound stupid or say the wrong thing, people won't like me."

Nina said little in class, and when I invited her privately to voice her views, she told me, "There's no point in saying what I think. People at school always say I have crazy opinions. I'm taking the summer off from being told to lighten up."

Shannon could not look anyone in the eye while she talked, and she sulked in the corner when anyone disagreed with her project ideas. Lottie commandeered a group project, refusing to ask peers for help because she feared angering them.

One afternoon at the Girls Leadership Institute, I watched Catherine struggle to complete an exercise in which she was asked to list her talents and strengths.

"What's going on?" I asked. "You have a ton of stuff you're good at."

She hesitated. "I don't want people to think I'm conceited," she told the group. Some of the other girls looked down.

"And if they did?" I asked.

"They'd think I was a bitch."

I began asking the girls how they felt about leadership. As I scrolled through a list of basic skills—public speaking, debating an opinion, and interviewing for a job—the girls' comments remained constant. "Getting judged" was their worst fear. Take a risk and put yourself out there, the girls told me, and people might not like you. "Someone could shut you down," Lottie said. "They could turn people against you."

The girls were no longer talking about their friendships. They were talking about critical, individual skills for leadership and life. What these girls feared about being strong in relationships was what they now feared about being strong on their own. What made them nervous about standing tall in their personal lives was precisely what made distinction at school nerve-racking to them. Their fear of disappointing or angering others, their intense need to please, had spilled over into their skills and potential as individuals.

When the Good Girl mentality migrates into girls' public venues—classrooms, extracurricular activities, and sports fields—girls learn many of the behaviors that will stunt their personal and professional success as adults. In 2007, high school students at Miss Hall's School for Girls in Pittsfield, Massachusetts, developed a national survey on personal authority and leadership for over fifteen hundred teens. The survey asked respondents to address ten challenging "leadership problems." Across a range of scenarios, the Curse of the Good Girl consistently diverted girls from doing the right thing. Overall, 60 percent of girls surveyed said they knew they *should* behave assertively in the conflicts, but only a quarter said they actually would. Many said they would defer to a friend's choice, go along with the crowd to do the wrong thing, or avoid the conflict entirely. The study concluded that girls "appear to define leadership in terms of friendship, which means that they can often compromise doing what they know is right for the sake of maintaining relationships." It found a significant "lack of alignment between what [girls] value and what they actually do."[4]

To remain "Good," the girls were splitting off from themselves, compromising their integrity, values, and authority.

Today, middle- and high-school girls indisputably outpace their male counterparts. Less than ten years from now, the statistics will reverse like a river's tide. By college, the ranks of female leaders will have thinned. When they become lawyers, the amazing girls will make up barely a quarter of law-firm partners. Only one-third of business-school students will be amazing girls. Instead they will earn between 75 and 90 percent of degrees in "caring professions": education, home economics, nursing, library science, social work, and psychology.[5] They will earn less and ask for raises less often.

The abrupt decline in women's career trajectories is hardly sudden, nor can it be blamed exclusively on men. Good Girls may enjoy success in high school, but as they enter college and move into the workplace, the rules of the game change. It is no longer enough to be smart and hardworking. The skills required to self-promote, negotiate, and absorb feedback are among the new criteria for success. Young women are ill prepared. Professional self-help books for women offer bleak inventories of these missing skills; the title of one of the bestsellers—Lois Frankel's *Nice Girls Don't Get the Corner Office: 101 Unconscious Mistakes Women Make That Sabotage Their Careers*—is no coincidence.

These books fill in the blanks of a girl's education. They introduce young women to the real rules for success. But by the first day of her first job, it's often too late. Good Girl habits are firmly in place. In this book I will show you how to identify and address the Good Girl behaviors in your daughter right now.

At stake is far more than girls' professional potential. In my workshops with mothers, women tell stories of sacrifice and silence, of automatic apologizing, of clipped tones used to hint at real feelings. They want a different future for their daughters.

We have become too focused on helping girls succeed by emphasizing the tangible items they can put on their résumé: a great GPA, a good education, and extracurricular and work experience. There is a less obvious but no less important inner résumé we must help girls develop, a set of skills that may prove most valuable for their success not just in the "real world" but in their day-to-day lives and relationships.

For nearly twenty years, we have lamented the loss of self-esteem in adolescent girls. The so-called Ophelia phenomenon has been only vaguely understood as a loss of voice and authenticity. In this book I provide the first catalog of skills and core competencies that are not fully developing in girls. I offer you a map to girls' crucial inner résumé and the strategies you will need to guide your daughter from Good Girl to Real Girl.

A Real Girl stays connected to a strong inner core of her thoughts, feelings, and desires. She is able not only to listen to who she is but to act on it. She maintains a critical balance: she can manage the needs of others without sacrificing the integrity of her own. A Real Girl can defend her interests in a relationship or advocate on her own behalf. Where a Good Girl might meet someone and automatically hope *she* is likable, a Real Girl will reflect on what she thinks and feels about the other person before deciding what to do next.

A Real Girl also maintains a balanced self-concept. Her aspirations unfold within a realistic awareness of personal limits. A Good Girl, whose identity is defined by appearances, tends to expect the unreasonable. She is often shattered by a mistake. Her investment in image curbs a taste for risk and adventure. A Real Girl, by contrast, can face her own blemishes, however painful; her limits and mistakes are as much a part of her as anything else. She has, quite literally, a *sense* of self.

A mother I met recently took issue with this approach. "I don't see the problem with raising Good Girls," she told me. "I've taught my daughter to be respectful and kind. She knows the difference between right and wrong." That's a good thing, I told her. But if we consider the Good Girl as only an ethical identity, we fail to see the other, less helpful lessons Good

Girls learn. For instance, if a girl is too respectful or too kind, she may become a pleaser. A girl who never seems to do anything wrong might be choosing to make her mistakes in private, becoming secretive, ashamed, or self-destructive.

There is nothing wrong with being a nice person, nor is it my intent to undermine the unique sensibilities of women and girls. But girls need to have the tools to say no, to ask for what they need, and to say what they think. Too many girls and women walk away from conversations muttering to themselves about what they really wanted to say. When kindness comes at the expense of truth, it is not a kindness worth having. And when generosity leads to silence or abuse, it is not a generosity worth giving.

My findings are based on interviews and observations of Girls Leadership Institute participants and girls at a handful of public middle and high schools I visited on the East Coast. Their names and identifying details have been changed. This book focuses primarily on middle-class girls, for whom femininity is often most constraining. But the Curse of the Good Girl is not an affliction of the privileged. One out of five GLI participants receives financial aid or a full scholarship. Nearly one third are nonwhite. Femininity is defined differently among different racial, ethnic, and economic groups; African-American girls will create a different Good Girl list than will their Latina peers. Still, no matter where they grow up, girls live in a world that defines them as caregivers. As such, girls are expected to nurture others, especially male partners, at the expense of themselves. They consume media that positions them as passive, sexualized objects and which privileges the Good Girl in film, television, print, and online. These influences play out in Girl World, the powerful peer culture that circumscribes girls' potential to be real with each other, and which every girl has to deal with despite the unique influences of her background.

Not all girls experience the Curse of the Good Girl identically. Some girls manage to avoid it altogether. Though I may use phrases like "Girl World" and "Good Girl," I do not assume this is a predestined or essential way of being for girls. I am describing a pattern of behavior that has emerged in response to cultural messages about how to be a socially acceptable girl.

The Curse of the Good Girl is timeless. It not only predates current trends in girls' disempowerment, it enables them. To break it we must give every girl the tools and permission to be herself, whoever that is. This book is a guide to helping girls reconnect with their true selves. Part I exposes the challenges society poses to girls' authenticity. In part II, you learn the strategies to help your daughter embrace her full potential.

I believe that a girl may be smart and driven, get good grades and make all the right choices, and still learn habits of mind and speech that form her very own psychological glass ceiling. For while girls may be permitted to do what they want—to fly planes, go to war, and slam-dunk—they remain unable to be who they are. When girls can no longer agree upon the answer to the question "Who is a Good Girl?" we will know they are free to be themselves.

## PART I

························································

# A MAP OF THE
# GOOD GIRL WORLD

*One*

# THE MYTH OF GIRLS' EMOTIONAL INTELLIGENCE

We have long assumed that just because girls have lots of emotions, they must be good at managing them. Of course, girls are deeply feeling creatures, the undisputed champions of, *I love you, you're my best friend, can you keep a secret?, let me get you a tissue.* They lavish their relationships with an intensity of feeling that ranges from passion to desperation to rage. We believe girls to be emotional experts,[1] yet as I will show you in this chapter, girls' emotional intelligence[2]—in particular, their ability to identify, express, and accept a complete range of feelings—is severely curtailed by the Curse of the Good Girl. If we allow myths about their emotional aptitudes to influence parenting and teaching, we overlook a gaping hole in girls' development.

During my summers at the Girls Leadership Institute, I live in close quarters with adolescent girls. I am an intimate witness to their conflicts, especially their decisions and thinking about relationships. I have found many girls to be emotionally illiterate at crucial moments of their lives, unable to identify what they are feeling, much less say it. Because they lack the skills for self-awareness and expression, their ability to state their needs and manage relationships is severely compromised.

The Curse of the Good Girl restricts girls' emotional intelligence. When girls are raised to be people pleasers, they learn early on that certain feelings are more acceptable than others. Just as parents distinguish between girl and boy infants by dressing them in pink and blue, they also employ different "display rules" that define for girls which emotions are appropriate. For instance, while parents typically train boys to retaliate in response to anger, girls are advised to moderate anger and prioritize making peace.

When emotions are ranked and valued, girls begin to question or even fear their most challenging feelings, often with destructive results to themselves and their relationships. They can dissociate from their inner emotional universe, avoiding the self-reflection required for smart decision-making. They also disconnect from peers, losing the ability to empathize with others' feelings.

Display rules are assumed to move from parents to children, but girls enforce strict rules about emotional expression among themselves. In interviews, girls described emotions as nuisances that made them stand out, not unlike an irksome pimple. Vulnerable feelings could create social disaster; they made you weak, a loser. Privately, girls described being locked in deep internal struggles with their emotions, many of which led to self-destructive behavior. In fact, what girls told me about their feelings might have come out of the mouths of boys.

Emotional intelligence is a portal to fulfillment in every area of life. Feelings are the raw materials of our needs, goals, and choices. We tell people how we feel in order to create change in our worlds. Yet one sophomore told me, "I never want to feel like I'm talking about myself or, like, being self-centered, so, like, saying, like, 'Oh, today I had a really rough day,' I feel like I'm being selfish by bringing that to the table, being a downer." If girls equate emotional self-expression with being selfish, weak, or worse, they may import their discomfort into adulthood, where the ability to state needs and make claims will define their potential.

We also tell people how we feel in order to be recognized and uniquely understood. When a girl is not entitled to express what she feels, she is by definition unable to be herself. That is, if a girl believes that only certain emotions will be rewarded by peers and adults, she will eclipse the parts of herself that fail to fit the bill. She may reveal herself only when she feels Good feelings or, worse, pretend to feel—and be—what she is not.

IN THIS CHAPTER I FOCUS ON THREE CORE SKILLS FOR emotional intelligence (EI): knowing, expressing, and accepting your emotions.[3] Emotions are almost always described in one word: happy, embarrassed, frustrated, and so on. They are different from thoughts, which are perceptions or reflections, and actions, which are behaviors. Knowing, expressing, and accepting your emotions are related skills: if you can't know your feelings, you can't express them; if you can't accept them, you probably won't express them.

*Knowing* what we feel helps us manage our relationships and internal lives. When Jasmine completed a group project at the Girls Leadership Institute, I supervised a special session where each girl offered feedback to her peers on their work. Two group members used their time to criticize the way Jasmine dominated group tasks. Jasmine had already gotten the chance to critique her peers; there was no "ganging up" afoot. But as she sat listening, her face hardened into an expressionless mask. She refused to look at anyone and, within moments, became unresponsive. The girls who had summoned the courage to critique her grew anxious, wondering if Jasmine planned to retaliate outside the session, turning their group work problem into social "drama." Indeed, Jasmine did not speak to any of the girls, or to me, for the rest of the day.

A more emotionally self-aware and articulate girl would know she was feeling not only furious but perhaps also embarrassed and hurt. Thinking about her anger might have led to more reflection about the incident or another course of action. Awareness would have helped Jasmine control her emotions, thoughts, and actions instead of having them control her.

According to author and EI expert Daniel Goleman, this kind of intelligence is the difference between "being murderously enraged at someone and having the self-reflexive thought 'This is anger I'm feeling,' even as you are enraged." Once a feeling is identified, a child can better locate its cause and begin moving toward a solution. Marc Brackett, a psychologist who studies EI, writes that knowing their feelings helps children "interpret and predict their own and others' feelings, motivations, and behavior."

When we lose awareness of our feelings, they pillage our minds: we ruminate, obsess, misinterpret, catastrophize. Overwhelmed, Jasmine was unable to receive feedback and improve her performance. She missed the chance to know herself more deeply and reflect on her sensitivity to failure. Instead her behavior signaled to her peers that their attempts to be honest would be futile, if not dangerous.

*Expressing* how we feel usually effects change in our lives, moving us through the situations that demand resolution. In the short term, expressing our emotions gets people to do (or not do) things for us. When I tell someone I feel hurt by her actions, for instance, I may get an apology. Say nothing and you may pay the price: Maddie feared challenging a friend who canceled their plans in order to spend time with her boyfriend. Two weeks later the friend did it again, leaving Maddie in the lurch again. Over time, emotional self-expression forms the basis of healthy relationships. Telling people how we feel helps them to know us, and our unique emotional cues teach others how to be sensitive to our needs.

When you *accept* your emotions, you validate your right to feel the way you do. In this way accepting your feelings is an act of self-affirmation. Emotions, after all, are at the murky core of who we truly are. Yet girls often pick over and judge their emotions the way they scour their every angle in a mirror. When a girl invalidates her feelings, she denies a core part of what makes her who she is. If she decides her feelings are less important than someone else's, she may silence herself instead of speaking her mind. To avoid her feelings, she may pretend to feel something else, embracing less authentic selves or personas.

## IT'S NOT A BIG DEAL

Dana, freckled, big-eyed, and wearing thrift-shop corduroys in July, lowered the magazine she was reading on her bed at the Girls Leadership Institute. When asked to describe herself, she said, "Weird in a good way," and it was hard to argue. At sixteen she had managed to become neither Queen Bee nor Odd Girl Out at a high school infested with brutal cliques. She was an unabashed member of the school's gay-straight alliance and had never worn makeup.

To look at Dana, you would swear that Ophelia had passed her by like the Bible's Angel of Death sparing lucky homes. Something about her unwavering eye contact and quiet carriage suggested she didn't care what you thought of her. In fact, when she arrived at camp, her mother made sure to inform me she was the "child who never gave me a day of trouble." Maybe, I wondered, I really had nothing to teach her.

One day Dana told me about Leo, a close friend from another school. Dana was upset because Leo didn't call her as often as she called him. As we talked, she said, "I'm probably making too big a deal out of it."

When she said this for the second time in a few minutes, I asked, "Why do you think so? Aren't you upset? Aren't these your feelings?"

"I guess," she said. But her voice seemed blank, reminding me of times in foreign countries when I have pretended to understand a native's question.

Where Dana's feelings should have triggered her to speak up, like an itch spiking across her ankle, they didn't. Like many girls, Dana feared the consequences of telling Leo the truth: conflict might end their friendship.

But Dana's real struggle was with something else: the emotions underlying the problem. As we spent more time talking, I heard her continuously trivialize and condemn her feelings.

Dana told me another story. On a Sunday afternoon, she sat in the backseat of the family car, smooshed between siblings, en route to a wedding. When her stepfather made a biting remark about an ethnic group, Dana bristled quietly.

"So how did you feel?" I asked her.

"Angry," she said. But she remained silent in the car.

"In my head," she explained, "I was trying to be like, 'Just get over it, it's not a big deal.' Stop thinking about it, you know, and trying to tell myself that I shouldn't be angry, that I didn't have a right to be angry, I should try to stop feeling that way because it would make things worse."

Dana told me her mother and father had advised her not to hate her stepfather. "[They said] I shouldn't hate him, and that I shouldn't feel this way, that I should just try to be nice . . . [so] I say to myself, 'Dana, stop being so negative, stop acting like you hate him, be nicer.'

"But it doesn't work that way," she told me. "Instead I just stop talking."

As Dana grew quieter, a voice inside her head became louder. *You're making too much out of this, you're just being a drama queen*, it said. The voice was a symptom of what psychologist Aaron Beck calls "self-monitoring" and "self-instruction," internal voices that tell us how we *should* feel and act. In excess, monitoring and instruction lead to intense self-consciousness and inhibition. People who are invested in a particular goal are most vulnerable to the behavior. In Dana's case, she wanted desperately not to feel angry.

To do this, Dana had to approach her feelings as if they were pathogens invading her body. She had to contain, if not destroy, her "bad" feelings. She knew she was angry, but she refused to feel that way. On some level Dana believed that if she didn't have to own her feelings, perhaps she didn't have to have them at all.

Dana listened to the voice inside her head. She began dissociating from her feelings, using physical language to describe the process: she said she felt "broken" and "carved out," that "something was really wrong with me."

> I'll narrate whatever is happening in my head as if it is already in the past. Instead of thinking about what is actively happening around me, I'll think about it as if I am telling it to someone or writing it down in a journal. . . . It leads me to disconnect with my surroundings in that I act like I am already past whatever is happening.

Describing her behavior around others when she was upset, she said,

> I guess I feel . . . empty, kind of—like there's almost no emotion there. Or that—aw, man—or, like, I stop talking a lot . . . and . . . I feel like I act really fake. That's a really big thing. I feel like I'm just acting normal and I'm really not at all. Everything's totally off in my head. In my head there's this whole negative down spiral, but when I speak, I pretend that nothing's wrong. It's amazing to me that no one picks up on that. I guess I'm good at it.

With Dana unable to direct her feelings outward—to say, *I need this from you, I am upset, I need this to change*—her thoughts grew more frenzied. "I feel like, I just keep saying, this is horrible, or like . . . um, I really don't want to do this," she told me. "I feel so horrible, and I feel, like, so wrong." Notice how Dana went from saying "*this* is horrible" to "*I feel* so horrible." She had begun to internalize her stress and blame herself.

Feelings fertilize our thoughts and actions. By denouncing her emotions, Dana lost confidence in her agency in the world. She grew passive, thinking about current events in the past tense. A hallmark of a girl's "hardiness," or firm stance under stress, is a "relationship to change in which one feels challenged and mobilized rather than defeated."[4] Dana had become little more than a vessel while her life unfolded around her.

As Dana denied her feelings, her true self began to fade. She became silent or fake: in her words, "empty." One day when Dana and I were walking to lunch, she said, "I'm afraid that by talking about how I'm feeling . . . someone won't want to take care of me." She quoted a song about not wanting to be a mess someone else would have to clean. "I worry someone will think I'm too much to deal with," she said.

Perceiving a choice between her feelings and her relationships, Dana chose to be liked by others. But the self she displayed was a mask of the person she thought others wanted her to be. The Curse of the Good Girl obscured and shamed the most important parts of who she was. By challenging her right to feel a full range of emotions, Dana had indeed learned to make herself smaller and neater; she would be no mess. But she was disappearing.

All this she did for her relationships; that they also suffered is a sad irony, and no coincidence. Dana began to resent Leo for not seeing through her cheerful façade to her real feelings of abandonment and hurt. Eventually she punished him, acting withdrawn and ignoring his calls. Dana believed he had disrespected her feelings when he failed to read her mind. In fact, it was Dana's disrespect for her own feelings that kept her from telling Leo the truth. Disconnected from her own experience, Dana was unable to empathize with his. In the process she created a confusing rift in their friendship.

At the Girls Leadership Institute, Dana learned to identify the voice in her head urging her to dissociate from her feelings. It helped her to see the voice as a "Good Girl voice," telling her what she should feel. She has learned to interpret the voice as a signal to pay attention to her internal experience.

But awareness of her Good Girl voice will matter little if Dana lacks the ability to talk back to it. Helping a girl like Dana express herself is not unlike teaching a person to play soccer or basketball. It's easy to shoot the ball when no one is around, much harder when someone tries to block your shot. We can teach Dana to know and say how she feels, but the trick will be learning to do it when the chips are down. Dana will need the confidence to recognize that all her feelings are important and that she will still be valued in relationship for having them.

Not all girls possess Dana's inner awareness or ability to participate in an internal dialogue. Where Dana tried to talk herself out of feeling the way she did, fifteen-year-old Taylor tried not to know her feelings at all. As with Dana, looks were deceiving: Taylor appeared intrepid and unself-conscious. She was the girl who asked how everyone was feeling, made endless eye contact, and was earnest and outspoken with friends. She was popular with peers and adults. At GLI she fearlessly dropped by my room anytime she felt like it to hang out, listen to music, and talk for hours about anything.

A few days after camp began, it became clear that Taylor was not eating. I asked her how she was feeling. "I don't know" was all she could reply. Then she mentioned that her parents were divorcing, and I asked again how she felt. "I don't know," she repeated glibly, tossing her head "whatever" style.

I pressed on, searching for windows into her emotional world. Like a suspect under interrogation, Taylor refused to surrender her feelings. "I don't know," was all she would say. After a while I realized that it wasn't the pouty choice of a sullen teenager. On the other side of *I don't know* were acres of emotions that Taylor had deemed unacceptable.

Days later she opened up about the divorce. "I didn't think I should be mad at my mom, because I didn't want to put all that tension in the household," she said. "I needed to be strong for everyone, and so I shouldn't have the emotions coming out like anger and sadness, because it . . . I just thought it just made it harder for everyone. It was easier for me to put on this happy face."

When asked how she felt, "I don't know" was Taylor's stock answer. It was a typical teenage retort that she could easily hide behind. But for Taylor, "I don't know" meant "I can't know."[5] She decided she simply could not—would not—feel her feelings. Taylor believed that her emotions made her selfish. She also thought her feelings were not as important as her mother's. If she did get angry, Taylor believed that her relationship with her mother would suffer indefinitely. The last remaining person in the house would become a stranger to her.

The more Taylor tried not to feel, the more she lost control over her behavior. Dana tried to empty herself of feeling by disconnecting internally; Taylor physically emptied and filled herself through disordered eating. Bingeing and starving in cycles, she would channel what she felt about her mother into that day's diet.

"I was so angry I would tell myself I didn't want the food," she told me. "Or I couldn't have it because it was bad for me, and that would make me angry, because I couldn't have it, and then I would go eat it." It was much cheaper emotionally to get angry at her own hunger than at the real source of her anger: her mother. "I was so thinking that I couldn't control my anger with my mom that I just controlled it with food instead. I knew I had the power not to eat, and so I didn't. I didn't have the power to not be angry," she said.

Without the permission to express herself unconditionally, Taylor did not possess critical skills to manage her emotional experience. The cost of her attempt not to "know" her inner life took its toll on her physical health. Just as water may change state and become mist or ice, Taylor's fierce attempts to dissociate from her emotions simply changed their form. The feelings had resurfaced as disordered eating.

## SHAME ABOUT EMOTIONS: I COULDN'T STOP THE FEELINGS

Maya hovered, still and silent, in a chattering group of girls. Her Laura Ashley floral T-shirt was tucked primly into ironed, pleated shorts. Her straight hair barely moved, and her smile was frozen and mirthless.

Her arms were rigid, rounding up into shoulders clipped too close to her ears. During a workshop exercise, when the other girls embraced as though being photographed, Maya stood on the end, her hand resting in the air just above the back of the other girl she would not touch.

Days passed, and this sixteen-year-old betrayed little beyond *I'm fine thanks*. When we finally began talking, Maya spoke as though issuing a disclaimer: I needed to understand how grateful she was to have every opportunity and resource available to her. Her mother always encouraged her. When Maya did something good, her mom bought her something special. Maya's mother called every day to check on her after school and ask where she was going, how school was, and what she wanted for dinner. When Maya had a bad day, her mom said she should try to be happy and forget about it.

The trouble began when Maya had a hard time being happy and forgetting about it. Her mood darkened gradually at first. Then a friend died tragically, and she couldn't stop crying.

Maya's emotional display made her mother uncomfortable, then angry. "My mom isn't a mean person," she told me quickly. "She wasn't doing it to be mean to me. She told me I need to stop and pull myself together and move on."

Maya was unable to move on, and one evening she evinced a rare flash of anger. Her parents gave her the silent treatment for days. "She wouldn't even turn her head to look at me," Maya said, remembering a night when her mother walked by and pretended not to hear.

As Maya told the story of parents unwilling to support their devastated daughter, she continued defending them. "My parents would do anything to try to make me happy. . . . [They] never denied me anything that I wanted," she insisted. She viewed her unhappiness as a sign of ingratitude.

I felt really guilty because I wasn't feeling happy. . . . I'm healthy, and I should be grateful that I'm, you know, healthy and strong. And I felt like

I was ruining my life because of, like, how I was feeling. I would get angry at myself. I felt like so many people would give anything to be in my situation and I should feel so fortunate to have the life I do have, but I wasn't happy about it. On top of my emotions, I was so angry at myself. . . . I felt like I was ruining my opportunities that my parents had given me.

Maya had learned from her parents that the only worthy version of herself was a Good Girl. The failure to adopt a sugary veneer would be met with frustration and anger, even silence. She was faced with a Faustian choice: take her emotions seriously and reject her parents or choose her parents and lose herself. She chose her parents, and her mechanical defense of them was final proof that their voices had replaced her own.

The more she tried to hide her feelings, the worse she felt. Unlike Dana, who told herself her feelings didn't count, and Taylor, who believed that her emotions would lead to loss, Maya decided that her feelings made her a bad person. "I think I felt that I was doing something wrong or that I was a bad person because I couldn't . . . I couldn't not feel them. I couldn't stop them," she told me.

Maya became depressed. She came home from school, ate, and went to bed in the late afternoon. She tried harder at school, pushing herself to socialize and pay attention in class. As she faded beneath the Good Girl exterior, she grew distant from her friends. People stopped waiting for her to go down to the cafeteria. Party invitations waned.

Maya couldn't concentrate. Her teachers were upset, and her mother, who had in sunnier academic times said that grades didn't matter, now assembled a team of tutors. When her father was hospitalized and Maya became even more distraught, her mother scolded her again. Her father wasn't going to die, she said, advising Maya to watch her as she continued with charity engagements. She carried on, Maya said, "pretending like our life is the best."

Maya felt she had lost everything: friends, academic success, her parents' approval. She began to cut herself as punishment for what she believed she had failed to accomplish. Echoing what has become a common explanation for self-injury, she said, "I couldn't take all this hurt or negative emotions and channel it outwardly, so I had to do it to myself."

Maya's parents drew an impossible emotional perimeter around her, letting her know that being happy and "about to be happy" were the only acceptable versions of their daughter. Her belief that she was a bad person stemmed from the sense that her feelings—and therefore her self—were serious disappointments to her mother and father. Maya could not separate from her parents as a normal teenager with a distinct identity; instead she manipulated herself into a reflection of their needs and demands. As she surrendered her feelings, she lost a critical anchor to herself. She saw herself only through her parents' eyes.

"I never thought I was perfect," she said. "I felt like I had to appear perfect." Above all, what Maya wanted were perfect feelings.[6] But the more she attempted to appear "Good" publicly, the more ashamed she felt.

At GLI, Maya felt the first support for her emotions and, when she went home, took the first steps to separate from her parents. Before GLI, she said, "I felt that they were perfect, and that I should do what they say, and that their way was the right way to do things, and that I should always bow down to them and hear what they say." Her belief in her right to have and to express different feelings instilled new confidence. A small space opened up in which she could define herself as an individual and find refuge from her parents' disapproval. "I recognize they aren't gods," she told me. "What they say, I don't have to do. They aren't always right . . . Now if they're upset with me, they'll have to deal with it." As she began taking her own feelings seriously, Maya grew more confident in her own perspective. Her sense of self was free to emerge dynamically in her relationships.

# LOSING CONTROL: THE EMOTIONAL HURRICANE SEASON

While Dana, Maya, and Taylor internalized their emotions, the struggle to manage feelings leads other girls to act out explosively. The tendencies to repress and unleash emotions are two sides of the same coin: in both cases, girls lack the skills to manage their feelings.

Adolescence launches an emotional hurricane season for girls. It's telling that Dr. Louann Brinzendine, a brain scientist, had three very unclinical words to describe the female brain at adolescence: "drama, drama, drama."[7] At puberty the prefrontal cortex is periodically "derailed" by stress, leading to a loss of self-control and an increase in impulsive behavior. "Hormonal surges at this age," she wrote, "can make a mild stress or seemingly small event feel like a catastrophe."

Daniel Goleman has called these losses of control over emotions "emotional hijackings," moments when people cease to behave reasonably and often say and do things they regret. Emotional hijackings return us to primitive aggressive states, and pubescent girls are especially vulnerable to them. They are known to become easily unreasonable, uncommunicative, inconsolable, or enraged.

Such behavior is often written off (and even mocked), labeled a "hormonal" moment of puberty with clearly unscientific innuendo. In fact, these outbursts speak volumes about the need to teach girls emotional-intelligence skills to cope and thrive.

Amplifying girls' mercurial adolescence is a culture urging them to enjoy many of the same opportunities, privileges, and social permissions as boys do. But parity may be driving new personality changes in girls. When Miss Hall's School asked girls how they would handle a series of conflict scenarios, a surprising eight out of ten said they would respond "reactively" in at least one situation, meaning they would escalate the conflict.[8] Notably, these were not "at-risk" or "problem" girls but high-achieving, aspirational young women. The study concluded that "in your face, get out of my way behavior is becoming more normative."

The study was a watershed in research on girls, dispelling the widely held assumption that it is mostly low-income girls, and often urban girls of color, who act out. Perhaps more important, it was a cultural beacon, signaling a shift in how we are raising girls.

The headlines bleat daily: "Girls Gone Wild," "Bad Girls," "Mean Girls," "Gossip Girls." The labels implicate girls as agents of their own (and our) destruction. But the spike in girls' aggression illuminates adults' failure to guide girls into appropriate uses of their newfound freedoms. We are telling girls to be stronger, but we have not helped them channel their power into respectful acts of self-assertion. The stars of reality shows and dramas like *Gossip Girl* have stepped in to fill the void. Appointing themselves girls' primary teachers in how to handle conflict, their lessons are of the "oh no she didn't" and "you took my man" variety. The result is that more girls are behaving aggressively, but not assertively.

Along with the increase in girls' arrests documented by juvenile-justice departments, professionals working with girls describe an emotional toughness less easy to measure. Veteran school counselors around the country told me stories of girls who are tense and tempestuous. Brenda, a counselor for over ten years in a mostly white, middle-class Kansas middle school, shook her head and gave a tiny, admiring snort as she observed some big differences between herself and her students during conflict.

"I'm a big 'sorry' person—I say it even when I don't need to say it anymore," she told me. "I say it because that's how I was raised." In her daily mediations of girls' conflicts, Brenda saw something else. "I'm seeing a lot of, 'I have no empathy for you. I can't put myself in your shoes. I don't care, it's all about me. This is how I've learned [to deal with conflict].'"

Brenda's colleague mimicked a girl she recently had in mediation. "Yeah, you can't deal with it? That's your problem. Whatever I did, you're not strong enough to deal with it? That's your problem." Counselors told me it wasn't always this way: their girls have become coarser.

As the pendulum has swung to the other extreme, girls believe they cannot make themselves vulnerable and say what they really feel. Some counselors observed that girls' tough exterior usually hid tender feelings, along with the fear that if they shared their emotions, they would be consumed—drowned, even—by their own vulnerability. For these girls, one counselor said, "It's either, 'I do this [act tough] or I'm completely crushed.' . . . It's not letting anybody inside or showing really how scared and frightened and insecure they really are."

In interviews, counselors echoed my observation that girls viewed emotions as weak or uncool. "It's almost like there's not a balance between victimhood and self-understanding. You don't have to be a victim to have some self-understanding and ownership and personal awareness," one told me.

Without a language or method to manage her feelings, Kayla often lost control over her behavior. Born in Colombia, South America, Kayla was adopted in infancy by a white, middle-class family in the Northeast. Tall and lithe, with beautiful dark skin and hair, she always smiled and hovered around clusters of louder, more socially dangerous girls. At thirteen, Kayla desperately craved approval from them.

Perhaps it was this insecurity that drove her to mask one feeling as another until she became overwhelmed by her emotions. Like Dana, Kayla thought she was controlling her emotions to preserve friendships. Unlike Dana, Kayla would lash out and often damage them explicitly as a result.

When Kayla was upset that her friend Stephanie did not save her a seat, Stephanie tried to talk to her. Kayla was angry and hurt, yet she was unable to verbalize anything close to this. Instead she barked at Stephanie, "I don't feel well!" and ran out of the room. Stephanie interpreted this as Kayla telling her off, got angry, and retaliated.

A few days later, Kayla received a disappointing care package from her parents. As she opened it in front of her friends, she began laughing to cover up the disappointed, sad feelings. The other girls took these cues and began laughing, too. Kayla then felt laughed *at* and ran from the room crying.

When Kayla cried, she hyperventilated, her hand trembling around her mouth as she breathed in gulps. Tears poured from her eyes. She could not speak. When I asked how she was feeling and if there was anything she wanted to say, she nodded but still could not muster words. Her emotions were overtaking her.

"Sometimes I try to feel one way, and I don't feel the other way," Kayla told me later. "I don't know why I laugh." When I pressed, she said, "I normally laugh before I start crying to stop myself from crying, because I don't like crying in front of other people." For Kayla, too much emotion meant unwelcome attention—and possibly consequences—from the girls whose acceptance she craved. Kayla sought out high-status girls who would not embrace tearful displays. It was only at home, Kayla said, where "I go to my room and break down in tears."

Although she rarely lost control with her friends, Kayla's family has borne the brunt of her pent-up or ignored emotions. When she did get angry, she said things she didn't mean "all the time. I say, 'Don't talk to me, just leave me alone, I don't want to talk to you, go away, shut up.'" Kayla beautifully described her emotional hijacking: "You're not thinking about what you're saying on the spot, and you don't know what's happening. You think it, but you don't mean it. Sometimes your mind doesn't stop before it comes out."

Kayla's restricted emotional intelligence left her with crossed wires: she physically expressed emotions that did not reflect her internal experience. When she wanted to fit in, crossing the wires was a choice. At other times the discrepancy between what was true and what she actually showed to the world left her with an explosive residue of unresolved feelings. At the Girls Leadership Institute, Kayla's favorite workshop was on the "I Statement," in which the speaker identifies an emotion she is having and explains what is bothering her. The most recent I Statement Kayla had used at school was with a peer: "I felt embarrassed when you told people I prank-called Caleb's answering machine."

The I Statements have given Kayla a protocol for getting her feelings out. Most important, they have given her permission to name and navigate the emotions that feel most chaotic. She still "loses it," she told me cheerfully, especially on the mornings she and her mom fight about Kayla's slow rise out of bed. They're working on it, though: she taught her mom about I Statements, and together they've been trying to use them.

Valentine's journey was more solitary. At sixteen she attended a highly selective all-girls public school, where many girls lived below the poverty line but nearly all attended four-year colleges. A Dominican resident of East Harlem, she divided her after-school time between homework and baby-sitting her younger brothers.

In middle school Valentine was a self-identified Good Girl: quiet, studious, a perfectionist. By high school she was struggling with her anger. By the time she arrived at the Girls Leadership Institute, anger was Valentine's default emotion and getting in someone's face her default response. She told me a story about walking to the corner store with her cousin one day after school.

> There's a group of girls, about five or six. I went to the store, and they called me slut. I just laughed. I went in and I laughed. I come back out, and after I passed them, they yell from a good length, "Slut" again. I was like, "Are you serious?" I was like, "Yo, what you talking about. How about you say it to my face and I tell you what I say to your face?" They started coming. My cousin was like, "We gotta leave, they gonna fuck you up." I was like, "She beefing with me, I don't care. I'm not going to pussy down." She kept talking, like, mad crap and I was like, "Shut up. Shut up."

Valentine did not fight these girls, but, she told me proudly, "If you have a problem with me, you better come say it to my face. I live in Harlem."

In her family's small apartment, Valentine enjoyed little time alone, and her young siblings frequently interrupted what scant privacy she had. She would scream at her brothers and then cry. The rage, she told me, "is like, oh my God, I just want to punch somebody. I can't do that. So I just, like, cry. Because I feel like hitting something or punching something." As her anger dissipated, she felt guilty for losing control. "This may sound a little weird," she recalled, "but I want to punish myself for being this way."

Valentine did punish herself; at GLI she revealed that she had been cutting. A few months after camp, we spoke about what learning emotional intelligence had given her. Before, Valentine's emotional range was like the vocal range of a singer who can hit only a few notes: she responded to problems with intense surges of anger or sadness. Unable to recognize other emotions and pursue more thoughtful coping strategies, Valentine had been confused and made unpredictable by her anger. Now, she said,

> [I] learned about angry mostly being a state of mind and something produced by disappointment and sadness and embarrassment. I think before that I didn't know that, I thought being mad was just there. It was something that if it was provoked, be careful, because we don't know what's going to happen. . . . That would distract me, I would make bad decisions.

Even when she is angry now, she told me, sadness "is the reality, is the truth of the person. If you don't know the truth, you're going to be confused." Valentine no longer cuts, and when she gets angry, she has learned that "instead of thinking about my anger towards whatever the situation is or the person, [I should] look beyond that to see what is exactly upsetting me." She has found she is angry much less often, and her boyfriend has noticed. Now her approach is to "let me see how I can face the situation rather than get mad and confused and all this other stuff."

Good Girl pressure delivers a sucker punch to girls' emotional intelligence. The Good Girl who emerges is an emotional bellwether, a projection of the feelings we have designated acceptable in girls. When girls cannot identify, express, and accept a full range of their feelings, they lose critical connections to themselves and their relationships. They are trained to reveal only the parts of themselves deemed Good and to avoid what remains. In extreme instances, when their most painful feelings lack an outlet, girls may compensate by resorting to self-injury.

The decline in emotional self-awareness and expression disrupts the mechanics of girls' relationships, which thrive on disclosure. In a social universe where intimacy is at a premium and insecurity abounds, chaos can result.

*Two*

# IS SHE MAD AT ME? GOOD GIRL
# COMMUNICATION RITUALS

The Curse of the Good Girl undermines direct communication in girls' relationships. It not only stifles the skills to know and express feelings, it prevents girls from engaging in emotionally honest conversations. Imagine two girls—let's call them Anna and Reena—passing each other in a crowded school hallway somewhere in the world.

"Hey!" Anna said, as Reena rushed by in silence.

*What did* I *do?* Anna thought.

Over lunch Anna caucused with two friends eager to speculate about Reena. When Reena passed their table, the girls stared. Reena was confused. She decided that the girls were talking about her. Anxious and angry, she approached her own friends for support. When word got back to Anna, another girl fight was under way.

To ask Reena if she was angry, Anna would have had to evince "bad" feelings like anger, hurt, or betrayal, exposing herself and their friendship to the possibility of conflict. The Curse of the Good Girl has deemed these emotions off-limits, leaving girls like Anna both unable to talk honestly with Reena and without a sense of permission to approach her in the first place.

When girls are unable or unwilling to pursue the answers to their most pressing interpersonal questions, they are forced to draw conclusions from dubious evidence: an unreturned wave, an ambiguous facial gesture, or a coy remark. They cannot ask, so instead they pretend to know, filling in the blanks by assuming what other people mean, think, and feel.

With no evidence that Reena was angry, Anna's mind had taken a big leap:

Fact: Reena did not respond to me.

Assumption: Reena must be angry with me.

In fact, Reena had never been angry with Anna. She had not heard her in the noisy hallway that morning. Meanwhile, Anna's assumption was pessimistic and wrong. It ignited a domino effect of negative feelings, ugly thoughts, and regrettable behavior—otherwise known in Girl World as "drama."

When girls use assumptions to steer their relationships, they do not fully engage with other people. They passively deduce the truth rather than seek it and imagine what is real instead of asking for it. When Anna acted on her assumption and invited her friends to speculate, she became a public, passive "victim" of a situation she could have potentially understood on her own. She was learning to settle conflicts indirectly and in a pack, and she could not practice dealing with problems independently. These habits damage the development of girls' interpersonal skills and inform how they approach day-to-day conflict as adults. In this chapter I will guide you through the underground world of girls' indirect communication rituals. When girls think clearly, they can make active, informed decisions and use their soundest judgment in difficult situations.

. . .

ASSUMPTIONS ARE A CASH CROP OF GOOD GIRL CULTURE. When girls are trained to avoid direct confrontation and keep the peace, they do not learn how to reflect about others' behavior and feelings, or to actively investigate why people might feel or act the way they do. Lacking the tools to get real answers, they simply guess instead.

Girls also lack permission to ask. When girls try to settle conflicts directly, they are often labeled as "mean" by peers and marginalized. By contrast, guessing games are richly rewarded in Girl World. Girls who make assumptions enjoy a glut of social support. Wondering aloud why someone is upset attracts pity and attention. By passively turning to others instead of confronting the people at a problem's source, girls get to remain "Good." Yet assumptions illuminate a troubling bind of the Good Girl life: girls try to remain Good and conflict-free by not asking questions, but this very ritual spins their conflicts out of control. The Curse of the Good Girl creates dead ends, no matter which way girls turn.

Declining self-esteem greases the wheels of assumptions: if you're insecure, it's easy to fantasize that people don't like you. Adolescence, a time of extreme self-consciousness, also plays a role. The painful, anxious obsession that "everyone is looking at me" can launch all kinds of delusions. Sixteen-year-old Rebekah said, "If your self-confidence is really low, you might be, like, 'Oh, they must be talking about me, they don't like this about me.' . . . You'll think something's wrong with yourself." Even more to the point, her classmate said, "If one girl thinks a bad thing about herself, she thinks everyone else is thinking about it. . . ." These girls size up situations through filters of insecurity and developmental self-centeredness.

Many girls also believe that the truth is hidden or sugarcoated, that what is said can't be taken at face value. I asked scores of girls to tell me if, in the last month, they'd had thoughts like, "She said she likes me, but I know she doesn't." They overwhelmingly answered yes. As fifteen-year-old Winnie told me, "The little things that people don't mean to say—I think they truly, seriously mean it." In such treacherous social waters, second-guessing is a conscious survival instinct.

The obvious question is, why don't girls just ask? There is an anxiety that pulses at the heart of girls' approach to conflict: the belief that face-to-face confrontation will terminate a relationship. "Are you mad at me?" may deliver the truth, but it is a messy question that trembles with tension and the potential for emotional blowup. The cost of straight talk can be wildly variable, ranging from a simple conversation to whole groups going to war. Girls often fear the worst. They know it's better to ask directly, a junior told me, "but then there's somebody right next to you, and it's a lot easier to just ask her, because maybe she knows." It's even easier to decide within the safe confines of your own thoughts.

## HOW ASSUMPTIONS WORK

Dr. Aaron Beck revolutionized psychology when he exposed our reliance on assumptions. He explained that while we can never really know what other people are thinking, we rely on signals they give us to clue us in to their thoughts and feelings. Most of the time, we do a pretty good job of reading others. The problems start when the coding system we use to decipher others' signals becomes defective.

Beck observed that when people were upset, they were more likely to incorrectly interpret others as being upset. He further saw that once people made assumptions, they became irrationally convinced that their guesses were absolute fact, even when they had no proof. The assumers passionately believed they were right about what other people thought or felt, making it all but impossible to convince them otherwise. Their thinking became "twisted" or distorted, triggering intense emotions and clouding judgment.

Beck also found that a person's assumption usually created the very result she wished to avoid. For example, Anna's assumption that Reena was angry led Anna to talk about Reena behind her back and stare at Reena when she passed. Reena, meanwhile, had never been angry with Anna. But when Anna acted on her assumption, Reena did get angry, bringing Anna's assumption to life.

Ironically, the better you know someone, the more likely you are to misinterpret her. Beck observed that "the more intense the relationship, the greater the possibility of misunderstanding." His studies of married couples and their distorted thinking were uncannily similar to the drama of girls and their closest friends. Yet no one has ever studied girls, who are exquisitely vulnerable to assumptions for several reasons.

The Curse of the Good Girl makes being nice at all costs the prime directive. This pushes girls to be dishonest about risky thoughts and feelings. Being untruthful can range from the mild "No, you don't look bad at all!" to the more severe "I'm fine, it's okay if you want to cancel our plans and go out with Maryana instead." A high-school junior explained,

> I think a lot of girls are self-conscious about how people view them, and they don't want to say things to make people not like them, so they might lie just to, like, say the right thing not to get people mad at them. Once you do that, though, whatever you're saying, you're just kind of thinking she's probably not really telling the truth, because I wouldn't want to tell the truth in this situation.

When a mist of distrust hangs over girls' interactions, it builds questioning into the act of listening.

Assumptions thrive in a social world where little is said directly. Girls' conflicts are often muted events, punctuated by cryptic body language and endless interlopers. The explosion of text messaging, social-networking sites, and instant messaging has only further fogged the channels of communication. When they are upset, many girls begin dropping hints with their bodies, pinching their voices or falling silent altogether. These are not aggressive acts but rituals of indirect communication, and they invite swarms of assumptions about what is really afoot.

"You can see it in their eyes," a seventh-grader told me. "Like, if Sam was mad at me right now, she wouldn't say it, she'd just kind of hint with her eyes, like, in a weird way. You can see in their eyes they're trying to, like, avoid you."

It's "the way you say it," a classmate volunteered. "The way someone says something."

"Be quiet," an eighth-grader instructed, explaining how she tells people she is upset. "Don't talk or answer questions. Or kind of like turn your head when they [walk by]."

"Ignore them," her friend said firmly.

Girls who reveal feelings mysteriously encourage others to fill in the blanks on their own. Where the truth is obscured, assumptions will flourish.

Making assumptions gives girls a sense of control over conflicts that develop unpredictably, accruing new players and attention every hour. When you suspect that someone is angry with you, fourteen-year-old Sarah told me, you get a terrible feeling in the pit of your stomach. "It's, like, the worst feeling in the world, because it means so many other consequences after that." You don't know what those consequences are; you just know they're coming. Filling in the blanks yourself gives you information you can act on, rather than just waiting for the chips to fall.

The company of friends offers a compelling incentive not to confront a person directly. Assumptions beget allies. "You take it to a place where you need backup," one girl told me. A budding conflict is juicy news, making you the center of attention among peers who crave fresh gossip. That can be powerful stuff for a girl who is anxious and upset.

Self-destructive or bizarre behavior can follow. Some girls like to predict the worst possible outcome of an assumed situation because, as one sophomore put it, "If we assume the worst, it won't be as bad. You can handle it better." You also get "pity and more attention," her classmate said. Others regularly assumed that conflicts were their fault, as if this would give them the "power" to solve the problem; one freshman said, "You always want to think [a conflict is] about yourself, and you're always doing something wrong . . . so you want to try and fix it." The trouble, she concluded ruefully, is that "you're not always wrong, you know?"

Assumers are frequently distracted from schoolwork and life, consumed by obsessive thoughts about a problem they are playing out in their own heads. Didi, a sophomore lacrosse player, told me about a game in which two girls from the other team were "like, whispering and laughing, and they kept, like, looking around." She couldn't take her eyes off them. "I'm like, Oh my gosh, they're talking about me. I was like, is it because we suck or something?" Eventually she realized they were laughing about something else. By then, Didi admitted, she had played a mediocre game.

# THE LANDSCAPE OF GIRLS' ASSUMPTIONS

## ASSUMING INTENTIONS: I KNOW WHY THIS IS HAPPENING

Ruby and Candace were high-school freshmen who had been close friends for two years.

"We're going to Great Adventure this weekend for my brother's birthday," Ruby said.

"Cool! I went there with Jess!" Candace replied. "It was amazing. We rode in the front seat of, like, every roller coaster. I had a huge crush on the guy who ran the stand-up one? So I rode, like, five times in a row and almost puked. I tried to give him my phone number, but Jess kept telling me he was gross."

Ruby sighed. Could she get one sentence out without Candace one-upping her? All Ruby said was, "Cool."

"Are you okay?" Candace asked quickly.

"Yeah," Ruby said, looking away as the first bell went off. "I gotta go."

Ruby doodled an angry, inky hole in her Spanish workbook. *Candace always wants to rub my face in the fact that she's closer with Jess than I am. She just wants to make me jealous.* By third period she could hardly concentrate. She knew she had to say something to Candace. *But what?* Ruby thought. *"Stop one-upping me, it's so annoying"?*

In study hall, Ruby told Carrie, another friend, about Candace. Carrie agreed that Candace could be self-centered, and Ruby felt a little better.

By lunch Ruby's anxiety had returned. She texted Carrie: "idk [I don't know] what 2 do about candace." But she accidentally sent the text message to Candace, who, Ruby told me, "texted me back all 'WTF?!'" Now Ruby had less than an hour before she would face Candace in math class.

When Ruby walked into geometry, she saw Candace, face streaked with tears, talking to a guy. Candace looked at Ruby, then quickly turned back to her conversation. *She's probably telling him what a bitch I am,* Ruby thought. Her anger surged like a white-hot bulb.

When Ruby sat down, Candace whirled around to face Ruby and whisper-yelled, "What did I do?" The teacher shushed them, and Ruby looked away.

They didn't speak for the rest of the day. That afternoon Ruby demoted Candace from her Top Friends list on Facebook. Candace took Ruby off her Top Friends and left a nasty comment on Ruby's page. Their friends read the posts and replied with comments of their own.

Two days later the girls reconciled a conflict that had run mostly on the fuel of Ruby's assumptions: when Ruby decided Candace was trying to make her jealous, she was guessing Candace's intentions without knowing the truth. Aaron Beck called this type of assumption *arbitrary inference,* or simply deciding, without real information, why people act the way they do. Because Ruby did not approach Candace directly to talk, she turned her guess into fact without knowing the true story.

Robust feelings of anger and anxiety grew from the seed of Ruby's unverified assumptions. Eventually she acted out.

**Ruby's First Assumption: Candace talks about her friendship with Jess to one-up me and make me jealous.**

*Ruby FEELS angry, frustrated, embarrassed, hurt.*
*Ruby LEAVES abruptly.*
*Ruby GOSSIPS with Carrie about it, intensifying the conflict.*

**Ruby's Second Assumption: Candace is talking to that guy about what a bitch I am.**

*Ruby FEELS embarrassed, enraged.*
*Ruby IGNORES Candace.*
*Ruby ESCALATES the conflict on Facebook.*

When they did finally talk, Ruby said she felt inferior when Candace talked about Jess all the time. Candace broke down and cried. "I just feel like everyone always has something to do. I don't want to be left out. I feel totally insecure," she told Ruby. With the blanks filled in, the conflict was over.

A frank conversation might have been stressful, but it would have yielded the truth. Ruby and Candace's story is surprisingly typical. I list some other common assumptions girls make below:

"SHE'S/THEY'RE LEAVING ME OUT." As any parent of a teenager knows, kids often make plans at the last minute, with the agenda changing five or six times in a few hours. It's easy to miss the latest update. When that happens, girls may assume they are being purposely excluded. As one junior explained,

Saturday-night or weekend plans, there's always that one thing where one girl might get left out by mistake, because she just wasn't home when the phone rang or something like that, or someone said, "Oh, I don't have any plans tonight [during] third period," and then, by later that afternoon, [she] had lots of plans . . . but she didn't have time to call the other girl and be, like, "Oh, sorry, I'm busy tonight." Things constantly come up.

The girl who finds out secondhand that her friend *did* have plans is left to wonder if "you were choosing them over me." This can lead to angry gossip that balloons into a full-blown fight.

"THEY DON'T WANT TO HANG OUT WITH ME." Jenn, a sophomore, was close with two girls who were best friends. She was constantly plagued by the fear that they preferred their own company to hers. "So I always assume," she told me.

They could be talking about French class or something and, like, this homework assignment, and how bogus it was, it sucked, and I'm, like, assuming, like, they're making plans to hang out without me, and then I get kind of, like, mad, because I know they have done that sometimes, so I just assume that's always what they're doing, and then I have to go off and be like, "Justin, oh my God, we *have* to do something this weekend because they're going somewhere without me." And then they'll be like, "Hey, do you want to go out on Friday, and you'll be like, "Oops."

Like Ruby's, Jenn's assumption led her to seek allies, gossip, and retaliate, only to discover her misinterpretation later.

"SHE THINKS SHE'S BETTER THAN ME." Fifteen-year-old Lisette was on the verge of telling her friend Kelly off. Kelly talked all the time about "how much guys love her and how, like, popular she is with guys." This infuriated Lisette. "She knows that guys don't really like me that much and that she is just, like, rubbing that in my face," she vented to me.

When I asked Lisette to consider another explanation for Kelly's monologue, she wondered if Kelly was just insecure about guys. "And, like, now that I think of it," she told me a few minutes later, "it is kind of sad that that's all she can talk about. That's the only thing she feels like she's really good at." As Lisette's thinking changed, so did her feelings: she was suddenly much less irritated by her friend and more sympathetic. That's the key to understanding the power of girls' assumptions: they are distorted thoughts that drive how girls feel and act, for better or for worse.

## ASSUMING THE WORST

It was Friday night, and Caroline lingered at the kitchen table, complaining that she had no plans. Her mother was tense after a long day at work, and she tried to find the right answer.

"I guess you don't have any friends then," she quipped.

Caroline was stunned. Later, when they talked about it, her mom apologized: she'd had a tough day, she was tired, it was a joke that came out wrong. Caroline couldn't hear it.

"For the next month," Caroline said, "I believed that she had always wanted to say those things and used being tired as an excuse to be honest." Caroline discovered she had similar suspicions of others in her life. Anytime she wasn't sure what someone meant, she assumed the worst.

"Whenever someone says something in a joking way, and then they're like, 'Oh, I'm just kidding,' I assume that's what they really wanted to say," Caroline said. "I assume they really want to say something." Beck called the consistent negative bias of one's expectations, observations, and conclusions a "negative cognitive set," the tendency to assume the worst about everything others say and do. Negative cognitive sets are most frequently found in people who are depressed and have low self-esteem. These individuals are fixated on what others think of them and blame themselves for what happens in their relationships.

Caroline was aware of her habit. "It all comes back to what I'm telling myself," she told me. "People are supposed to have good self-esteem, so imagine what other people think who aren't even supposed to like me. I'm supposed to like me, and I feel this way. You're not even supposed to like me, and you must feel this way."

Caroline told me she assumed the worst because she believed there were terrible parts of her that no one else could see. Even if people denied it, what they said was probably meant in a bad way, as it should be; she deserved it. Caroline's commitment to her own tortured self-image prevented her from challenging her mistaken assumptions. At the time of writing, she was seeking treatment for anxiety and depression.

## ASSUMING EMOTIONS: I KNOW HOW SHE FEELS

As a teenager I spent countless hours trying to figure out how my friends really felt. I would catch up to a friend I was worried about in the hallway. I would say "hey" in the most unassuming way I could. I deconstructed the tone of my friend's reply the way other people taste wine, searching for notes of anger or dismissal, for finishes of frustration or annoyance.

Sometimes I summoned the courage to ask, "Are you mad at me?"

Usually the friend said no. But as I watched her back recede down the hallway, I filled the silence that followed with my own stories about why she was angry. I filled long periods of history and precalculus with those stories. But I never knew for sure how my friend felt. I just assumed.

Guessing others' emotions is an anxious social ritual in Girl World, and a dangerous one to boot. In particular, the assumption that another person is angry takes conflicts from zero to sixty in a few short moments.

It starts, as it did with Anna and Reena at the beginning of this chapter, with simple body language: Anna interpreted Reena's silence as anger. In a world where so little is spoken directly, girls rely disproportionately on facial expressions, eye movements, and gestures to tell them how someone is feeling. "I admit it," a junior told me,

> when a girl gets up and leaves [without saying good-bye], I go, "Oh my God, guys, she's mad at me," you know, and then gossip starts. They ask, like, why and [I tell them] my friend and I were in a fight before. . . . I was, like, "Oh, she's mad at me again." Then my other friend gave me an example. She was, like, "Oh, yeah, she was really mean at the lockers." . . . And then [drama] starts.

The trouble is that body language is often ambiguous, if not unconscious, making it a notoriously unreliable reading of another person. Aisha, an eighth-grader who was certain another girl was talking about her after she left the lunch table, confronted her aggressively. "I went up to her, and I was, like, 'Why are you talking about me, why are you talking about me?' And that started, like, a huge, big fight between us both." Aisha was wrong—the girl wasn't talking about her at all—and she spent days trying to reconcile.

Even the smallest of gestures can feel like acts of war, triggering a surge of adrenaline and a defensive response. "It's like this fight-or-flight instinct," one girl told me. Frantic wondering if others are talking about you is constant static in the radar, a monumental distraction, and it happens everywhere: classes, hallways, sports fields. Most pernicious, it seems, is the universal posture of two girls bent into an inverted V, whispering and occasionally staring, with only a few words or murmurs escaping the huddle. Standing that way certainly can be an aggressive act, but girls tend to assume that it always is: by this "logic," if someone is talking and happens to look at you, she must be saying mean things about you.

Girls also assume their peers' emotions by blaming themselves for their friends' bad moods. For instance, if a friend comes to school upset about something—she overslept, her parents are fighting, she's feeling down—her friend may automatically interpret her change of mood as a conflict between *them*. Rebekah explained,

> You just kind of end up thinking they're mad at you, because usually they'll talk to you all the time and then all of a sudden they're just, like, snapping at you. And then you don't really feel like bothering them, and you're like, "They're . . . mad at me."

Girls usually follow up by seeking allies for comfort and defense and, in this, way create conflicts from whole cloth.

Once a girl realizes she has misinterpreted another girl's emotional state, it's often too late. By then she may have riled up an army willing to fight the supposed opponent or gone on record saying mean things about her. "And then when you find out it's wrong," Padma, an eighth-grader, explained, "you're like, 'Oh, well, I just said all that stuff to somebody. What do I do?'" For Janie, her classmate, embarrassment is the worst part. "I'll think one thing, and then it'll be the complete total opposite, and it makes me feel really stupid," she said. "Like, you're like, 'Oh, God, how could I have thought that?' And then it just kind of makes you feel like— Oh, God, it's humiliating."

Girls pay for their mistakes with the time they spend fighting and reconciling, the boiling emotions that distract them from their work and hobbies, and the unhealthy habits of relationship they learn. Although assumptions can be specific to a moment, girls also operate under more general assumptions that define their social interactions. One of these is the belief that your closest friends should know how you're feeling. In other words, just as girls try to read others' minds, many assume that their closest friends will magically read their own.

## SHE SHOULD KNOW HOW I FEEL

The belief that others should know how you feel without your telling them is another destructive by-product of the Good Girl curse. According to the Good Girl rules, being direct about your bad feelings is selfish, a conscious choice to put your own feelings ahead of someone else's. Waiting for a friend to guess your feelings takes the pressure off having to communicate yourself. A freshman who never told her boyfriend when she was upset explained, "I feel like sometimes if I put myself out there that—I don't know—I don't want him to think it's all about me and my emotions or whatever." Her classmate added, "You want people to figure it out. You don't want to be begging for attention, like telling them that." If the other person "discovers" your feelings, it seems to make them more acceptable in the first place: the situation was so significant and obvious that it spoke for itself, without the upset person's even needing to say anything.

Sixteen-year-olds Passion and Evie were best friends at the Girls Leadership Institute. A few weeks after camp ended, Passion told me she had a problem.

> This weekend I talked to Evie on the phone, which was cool because usually we only talk online. As usual, Evie went on and on about herself, her boyfriend, blah, blah, blah. As usual, she never asked me how I was doing. The conversation was always about her. I just sit there on the other end and go, "Uh-huh, uh-huh . . . wow . . . uh-huh. . . ." She could probably have a mannequin sit there with a tape recorder making those noises and she wouldn't know the difference.
>
> I try and drop hints—I tried being a little distant tonight, but she was so into herself that she didn't even realize what I was doing. I know we just met at camp and we live in different cities, but I really felt like we connected in such an intense way. I totally felt like she was my spiritual twin. I get that it's hard to be as close now as you are at camp when you live

together and stuff. I shouldn't have to explain to her how I'm feeling or how to be a friend. That's what friends are supposed to know. Maybe she's not the person or the friend I thought she was. Tonight she IM'd me online, but I ignored her.

Here Passion decided that if Evie didn't magically know how she felt, and if her hints were not sufficient, Evie was not a good friend. Passion punished Evie with coldness and the silent treatment. Eventually Evie got confused, then angry, and a minor problem spun into a major conflict.

The alternative is to ask directly, but girls say attempts to verify assumptions are dangerous. "Once you start telling about a problem you have," a seventh-grader told me, "then another problem might come up, and you start talking about that problem, and it makes more problems you have with your friends."

To say it without saying it, girls drop hints, an appealing incentive in a peer culture skittish about open conflict. But miss these mysterious signals and your silence may communicate indifference or retaliation. When girls believe that their call-and-answer ritual is failing, they grow frustrated and can explode without warning. "One thing they say could just completely send you," said one junior. Feelings are repressed or misdirected to others. As girls wait and wait for the person to get a clue, their anger intensifes. "I shut 'em off," Rhonda, a freshman, said. "I want to make 'em feel bad because, like, they made me mad. It's like getting back at them."

Expecting others to know how you feel creates a distraction too convenient to be coincidental. When a girl can blame her friend for not magically knowing how she feels, she doesn't have to name the real problem. In this way she can avoid the risks of sharing her feelings: rejection, challenge, or retaliation, for instance. But by imposing the unfair expectation that a friend should be able to read her mind, her relationships become frustrating and distant.

These habits of indirect communication do not confine themselves to girls' personal lives. As I show in chapter 4, girls frequently make negative assumptions about coaches and teachers. By adulthood, young women use hints liberally in the workplace to communicate. Former CNN executive Gail Evans recalled an employee who wanted an assignment in Paris. Her strategy for landing the job was to mention how much she loved travel, that she had signed up for French lessons and loved French culture. Finally "some guy down the hall" drove his point right up the middle of the conversation. He pitched Paris and got it. When the woman protested, the boss said, "I didn't know you wanted it."

The personal costs persist into adulthood, especially in marriage, where women often criticize spouses who fail to see the hidden message of a slammed kitchen cabinet, a monosyllabic reply, or a heavy sigh.

IF GIRLS WERE TO RANK THEIR PRIMARY LIFE NEEDS IN ORDER of importance, most of their lists would run something like this: friends, air, water, food, Facebook, Instant Messenger, phone. Girls are deeply relational creatures, whose lives and stories are dominated by the people they sit next to, the parties they go to (or don't), the people they love the most, and the ones they can't stand. Girls are like seismographs, sensing the tiniest shifts in their relational landscape.

Yet their social world is riddled with disconnection. The Curse of the Good Girl restrains girls from exploring their most challenging emotions, turning the volume of self-expression down like a knob on a stereo. So much silence leaves much to be imagined, and girls do: they make anxious assumptions about what people mean, what they feel, and why they act the way they do. Their assumptions send relationships off well-lit roads where the truth is spoken and into rocky, dangerous territory where it is only guessed.

A thin substitute for truth, guessing confers the illusory impression of control: you write the script instead of dealing with the face-to-face fact-finding that is unpredictable, messy, and genuine. The dominance of assumptions is a sign that girls are unable to move beyond wondering about interpersonal problems and into acting on them. Assumptions lull girls into believing they can avoid conflict, yet it's precisely these maneuvers that ripen into anxious, angry blowouts.

When girls decide to pursue the truth directly, the question "Are you mad at me?" reveals far more than what another person might be thinking or feeling. The answer brings the potential for conflict and, more profoundly, the difficult truths girls learn about themselves. Conflict unearths our most frustrating mistakes and limits. It demands the kind of honest self-reflection that Good Girl pressure undermines.

*Three*

# THE GOOD FIGHT:
# GIRLS IN CONFRONTATION

Sooner or later assumptions give way to confrontation, Girl World's bogeyman. Taken to task for their social missteps, girls are accountable not only to the person they have wronged but to the Good Girl persona they have invariably betrayed. The Curse of the Good Girl puts girls into wildly improbable double binds: be nice all the time and friends with everyone or else be labeled mean; do everything right or be wrong. The curse has created a peer culture where taking responsibility for mistakes indelibly marks your reputation and where the rules for social success are at odds with being honest. The ruthless criteria for being Good make any kind of self-examination feel like a personal failure.

Under such absolute terms of being, confrontation is experienced as a major violation: if I am not nice, I must be mean, and if I am mean, I am not Good. In the face of conflict and criticism, girls resort to all-or-nothing thinking, an approach to life in which things must be one way or another, with no in-between. Self-concept is regularly divorced from reality: a mistake must define the way I think about myself and how others view me. Extreme responses to confrontation, including lying, denial, and crying, often result.

Relationships uniquely illuminate, and often trigger, our particular sensitivities or limits. Confrontation offers the opportunity to address our roughest edges and develop as individuals and in relationship. Good Girl pressure suggests the opposite: confrontation, and the weakness and faults it exposes, contaminates the Good Girl persona. In a peer culture guided by this principle, the need to appear Good becomes a survival mechanism that ultimately costs girls their integrity in relationship.


GIRLS DRAW FROM AN ARSENAL OF TOOLS TO AVOID TRUTH-telling during confrontation. Some respond to the initial moment by raising their voices defensively or crying. Others keep calm, brushing off the issue with a quick "just kidding." To deflect responsibility, girls bring up peers who "agree" with their side of the story, invoke a person's past offenses to justify their own, and use apology as a tool rather than a gesture of regret. The sum of these maneuvers is a wholesale loss of truthfulness in relationship.

Some girls use denial as a swift, low-cost antidote to confrontation. One seventh-grader put it simply: "Like, sometimes you don't want to break a friendship or something, so you just try to hide [what you did wrong] and act like nothing happened." These girls see a choice to be made between truth and friendship, and they often choose friendship, even at the expense of their own needs and values.

In Girl World, owning a wrong can be incompatible with a good reputation, carrying consequences that reverberate across a girl's social life. In the digital jet stream, girl dramas make headlines, and nobody, a middle-schooler told me, wants to be seen "as a liar or thought of in, like, a bad way."

A good reputation is paramount for girls—it's the "only security they have," a sophomore told me—and it is the most powerful predictor of friends. Truth-telling can wreak havoc on the way others perceive you, broadcasting imperfections of self and relationship. A junior told me,

> If somebody finds out you're doing [something wrong], then people are going to lose respect for you, and then their friends are going to lose respect for you, and then their friends are going to lose respect for you. So through the grapevine you're gonna end up, like, not having any friends, because everyone's told each other and nobody you know wants to associate with that kind of person.

One freshman put it bluntly: "I think that whenever I have a conflict, it's like I'm having a conflict with twenty other people. . . . If you're mean to her or you hurt her in some way, that will return back to your friends, and it will be, like, 'Why were you so mean to this person?'" As a result, a sophomore said, "Girls are a lot more careful about what they say or how people perceive them. They have to do a lot more work to be seen as good."

Failures stipple a self with the scars and scrapes that make us who we are. When girls sequester their shortcomings, they secrete away core parts of their developing selves. Tasha, a ninth-grader, refused to own up to mistreating a friend. She told me, "If I really told her what I did, I knew she wouldn't be my friend anymore. In my mind I was pretending like I never even did it in the first place, so I just denied it." Tasha's denial was not merely a matter of harboring the truth internally while telling others a different story, or using the lie to preserve her Good Girl reputation among others. Her mendacity was an attempt to revise who she was. Lying did not only divide her from others; it made her a stranger to herself.

I am not saying that girls are duplicitous creatures by nature, nor am I saying that girls are more apt to lie than boys are. In fact, girls seem to know better than their behavior suggests. As I noted earlier, the study by Miss Hall's School found that while girls consistently identified the "ideal" way to respond to a conflict, Good Girl pressure regularly drove them to an "actual," often regrettable, response. The "actual" response belied their fundamental instincts and what they knew was right. That girls consistently see two ways to respond—one that is right and another that their context demands—is powerful evidence that the state of their integrity is a product of culture, not nature.

Relationships are a girl's primary classroom, and what they learn about responsibility in relationship forms the foundation of lifelong habits. Honesty is as much a skill as it is a value. Admitting a wrong is a high-stakes, nerve-racking experience; the longer girls go without these formative moments, the more terrifying they will seem. In confrontation, the need to be seen as Good—and the fear of being exposed as Bad—will pull girls' strings like a puppeteer. If girls feel they cannot be straightforward about their mistakes, they will hide them and take their true selves underground. And if they feel unable to own mistakes, they will not feel comfortable learning to make them.

True freedom of the self is permission to make a mistake without feeling obliterated by it. This sort of internal balance is central to developing self-confidence. A young person can reach her full potential only when she feels the agency to take the risks that can result in great triumphs, but that may also backfire along the way.

# SHAME

To live a Good Girl life is to walk an internal tightrope. With one's self-esteem tied up in wildly unrealistic expectations, mistakes become emotional free falls, leading girls to question their fundamental self-worth. This can oxidize everyday, bearable guilt over error into ugly feelings of shame, producing the extreme responses to fault that erode girls' integrity.

At a Girls Leadership Institute workshop, twenty-five high-school girls sat in heavy silence. Each girl had repeated a challenging but legitimate criticism she had received, just as she heard it. Some recalled moments with parents, some with friends.

One by one they recited, "When are you going to stop doing this?"

"Why did you tell my secret?"

"You're not working hard enough."

"I'm disappointed in you."

I asked the girls to list their emotions, thoughts, and actions around the experience. What did you feel when you heard this? What did you think when you knew the person was right? What did you do, or want to do, when you realized you had made a mistake? Here is an excerpt of the list they made on the classroom white board:

| EMOTIONS | THOUGHTS | ACTIONS |
|---|---|---|
| • Scared | • I am a bad person. | • I want to quit. |
| • Sad | • I am a bad friend. | • I cried. |
| • Hurt | • I'll never be trusted | • I denied it. |
| • Stupid |   again. | • I apologized. |
| • Humiliated | • I'm stupid. | • I snapped back. |
| • Ashamed | • What's wrong with me? | • I got defensive. |
| • Unwanted | | • I want to be alone. |
| • Guilty | | |
| • Angry | | |
| • Worthless | | |
| • Overwhelmed | | |

The girls named this chart, half jokingly, the "Death Board." I called it the "Shame Board."

Shame involves feeling helpless, incompetent, and reclusive. It's the sense of "How could *I* do that?"

Shame means you feel you are a bad *person* for what you have done. It's not that the thing you did was bad, but that *you* are bad for doing it. The psychologist Erik Erikson described shame as a moment when "one is completely exposed and conscious of being looked at." Shame feels like wanting to hide your face and disappear. Physically, it looks like a body closing in on itself.

Shame is found in large doses in girls who overreact to and deny their mistakes. Ashamed people are known to deny their bad behavior as a way of protecting themselves. They externalize, or view their behavior "as un-characteristic of the self, by minimizing the self, or by excusing the self." Because it's so threatening to the self, a person may cope by pushing that knowledge outside him- or herself, leading to surges of anger, humiliation, hostility, and denial. As I mentioned earlier, a girl invested in being Good is exquisitely vulnerable to such self-protection; denial, according to one researcher, may be an attempt to "re-empower the self by placing blame outside of the self."[1]

Shame is also evident at the other extreme: self-lacerating letters of apology that GLI campers have sent me, for example. Last year, in re-sponse to a reprimand, the ruthless language of shame was on display. "I think I have a serious trust problem, I'm not good enough to have relation-ships with good people, and that I'm a bad person," wrote one girl. It's worth noting that some of what I call the "Good-est" Girls—the ones who fit the Good Girl bill to a tee—are the ones who, when disciplined, are so overcome by emotion that they often leave the room to weep, forehead to knees, in a place they clearly don't want to be found. These girls' merci-less self-concepts provide no room for error, and because of this, their rock-hard exteriors shatter easily. They come apart in the face of anything that undermines their Good Girl image.

Shame is a virus that creates paralysis in its hosts. When you're busy telling yourself what a bad person you are, you expend most of your en-ergy obsessing over your self—not what you may have done wrong, not what you can do to fix it. For this reason, shame creates a moat around girls' potential. It limits their ability or willingness to face challenges. It makes them want to be alone, isolating them from friends, their most important buffer against stress. Shame is therefore a major threat to girls' resilience.[2]

# I DIDN'T DO IT

When I asked girls to name one thing they wished they could change about confrontations with their friends, their answers were unflinching: I wish I could just express my problem and be listened to without a defensive or diminishing response.

An unusual number of girls described gently attempting to express a problem, only to be met by a hot blast of invective. "One thing that really bothers me," a seventh-grader said,

> is when you try to talk to another girl about a problem and they'll just start cursing you off. Someone's trying to, you know, have a serious conversation, and they just . . . say all these mean things. I'm like, "I'm just trying to talk to you. I'm not trying to say anything mean." And then they get really angry at you, and then they won't talk to you, and they walk away.

Girls who react like this seem to interpret any sign of a grievance, even gently rendered, as an act of war. They begin, as one sophomore said, "*flipping* out."

"They keep interrupting you," a freshman told me. "You can't get your thought out. You can't say what you want to say, because they want to defend themselves. . . . If you say one thing, they're like, 'I didn't! I didn't!' It's really frustrating." Some girls become so anxious when confronted, or are so fearful of even the slightest appearance of wrongdoing, they must shut down the other person wholesale. The response either drives the confrontation underground—online, behind backs, into angry looks—or ends it explosively.

Such behavior is becoming increasingly common. As I showed in chapter 1, a surprising number of girls surveyed by Miss Hall's School said they would respond to confrontation "reactively"; that is, they would escalate the conflict. These were not "at-risk" or "problem" girls, but high-achieving young women.

The constant pressure to maintain a Good Girl façade drives outbursts like these. Girls spend an awful lot of time curbing the uncomfortable emotions surrounding conflict. By the time two girls talk directly, dark feelings may be bubbling dangerously beneath the surface. Sarah told me she had two personalities: at home she could be "totally mean," while school demanded a Good Girl front. Sometimes she failed to divide her emotions evenly between her public and private worlds:

> So I feel, like, for me, in [confrontations], I think that my friends could say I could sometimes be mean to them, straight up, and it's because I need to, like, let it out. So I think that I go to extremes either way, because there's so much bottled in this social environment with your friends. And then you get away from that in a different environment, and it all just, like, comes shooting out, and it's hard to contain.

When permission to be authentic is intermittent, emotions don't always honor the schedule.

The need to appear perfect around others may also trigger denial responses. When there is no room for the errors that confrontation exposes, any kind of dispute feels catastrophic. Instead of fighting back, some girls deny fault outright, whether to avoid a fight or to protect their self-image. "Everyone's trying to be better," a junior told me. "I think that by showing your weakness and having everyone acknowledge it, then it's [making you look bad], and you want to deny that." When a girl builds her identity around being Good, an accusation is not just a threat but a challenge to her very sense of self. A junior explained,

Like, if I did something, you kind of know that you did it, but you don't want to admit it to yourself and you don't want to admit it to them, because then it makes it so much more true in your own eyes, like, "Oh, wow, I'm a really big B, because I just did this to this girl that I really like. I'm her best friend, and I just did that? Like, what kind of friend does that?"

This girl perceives whatever wrong she has committed as having global consequences: her mistake, in her eyes, makes her a "bitch" and a bad friend. By these extreme standards, her behavior feels incompatible with who she is. Denial, for her, will have little to do with the issue she is confronted with and everything to do with restoring her sense of self.

The fear of being wrong plagued fifteen-year-old Caroline as I sat with her, listening to her tick off a list of mistakes she hadn't apologized for. She wondered what her friends would think if they knew.

First there was the school overnight orientation, filled with new-student anxiety and forced bonding. Caroline was miserable but promised her friend she would stay with her. Soon the stress of having to fit in was too much. No one spoke to Caroline, and she called her parents and left. When her friend confronted her the next day, Caroline recalled, "I was like, 'I told someone to tell you. I don't know what you're talking about. I'm not at fault here.'" She did not apologize, she explained, because "in order to apologize, I'd have to apologize for not knowing how to socialize. I don't want to confront that issue."

Caroline was savvy. She knew the Good Girl version of apology. "The little things—please, thank you, da-da-da—I'm a manners maniac," she said wryly. "But, like, the hard things, I can't really, like— I don't know." To say she's really sorry, she said, would mean saying, "I'm sorry I didn't come, because I didn't want to be alone, because I have this issue as being seen as a loser. Because if I did open up, my insecurities would be never-ending, and they would intimidate people."

Caroline was convinced that one incident would permanently define her; it would pronounce *who she was*. Every mistake meant you had "issues," and people, she assured me, didn't want to know that part of her. Apology amounted to an admission that these parts of her existed, a public warning that trumpeted her as an untouchable. Most important, Caroline's anxiety isolated and silenced her, leaving her unable to repair her mistakes.

Some girls told me that denial was the only safe alternative, because they felt punished by peers when they tried to be honest *and* when they tried to avoid confrontation altogether. Rebekah, a junior, articulated a troubling double bind of truth-telling among girls.

> If you're honest, you get the reputation of being a bitch, because you're just, like, PMS-y all the time, so you don't confront people, and [then] you're a bitch because you're hiding your feelings. . . . So it's just easier to, like, lie and completely forget about it. Either way you're going to be considered an angry bitch because you don't talk about it or an angry bitch because you brought it up.

Rebekah described a peer culture unforgiving of conflict in any form, a world where erasing what happened by denying it was the only viable option. Her classmate, Adrianna, told me resignedly, "I think it's easier to deny things than to deal with what would happen and what people would think of them."

When a girl cannot deny what she's done but still wants to avoid facing the problem, she may use one of two strategies to save face. First, she may read the person who confronted her a list of her priors: that is, she will lay bare the other girl's past offenses to justify her own. An eighth-grader explained that "they'll just, like, overpower you with what you've done, and it just . . . you go around in circles. Well, you did this. Well, you did this. Well, you did this. And it's really . . . it goes nowhere."

Girls explained this behavior, in which they make their friends "feel bad about something they did," as a bizarre relationship-saving device. "That's your friend," said a junior, "and you don't wanna lose them, so you try and think of, like, something they did wrong. Make it kind of even, I guess." The recrimination of both girls seems to cancel out the crimes of each. If neither of us is Good, no one can be punished. Equality is restored.

But like the single bullet of a firecracker bursting into hundreds of points of light, the back-and-forth summoning of old mistakes spins a single problem into many. "[Girls] sort of make it a battle instead of just, like, a conversation," fourteen-year-old Sarah said. "It's, like, who can play their cards the best, instead of how can we figure this out together." In the bid to ensure that no one is labeled "Bad," confrontations become competitions instead of conversations.

Another popular way to deflect an accusation is to invoke the ghosts of other girls on "your side." A middle-schooler explained,

> You go up to someone and you'll say, "You've really been leaving me out a lot with your other friends," and then she'll say, "Well, you haven't been acting like a friend either. You've been so mean to me. And So-and-So agrees with me." [I respond,] "Well, I'm not talking about her. I'm talking about you." . . . [She replies,] "She agrees that you're being a real brat about it."

Having another person on your side adds heft to your argument; suggesting peer support increases your Goodness. It also hints at a steeper message to the opponent: if you persist in this conversation, you may lose both of us. It feels, a sophomore said, like "now you're fighting with two people."

## NO OFFENSE, BUT . . .

"Just kidding" and its cousin, "no offense,"—as in, "No offense, but could you go away?" "No offense, but that shirt is not flattering," and "No offense, but my parents think you're weird"—have become staples of Good

Girlspeak. The phrases are the adaptive responses of a peer culture aspiring to an impossible ideal: 24/7 niceness, with little tolerance for real feelings. The crude, inelegant utterances that follow "no offense" or precede "just kidding" reveal how little practice girls have speaking truth in relationship. They illuminate a glaring absence of permission to share honest thoughts and feelings.

"It's, like, sort of a Get Out of Jail Free card," Iris, a junior, told me. "You can be totally mean and hurtful. . . . You can say whatever you want, but then you're just like, 'Oh, no offense, *it's all right*'" (my italics). Kim, Iris's classmate, said,

> You really wanna say it, but you don't want to be blamed for saying it. It sounds, like, a little weird, but, no offense, Anna [looks at classmate], but I don't really like your shirt. I'm saying it. I want to say it, and I want to voice my opinion, and I want to let everyone else know it, but I don't want . . . Anna to turn around and be, like, "Oh my God, I can't believe you said that," 'cause I'll be like, "Oh, but I said 'no offense.'"

"No offense" allows truth and relationship to coexist: "I want to voice my opinion, but I don't want Anna to be angry." The phrases are verbal fulcrums, feeble attempts to balance girls' need to tell the truth with the need to be seen as Good.

When someone says "just kidding" or "no offense," the listener is expected to agree without comment. Resist and she will hear some version of the script countless kids have been cornered with: "What's your problem? Can't you take a joke? Don't be so sensitive, chill out!" The person with the problem is silenced, and she learns that refusing to go along with the "joke" means losing her spot in the group. As one sophomore told me, "the other person's in trouble if they're upset about it. You know, like, 'I was just joking around, no offense, come on.'"

On the surface the phrases appear innocuous, cute little jabs that aren't supposed to leave a mark. But they contain an invidious logic about human behavior and personal responsibility, something along the lines of, *If I didn't mean it, it didn't happen.* If I didn't *intend* to hurt you, the *impact* didn't occur. If I said "no offense," there can't be any offense. If I was *just kidding,* you can't be mad at me. I can't get in trouble. "You say 'just kidding,'" Sarah explained, "or 'whatever' because you want to fix something that you just broke." The phrases are supposed to erase the consequences of your behavior and restore Good Girl status.

This logic is dangerous for two reasons. First, it allows girls to disengage from personal responsibility, to deny their wrongdoing by denying their intent. What begins as a linguistic maneuver to avoid hurting someone's feelings becomes a habit of not owning up—indeed, of lying. Second, when a girl tells another girl not to be offended or that her words were meant as a joke, she is essentially telling the other person how she *should* feel—something like, "I said 'no offense,' so you can't be upset. You should be okay with what I said." The casual undermining of others' emotions signals a lack of respect in relationship.

I am not saying every instance of "just kidding" is a problem. Teasing is an important part of interpersonal and individual development, and it's fun. But "no offense" and "just kidding" are used for far more than joking. Girls are skirting as close as they can to saying what they mean, only to pull back at the last second. Good Girl pressure is leading girls around healthy truth-telling, causing them to protect relationship and appear Good at the expense of personal integrity.

# CRYING

Girls were remarkably outspoken about the tendency to cry when confronted. Crying is a response to confrontation that appears heartfelt but in reality terminates meaningful discussion. Tears send a public distress signal that rallies support to a girl's side. By appearing helpless she can continue to be seen as "Good" by others, gaining the upper hand and making the person with the problem seem like the Bad Girl. An eighth-grader explained,

> Like, crying is one of the ways they get other girls to gang up on you, because, like, everyone feels really bad. Like, when you have a fight, often other people don't really know about it, but if someone starts crying, everybody walks over to them. "Are you okay? Are you okay? What happened? What happened?" And then it's like, [voice turns sinister] "You made her cry. What did you do?"

Girls describe the phenomenon with frustration and resentment. Tears provide a quick exit from a conversation, silencing the person articulating the problem. The crier's well-being becomes the center of attention. The only socially safe choice is to table your grievance and give the crying girl comfort, lest you be seen as mean.

For most girls, crying is hardly deliberate. More often it is an expression of helplessness. Girls who cry may not know what else to do, and their tears suggest that confrontation is frightening, incapacitating, or both. Above all, crying indicates a lack of taste and skill for conflict. When girls habitually respond to confrontation with tears, they do not learn how to address another person's concerns in relationship. They use emotional display as a substitute for honest conversation.

They also teach their peers to avoid sharing difficult thoughts and feelings. A sophomore whose friend consistently becomes "hysterical" told me that her friend's tendency to overreact "makes me feel like I can't be honest with her, because I don't want her feelings to get hurt anymore."

## APOLOGIES

The Curse of the Good Girl also erodes truthfulness at a conflict's end: the apology. "I'm sorry" is often misused to reverse damage to a Good reputation, repair a relationship out of fear of its loss, or express power. When that happens, apology is employed more as a tool than as a gesture of genuine regret, and its true meaning and purpose are distorted.

Although there is nothing wrong with wanting to repair one's image or a relationship, the problem comes when these motives exclusively drive an apology. True remorse takes a backseat to Good Girl survival strategies. Girls lose touch with the critical truths of what happened and who was responsible. Most important, they lose the opportunity to develop an honest relationship with their own limitations as people, worrying instead about the larger social cost and what others will think.

Elena, fifteen, told me how she recently used apology to demonstrate her selflessness. "I am doing it for others," she explained, adding, "I have grown up trying my best to put others in front of myself, and it is very hard to do otherwise." That Elena apologized for her conflict, even though she told me she believed she was not at fault, signaled she was less concerned with remorse than with her public image. Fifteen-year-old Jamie told me her frequent apologies projected a kindness that made people trust her more. For these girls, taking blame was a badge of Good Girl character and a means to maintain, if not accumulate, friendships.

In fact, girls use apology to affirm their niceness in situations having little to do with confrontation. According to linguist Deborah Tannen, adult women use apology as a "ritual way of restoring balance to a conversation." Apology is not necessarily an assumption of blame, but is intended to express understanding and caring about another person's feelings. I see this when girls hit tennis balls out of bounds at GLI three, four, five times in a row, and shout a sheepish "Sorry!"

Their apology is supposed to comfort the other person chasing down their ball. "Sorry" signals their awareness of breaking Good Girl rules: *I asked you to do something for me by making you chase that ball. I made a mistake. I didn't do everything right.* Tannen says that such apologies really mean, "I'm sorry that happened." I think their meaning can be even more casual, a kind of slang for "Excuse me." The apology becomes a way to affirm and express one's Good Girlness.

Tannen says that women may also apologize because they expect the other person to reciprocate, restoring equality and coherence to the relationship. Fourteen-year-old Beth confirmed that apologies often compel other girls to step in, apologize in return, and repair the friendship. In an e-mail she wrote,

> I think many times girls take on blame for problems they know they didn't cause to get a reaction from someone else (a.k.a.: "No, it's not your fault, it's mine" or "You can't blame yourself for this. . . ." etc.). Girls can manipulate blame to make someone else say something, or admit to causing the situation. Other times, girls might take on extra blame for other reasons: to get sympathy, to be noticed/in the center of attention. . . .

This type of apology, used to trigger a reassuring response, is reminiscent of the girls who say "I'm so ugly" in order to hear the automatic salve, "No you're not! You're pretty!" But just as you would never expect a friend to say, "You know what, you do look kind of heavy," a girl who uses apology as a ritual does not want her friend to say, "I accept your apology." The girl wants her friend to say she is sorry, too, or that "it's okay." Tannen writes that anything else would be a "misfire," leaving the apologizer in the vulnerable position.

"Sometimes," a sophomore told me, "people will just apologize to get a situation over with. Like, even if they're not really sorry, they'll just apologize anyway. 'Gosh, I'm sorry, can't we just leave it at that?' Even if they'll end up doing it again." This brand of "sorry" is less an epilogue to a confrontation than an abrupt interruption of it; it becomes a way to extinguish a problem before it has been properly expressed. These girls use "sorry" the way wizards cast spells: the word is supposed to make a confrontation vanish.

There is an incentive to all this. As with girls who cry during a confrontation, apology actually affords control over a situation. When you say you're sorry, even if you didn't do anything, at least you know where you stand. "Sorry" is a place you can point to on a map, allowing you to draw a line in the frequently shifting sands of girls' conflicts.

Self-blame also draws a curtain over the messiness of a fight, especially the painful reality of a friend's betrayal. In an e-mail Jamie wrote that for many girls it's "easier to recognize that they did something wrong than to feel like other people let them down. It lets them keep at least feeling like they trust the person that was in the wrong, like a defense mechanism." Jamie admitted she did this, too. By waving a white flag, she could avoid a difficult truth and spare a friendship, even if it meant paying later within the friendship itself.

Which she often did. More people trusted Jamie when she apologized often. The trouble was, Jamie told me, she trusted herself and others less. She began questioning her relationships: what did it mean about her friends if they refused to own their mistakes and if she faked owning hers? She began to lose the distinction between when she was really wrong and when she was just pretending.

I heard this from many girls. Constant self-blame, real or not, left girls uncomfortable and anxious. Elena explained in an e-mail that her habitual, inauthentic apologizing often left her "with an aweful [sic] feeling in my stomach of judging myself as a bad person for the things I take the blame for. It is almost as if I start to believe that I did the things I took blame for that I didn't actually do. . . ." Her Good Girl attempt to comfort others with a false apology came at the cost of her internal well-being.

Low self-esteem makes it easy to assume blame automatically. Fifteen-year-old Taylor took the blame when she lacked confidence or faith in herself. "Sometimes I feel that I am not worthy of having a right opinion or doing the right thing, because I can't do anything right," she said. Her perception that *she* was incapable, rather than just a part of her having a problem, suggested that shame drove her behavior.

Frantic flurries of apology are stopgap solutions; they may silence the person temporarily, but resentment will linger beneath the surface. One sophomore told me,

> If you keep saying you're sorry, and you keep doing it again, it just, like, doesn't mean anything after a while. You don't change your act. When you say "Sorry," I'll be like, "Okay," but I'm not really going to believe you. So it's not like a real sorry.

Too-frequent apologies erode trust in relationships, making girls second-guess each other. Like a word stared at for too long, such apologies turn into nonsense.

"Sorry" may bear a particular message or purpose when used among girls, but it remains a word that divests a person of power. An apology makes a person vulnerable and is, in many respects, a revelation of weakness. The excessive misuse of apology works easily among friends, but girls will not always be playing and working among one another, enjoying the easy shorthand of their accepted social vernacular. When they enter a world in which apology means what it is, "sorry" may subordinate girls in relationships of all kinds.

Indeed, when girls apologize excessively in their social lives, the habit can bleed into other areas where girls need to appear strong. Kelsey, a sophomore, told me how her constant apologies to save a friendship affected her.

> So it got to a point where if I did any little thing wrong, I had to apologize for it over and over again. So if in school I messed up on a project or wrote a word wrong on a poster, I would be like, "Oh, I'm sorry, group, I'm sorry." If I was playing a sport and missed a shot, I would apologize for it 24/7. . . . I couldn't really change no matter where I was. It didn't matter what environment I was in. I was consistent with the whole apology thing.

Kelsey had begun using apology to restore relationship with her friend. As its use became more facile, the word crept into her daily interactions, making her appear "sorry" for everything.

In her study of women and men in the workplace, Deborah Tannen observed women apologizing habitually. Their behavior left negative impressions, suggesting, she wrote, that "this person apologizes often and that others don't." The implication, of course, is that the women had something to apologize *for*.

The Curse of the Good Girl prohibits conventional expressions of power, and some girls use apology to assert control in a relationship or group. Refusing to apologize is an indirect means to assert control. Whoever has more friends, and more high-status friends, will be on top. By refusing to apologize, you suggest you can afford the loss of a single friend more than the other girl can. It also allows you to bypass conflict and the messy discussions Good Girls are supposed to avoid. In this context whoever apologizes becomes a "loser" and the "smaller person"; when someone is right, it means she is "better than you."

Katie, an eighth-grader, was living this dynamic. She told me that her best friend's refusal to apologize meant her friend was "stubborn all the time. Like, she always has to have it her way." Katie described herself less as a peer than a subordinate: her best friend "won't give me the time of day to listen to me to see if I'm right, because I'm never right. I'm never right, she's always right." Katie was frustrated. "You, like, almost have to watch what you say, like, all the time, and it gets sort of annoying after a while, because if you say something that will offend her or get into a fight or something, she's not going to want to make up and say sorry even though she said something to hurt you." In this relationship the refusal to apologize was a weapon that censored Katie and kept her in her place.

Kelsey, a sophomore, told me about a friend whose refusal to apologize was absolute torture. . . . It ate away at you, like I must have done something wrong. It sort of like tricks you into thinking that you are in the wrong and that it is your fault, because if they're not saying sorry, you think you have to fix the situation. You're like, "I guess they are right, I'll step forward and I'll be the bigger person." But if you step forward every single time, it's just like showing you are weaker than them, almost.

Apology was a test of wills, a way to win. For Kelsey, it became a code for surrender.

With their reflexive willingness to apologize, Katie and Kelsey communicated that they could be counted on to take blame and therefore be taken advantage of; this made it easy for their friends to minimize or disregard their own behavior. Because their apologies were predictable, there was little incentive to change behavior. Elena told me that the momentary benefit of her premature apologies—feeling good about herself—was offset by the fact that, in the long run, "my friends seem to never learn from their mistakes. . . ."

When girls use apology as a way to show power, confrontations are resolved according to who has more of it. By this logic the person who apologizes is not only wrong but a "loser," and whoever is apologized to becomes a "winner." This despite the fact that the "loser" may have done little wrong in the first place. When a conflict's resolution is about power, the question of right and wrong is sidestepped, creating a profound distortion of what apology is meant to be.

IF GIRLS HELD THEMSELVES AND ONE ANOTHER TO MORE RE-alistic standards of behavior and friendship, extreme responses to confrontation would surely subside. What girls need is a careful balance between self-concept and the mistakes they will inevitably make. That is, a girl's fierce denial suggests a refusal to admit a mistake into her idea of who she is, a slamming and bolting of an internal door. A meltdown, by contrast, is a mistake that consumes the self, a kind of drowning. Ideally, every girl should possess the knowledge that she is made of many parts: some of them she is proud of, while others are still evolving. A mistake must be held within the self as a single part of many she possesses. Rather than be defined by any single mistake, the developing sense of self should be fluid and fungible, and most of all forgiving.

This same approach must be embraced by the girls who cluster around a conflict's edge and fan its flames. Bystanders—a poor name for the very active role peers play in girl conflicts—ramp up the fear and anxiety girls experience around dealing with mistakes. So long as girls continue to talk and type about other girls' failings, the cost of honest self-expression will continue to rise. Likewise, girls will feel pressured to avoid honesty in the first place.

I frequently ask girls to consider their role as Good Girl police when they judge each other for mistakes. That is, just as girls police their peers with terms like "slut" and "bitch," responding to the culture's definition of what is feminine, girls are also policing peers when they punish each other for not being completely "Good." They force each other to comply with the same impossible rules they struggle with themselves. It is a self-reinforcing, destructive cycle.

Girls' integrity in confrontation, from the first moment to the concluding apology, is riddled with damaging Good Girl influences. The need to be nice at all costs pressures girls to avoid coming clean about their mistakes and enforces unforgiving standards of personal conduct. Many girls perceive their mistakes in relationship as catastrophic, for either themselves or their public image, and shy away from the truth-telling so critical to authentic relationship. Bogged down in shame or distracted by what others will think, girls are unable to convert feelings of remorse into positive action or genuine apology. They do not learn to accept their limits with a sense of humor.

What girls learn in conflict with their intimates becomes the template for how they negotiate the world. As a girl gets older, she will have to confront not just social mistakes but academic or athletic errors. When that moment comes, many are unprepared.

# Four

# ALL OR NOTHING:
# GIRLS AND FEEDBACK

Girls' resistance to peer confrontation resurfaces in their relationships with teachers and coaches. Constructive feedback is face-to-face bad news from another person and too closely resembles the interpersonal conflict Good Girls aspire to avoid. When girls import their fear of mistakes to performance evaluation in school, clubs, and sports, they perceive negative feedback as catastrophic for relationship, a painful moment of disconnect between two people.

"Taking it personally," a proclivity that accompanies girls into adulthood, suggests that girls are applying one definition of relationship—friendship—to their interactions with teachers and coaches. That is, girls who personalize criticism expect teachers to abide by the same social rules as their friends: hurtful truths destroy relationships, and confrontation must be avoided at all costs. Operating under this single definition of relationship, feedback is frequently interpreted as a personal affront. The all-or-nothing thinking that marks girls' approach to conflict becomes the template for their response to athletic and academic error.

Indeed, many teachers, coaches, and counselors walk on eggshells when it comes to evaluating girls. The concern of these adults, and girls' struggle to handle their feedback, is a largely untold story in girls' development.

It's a story that needs telling: when girls can't handle criticism, it affects how teachers and coaches talk to them. Fragile girls get less specific feedback and more sugarcoating, so they get fewer chances to improve their performance. Skin stays thin. Discomfort with criticism is, by extension, discomfort with being wrong, which can lead girls to play it safe, avoiding situations where risk is required and failure is possible. Girls may shy away from situations that aren't a sure thing, hewing carefully to the areas where they know they can do well.

When they deny criticism or become defensive, girls develop poor habits around failure and challenge. They grow unwilling to face or admit their shortcomings. They don't go with the flow or adapt under the stress of change, so they may quit teams, give up, or grow a chip on their shoulder. It's boys who often learn in crisper, less uncertain terms what needs to be fixed—and who get used to being told they're not always right.

Girls' experiences with feedback are direct training for how they will negotiate evaluation as adults. In fact, girls' discomfort with feedback may be the clearest signal yet of a glass ceiling forming in adolescence. Current bestselling books for businesswomen promise readers strategies to overcome taking feedback personally, a phenomenon considered a major barrier to success. That girls evince similar trends suggests we have a window of opportunity to teach new, healthier habits.

## GIRLS AND CRITICISM

Bethany had played soccer since preschool. At sixteen, she was part of an elite group of athletes in Bergen County, New Jersey, being watched by college coaches early in their junior year. At a tournament where she had played with usual élan, an opponent suddenly scored off Bethany's error.

Coach Joe Barringer said nothing—it wasn't the end of the world—but moments later everything was different.

"She loses total composure," Barringer told me. "She cannot recover." Bethany was so devastated by the mistake that her playing went into a tailspin. Although the team recovered and continued to play well, Bethany fell out of sync. Her coach benched her—"she was worthless to me on the field at that point"—and Bethany refused to talk to or look at anyone.

Barringer expected this. It was the usual with Bethany. He told me,

> When she messes up on the field, she will not talk to you. You can sit there and talk to her and say, "It's okay, you made a mistake, we want to get it better." She tunes you out. She's heaped so much criticism on herself. She's so uptight she cannot even hear what you're saying. She'll look at you and nod.

Bethany, her coach told me, was her own worst enemy. At this moment, he explained, "I lose her. That kid's lost."

When it comes to hearing that you've done something right or wrong, there seem to be clear sex differences. When girls fail, they blame their lack of ability, while boys figure that external factors—say, a windy day when they missed a tennis shot—were the culprits. More to the point, girls seem to let failure permeate within; they blame themselves, while boys let it roll off their backs. As a Division I women's soccer coach explained, if you tell a group of boys they're playing poorly, "the guys are turning to the guy next to him and saying, 'He's talking about you, you jerk!' Give the same speech to the girls," he said, "and they turn to each other and say, 'He's talking about me!'"

Girls may have a stronger reaction to criticism because of the type they receive. In a study, psychologist Carol Dweck found that while boys got more feedback than girls, it was different in kind from what girls heard. Boys were told to "calm down" or "work harder," comments easy to disregard. Girls, on the other hand, heard critiques related to ability, making it harder for them to discount. Some suspect this trend has led boys to develop thicker skin. Because girls get criticized less often but more deeply, they take it to heart.

Among peers, Good Girl mores provide little support for frank exchanges. Left to their own devices, girls don't spend much time exploring hard-to-hear truths; if they do, it's often of the "Do I look fat?" "Of course not!" variety. Boys, on the other hand, are more openly dominant with each other and comfortable with a rough-and-tumble exchange of demands, interruptions, threats, and refusals.

Criticism, especially when offered by peers, heaves a boulder into the still waters of equality that girls like to pretend exists. Good Girls, expected to be modest, caring, and humble, learn to avoid hierarchies of skill and ability. Criticism implies that one person is better at something than another, a dangerous prospect in a world that punishes girls for thinking they're "all that." Some girls contemptuously described feedback as a sly way of saying you were "better" than someone else. They did not say "better *at*," but "better *than*": they left the specific critique behind for the larger belief that "she thinks she's better than *me*."

For many girls, criticism is the knowledge that you have failed not just some*thing*, but some*one*. It feels like letting another person down, a violation of Good Girl rules. Zandra, a sophomore at the Girls Leadership Institute, said criticism from an adult made her "feel like I've made [someone] unhappy in some way and that I've upset them, and I, like, take it personally as something I'm doing wrong, and, like, I don't take it as I can do better. I take it more as, like, 'Oh, I did this wrong, how am I ever going to fix it?' type thing." Isabel's fear of disappointing others led her to refuse feedback outright. "You don't ever want to admit to yourself that I'm wrong. . . . Like, disappointing other people around you makes you so upset that you can't even handle it, so you just . . . can't admit you're wrong."

When individual performance becomes knotted up with approval from others, one ceases to develop independently. If a girl's reaction to failure is instant focus on someone else, it stands to reason that her life's pursuits may be equally burdened with this concern. Natalie, fourteen, loved basketball, but she lacked the aggressiveness on the court that would make the difference between good and great game. Her mother, also a coach (not Natalie's), explained,

> Her biggest thing is that she doesn't shoot the basketball. Because if she misses, it's devastating. She'd rather not shoot it and be told, "You need to shoot the ball," than take five shots, miss four, and be told, "You missed four out of five." . . . It's more devastating to her to be told, "You didn't do well when you tried," than saying, "You need to do it a little more often."

Natalie's fear of being corrected hemmed her in, preventing her from taking the risks crucial to changing her game. Her playing was as plainly marked by the need to please as it was by a faulty follow-through on her jump shot.

## SHE HATES ME

If girls believe that a mistake is a way to let someone down, they are equally likely to feel betrayed by their assessor. When girls take criticism personally, they interpret a comment about an *issue* as a sign that something is wrong with a *relationship*. "If you say something critical of me, it means you don't care about me," a school counselor explained. "They put that interpretation on it."

The classroom has always been a relational place, perhaps even more so now that teachers are expected to combine social-emotional learning with traditional methods of instruction. Teachers helm birthday celebrations, mediate peer conflict, and provide emotional support. Boundaries can blur. Carey, a high-school English teacher, said that "the whole school experience is personal. Girls especially spend so much time talking about their teachers, fantasizing about their teachers, imagining what they do outside of school. . . . That's the norm. 'I saw you on the bus, and this is what you were wearing and doing and reading.'" As the teacher-student dynamic strays from the professional to the personal, it can be easy for girls to default to what they know well: liking and being liked by others. The upshot is that what one does becomes inseparable from how well one is liked.

When I asked one sophomore to explain girls' sensitivity to feedback, she replied, "Girls are more like, 'I need to get good grades, I need everyone to like me, I need, like, everything. I need everyone to be nice to me.'" Notice how she conflated the *absence* of criticism with being *liked* and having others be *nice*. In this way the terms of her relationship with teachers and coaches become no different from what she seeks with other girls: conflict-free, "nice" relationship.

When girls interpret feedback as a personal conflict, their reactions can look a lot like retaliation. Carey told me that "there's definitely crying. There's giving the teacher the silent treatment and just being sullen and hurt and not participating and feeling that . . . *they've been betrayed by someone that they trusted*" (my italics). As another high-school English teacher told me, "When girls get a good grade, they say, 'I got an A.'" When they get a bad grade, they say, '*She gave me* a C.'" Many teachers described how girls simply stopped participating for a while after difficult feedback, interrupting their productivity. Others told me about middle-school girls ganging up on them with aggressive body language during class, and even holding long-term grudges. Feedback did not interrupt the participation of male students to the same extent, they said.

Theresa, a New Jersey school counselor, told me chunks of her days are spent counseling girls upset with teacher feedback. "They want me to do something about it. 'They gave me a bad grade,' or 'She hates me,' or 'She doesn't like me.' . . . They also have that almost arrogance about them—they're going to come tell me, and then I'm going to get the teacher in trouble." In these cases the girls almost regarded the teacher as a peer to incriminate.

To be sure, some girls used the "teacher hates me" defense as a way to avoid responsibility for a mistake. Said one freshman,

> I don't want to accept the responsibility that I did write badly and I did it at the last minute so I obviously didn't spend that much time on it. [Saying the teacher hates you] kind of gives you a reason to, like, push the feelings aside so you don't have to accept it, you just want to push it on them.

The decision that someone hates *you* makes it easy to deflect the content of feedback, creating an "us versus them" mentality that demonizes the teacher and releases the student from responsibility.

## ALL OR NOTHING: "I'M DOING SOMETHING REALLY WRONG"

When all-or-nothing thinking guides girls' response to criticism, the highest performers can be easily derailed. Lily was a thirteen-year-old blur of braces and verve. She was one of those "amazing" girls, her schedule swollen with activity and enrichment.

When asked to describe herself, Lily told me she was rarely corrected by adults. "I don't do bad things, I'm just Miss Perfect," she said. But with her self-esteem perilously balanced on her excellence, she could only interpret failure as catastrophic.

While counseling her on a project, a faculty adviser told Lily she wasn't spending enough time working after school with her team. Kindly but firmly, the teacher asked if Lily could try to make more time to work because of pending deadlines. The feedback crushed her.

Lily shared her thoughts with me after hearing from her adviser.

> This is bad, I'm doing something really wrong. . . . I was insecure and embarrassed when people were talking to me. I felt caught up in it. . . . I felt a little alone, like I was the only one they were giving criticism to. . . . I felt like a bad person.

Lily shamed herself when she made a mistake, becoming upset not only about her performance but about who she was as a human being: "It must mean that I was a bad person." She reached her heights at a steep internal price. Her Good Girl thinking forced her to walk an unforgiving line; one misstep would plummet her to the snapping jaws of failure.

Lily's sense of self was so dependent on appearing perfect that she could not tell the difference between a critique of an action and of her self. The impact on her productivity and focus was immediate. Overwhelmed by negative thoughts, she was unable to set positive goals and fix her problem. Her unreasonable expectations kept her shackled to failure, preventing her from shaking off a mistake and moving forward quickly.

And that's the rub: as we learned from the earlier observations of Bethany's coach, all-or-nothing thinking often worsens the performance of the girls who are so capable and driven. Brooke, an accomplished sophomore softball player, explained how "you're having a really great game or whatever, and then one thing goes wrong, and all of a sudden the other team is winning. All you can think about is that one thing that went wrong. That if it didn't happen, you would have won." Brooke said that even one mistake ruined the rest of her own game. To make matters worse, when she was at bat and didn't hit well or struck out, "[If] I don't get it, I feel like the whole team is so disappointed in me, and then that's all I can think about. I don't think about everything else that I did in the game that was good to help the team."

All-or-nothing thinking does not only manifest in emotional blasts. Caroline was whip-smart and serious, barely cracking a smile when the other girls laughed in workshop. When she wrote notes, she didn't sign them with smiley faces, hearts, X's and O's, or Love ya!"s. There were no girly frills, just "Caroline."

One day, in an uncharacteristic moment of openness, she told me, "My friends and family are scared to confront me, because I'm so good at denying stuff. It separates me from them."

Caroline explained that when anyone tried to confront her, she projected indifference or cracked a joke. She told them, as she said, "Yeah, whatever." Later she told me, "I cannot be criticized about how I interact with people. . . . [If someone does,] I will be like, 'Oh, okay, please leave me alone so I can cry now.'" Either way, she told me, "I think both responses make me look like a jerk to a certain extent."

I introduced Caroline in the last chapter. She refused to apologize to friends because she feared the implications of being "wrong": her mistakes, she was certain, would make her unlikable. Interpersonal criticism so overwhelmed Caroline that it caused her to shut down completely. Rather than react to it, she simply removed herself.

Now the lessons of Caroline's social life had become the template for her academic relationships: what began as the refusal to apologize to friends was now the refusal to meet with concerned teachers. When exams came back with disappointing grades, she told me, "I can't go over the problems, because I can't sit there and say, 'I got number fifteen wrong, I got this wrong.'"

I asked her why.

"I can't do that, because by just looking at my percentage, I've already unleashed an entire self-criticism. I just have to put it away or it will never end."

In Caroline's all-or-nothing approach to life, she hit every ball out of the park or struck out. She ruthlessly evaluated her self and her behavior. "If [I make a joke and] someone doesn't completely pee their pants laughing,

I'm like completely depressed the rest of the day. I'm like, 'Oh my God, they hate me, they think I'm, like, the weirdest person ever.' Everything [I do] that could be perceived as a little weird or less than amazing, it just seemed horrible to me." The same now applied to her schoolwork; one mistake and she had to flee, lest a teacher discover the full extent of what she was sure was her own mediocrity.

Girls who respond to feedback defensively appear to shirk the significance of their behavior, but the internal scene is dramatically different. When your self-concept rides on being seen as flawless, being wrong isn't an option. Ironically, Caroline's anxiety about her limitations prevented her from correcting the mistakes that haunted her. Denial surrounded Caroline like a moat, keeping her from reaching multiple areas of potential, locking her into vigilant, but ultimately circuitous, self-examination.

All-or-nothing thinking is a problem of perspective. Caroline and Lily look at their failures through distorted funhouse mirrors: the specter of the Good Girl they believe they must become is grossly enlarged, dwarfing the space in which they can comfortably be themselves, struggling, as we all do, with new challenges. When they fail, the girls speak to themselves, punishingly, in the voice of the Good Girl they have betrayed. The Good Girl voice pries Caroline and Lily away from their real, flawed selves, whispering that who they are isn't Good enough.

Girls like Caroline and Lily are constantly performing, as much for the Good Girl they think they should be as for the adults and peers who look on. They have spent their lives growing internally dependent on external rewards: pats on the back, A's, club presidencies, Most Valuable Player trophies. They become more concerned with how they appear and should be than with who they are. What others think and feel replaces what is true for them.

If they had the mental space to consider their own thoughts and feelings, Caroline and Lily could begin to know what each wants and expects for herself. I have seen more than a few girls discover their voices only to realize that they actually didn't want to do gymnastics four times a week or ride a bus every other weekend to a daylong debate tournament. Alternatively, some girls find that when their pursuits belong to them, and not others, they can face their mistakes with more balance and compassion. This kind of self-awareness is a form of ownership and personal responsibility over one's life. It is the real stuff of a strong self. It can buffer girls against the Good Girl voice and, eventually, drown it out.

# PARENTS

Girls do not develop their responses to criticism in a vacuum. Parents seem less willing than ever to abide an ordinary, mistake-making child. This shift in the culture is leaving its mark on how all children handle criticism, as pressure to overachieve turns feedback into a moment of failure rather than opportunity. Like a storm front, Good Girl pressure is mixing with what psychologist Wendy Mogel calls an "outbreak of specialness," where parents are satisfied only if their children are gifted and exceptional (or diagnosed with a treatable problem that the right pill cocktail can restore to excellence).

The culture of specialness prevents an organic pursuit of learning for all children. The price, as one teacher put it, is that "some students are just not focused on growing from the feedback and getting better. They're just focusing on the numerical [grade]." Psychologically, Carey, the English teacher, told me, "they often feel that if they try what they think is their best and don't see the results they want, they've failed." More and more, parents measure success by ends, not means—and so do their children.

Parents' investment in excellence has made them major players in the minutiae of their children's lives. Some parents, under the guise of being advocates, have become aggressive toward the teachers and coaches who criticize their children. In my interviews I heard stories of belligerent phone calls to schools; assurances to girls that they were right, the teacher or coach did in fact hate them (or was wrong, unqualified, or both); and informal campaigns to ensure that parents of younger students kept their children out of the offending adult's class or team the following year. Parents of both sexes are involved, but girls' sensitivity to criticism may make parents of girls a stronger presence.

Educators used to offset their modest wages with a large helping of public respect. Not so anymore. An English teacher told me wistfully, "When we were in school, if something was wrong, it was you. You were wrong."

Now, a thirty-six-year veteran told me, "The parents come back at us. When we started teaching, that just didn't happen. You were considered professional, and if my opinion about your paper was this, that was accepted because I'm the teacher and I'm the professional. And now it's everything is second-guessed." Many teachers, especially those in more affluent communities, believe they are treated no better than a customer-service representative at a store. They are selling a product, and the parents are paying customers. When the parents aren't happy, they complain. Their children watch and learn.

Parents who challenge the professional expertise of teachers and coaches teach their children to disregard authority when it doesn't meet their goals or satisfaction. When girls come home distraught, their emotional version of events is often absorbed by parents as a definitive account. At a midwestern public school, a teacher who also coaches explained,

> If I call in a student, a senior, and say, "You are struggling right now. If you don't get your grades up, you could fail," I get a parent phone call. "Why are you telling my daughter that she's dumb?" "She's failing the class," I say. Or "Why are you telling my daughter she's not any good at volleyball? Or basketball?" I say, "Well, I didn't tell her that. This is what I told her."

It doesn't matter what she says, the teacher told me. "Constructive criticism is, in my experience, immediately turned into negative criticism. The kids go home, tell the parents, and Mom and Dad are knocking on my office door, or I get a phone call."

Minka, a middle-school teacher, recalled a parent whose daughter was upset by the comments on her paper. "She feels like you hate her, so she's not going to discuss this with you. So how can I help her be a better writer?" she recalled the woman saying. "I'm thinking the first thing you can do as a parent to help her be a better writer is to help her get past the fact that she thinks these comments are about her as a person or her character or about how I feel about her in any way," Minka told me wryly. "These comments are strictly about her sentences." But the mother was firmly committed to her daughter's version of events. In moments like these, parents cease to be partners with teachers and coaches. They become unthinking agents of their upset children, indelibly marking the parent-teacher/coach relationship with mistrust and tension.

In his book *The Optimistic Child,* Dr. Martin Seligman argues that parents who try to fix their children's problems in the name of building self-esteem teach lessons in helplessness. When a parent shields his daughter from the conversation she should be having with the teacher herself, the lesson she learns is this: "When things don't go as you want, give up and let someone else rescue you."

When they erupt emotionally to negative feedback, parents eclipse their daughters' opportunity to practice a more rational response. As children learn to walk, parents grasp the importance of modeling a healthy response to failure: meeting a toddler's tumble with a look of fear signals danger and causes the child to cry, while a calm reaction gets baby back on her feet. The same prescription could be suggested for helping girls deal with feedback. A parent who lets emotions guide his response prioritizes his own feelings over the obligation to teach a child how to handle stress.

When parents go around the teacher to call a colleague or a superior, they model a toxic recipe of indirect conflict and disrespect for authority. As a school counselor in New Jersey told me, "[Parents] will criticize everything from grades to a comment a teacher has made in class. The interesting thing is, I say, 'Have you talked to the teacher about this?' 'Well, no, that's what my daughter says.' 'That's what my son says.'"

The sensitivity of girls and their parents to criticism is affecting how teachers and coaches teach. Many educators paused suddenly when I asked if girls or parents influenced their feedback. Some clearly hadn't considered the question until that moment, but others looked downright guilty. It was apparently the first time anyone had pointed to the elephant in their classrooms: many of them were showing girls the kid gloves, ensuring that they would continue to struggle with feedback.

"I think [my summary comments on English papers] are much more peppy than they should be," Debbie, a teacher at a girls' private school, told me. "The comments become more gentle, more enthusiastic." Her feedback was once so timid that a parent read her child's paper, along with Debbie's comments, and asked how Debbie could possibly call the paper "good work." "Maybe I sometimes went too far," she concluded.

With girls, a middle-school coach told me, "you'd spend a little more time, you know, cushioning their emotions." Patty, a middle-school teacher in her fifties, said,

> I feel like a lot of times I'm tiptoeing around. I'm thinking beforehand, you know, how am I going to word this, definitely give them positive feedback before I get to the criticism or suggestion. And then I question myself whether I am doing them a favor or not by, you know, tiptoeing around the issue. Not just being more up front and direct.

Susan, another middle-school teacher, said, "Before I start that criticism, I would think in my mind very quickly how to phrase it, whereas [with] a boy it would be, 'Sit down! What is this?!' . . . With a boy I can just hand it back and say, 'Do it!'" The teachers' acute awareness of differential treatment, though concerning, also suggested they were invested in changing the dynamic.

Some teachers said their anxiety about aggressive parents had softened their feedback as much for boys as for girls. "Once you write something down, that's when a phone call can potentially come," Carey told me. "Teachers are afraid to critique as much as they want to and or should, because there's a fear of repercussions for them from parents." Teachers' nerves are on edge while they're grading a paper: a Boston teacher told me that, with certain students, "I'm thinking, how is the parent going to react to this grade, and you know, I already have my case. I'm just grading a test, and I know what's right and I know what's wrong, but somehow it's become this emotional thing."

In her book *The Price of Privilege,* psychologist Madeline Levine describes an epidemic of young patients buckling under the stress of adolescence. Their families were not struggling, nor were her patients victims of trauma or abuse. The parents were affluent, professional, and high-achieving, and they frantically protected their children from challenge or disappointment. The adolescents, meanwhile, were disconnected, passive, and alarmingly vulnerable to depression and anxiety. Affluent teens, she concludes, had become a new at-risk population.

The pressure to achieve, along with parental overinvolvement and a lack of discipline, had "impoverished" the teens' internal lives. Their focus on others' approval was suffocating the teens' ability to "find the time, both literal and psychological, to linger in internal exploration: a necessary precursor to a well-developed sense of self," she writes.

Levine illuminates a central paradox of development: that in order to become our best self, we need to learn how to fail at that very task. The Curse of the Good Girl suggests the opposite: girls must spring full-blown from the head of Zeus as their best selves, with no stops along the way. This brutally inflexible set of rules now intermingles dangerously with the advent of the "helicopter parent," creating two powerful cultural forces prying girls away from organic self-development.

I recently worked with Monica and Peri, a mother and daughter from New Jersey who told me about a horseback-riding lesson that made Peri want to quit riding. The instructor had been hard on her, and since then, Monica confided, she stood watch at every lesson Peri had. "I mean, [the instructor] was pretty *abusive*," Monica told me urgently, though she had not seen the class in question.

When I asked how Peri was being helped by her mother's hovering presence at the ring, Monica said, "She wants me there. It makes her feel better." As we talked more about Peri's history with feedback, Monica suddenly said, "Well, she *does* sometimes say that I'm yelling at her when I'm not, or that a teacher did when I know that didn't happen."

Monica wanted to know what I thought. I told her what I've told many, many parents: You have a tough choice when it comes to helping your child deal with misfortune. You can solve the problem of hard-to-hear feedback by fighting with the teacher or undermining the coach, giving you the immediate, short-term satisfaction of alleviating your child's pain. But you risk paying a long-term cost—raising a child who can't cope with criticism on her own.

I won't make any bones about it: the alternative is much harder. Remaining compassionate while letting a child's pain run its course can be excruciating, especially if you're worried that a coach's benching her or a low grade will endanger her eligibility for a reward. But you collect your reward later in the form of a daughter who knows her limits and therefore herself, who has experience dealing actively with her own failure, and who understands, in a real, lived way, that mistakes do not define her potential or her self.

Success is built on a paradox: the more concerned about failing we become, the less we are able to achieve. Good Girl perfection is success with a ceiling. Its pursuit offers little room for the risk and adventure that yield exhilarating leaps in growth.

*Five*

# GIRL MEETS WORLD: BREAKING THE GOOD GIRL GLASS CEILING

The Curse of the Good Girl is compromising assertive self-expression in the classroom and on sports fields. It's not that girls aren't participating, but rather the way they are doing it, that is cause for concern. Three social customs that emerge from Good Girl pressure—the belief that conflict is personal and ends relationship, the injunction against claiming one's strengths, and the indirect aggression girls are infamous for—have formed a blueprint guiding girls' day-to-day participation in school and sports.

In their survey, Miss Hall's School for Girls found that girls defined "leadership in terms of friendship"—that is, they applied the rules of friendship across a wide range of challenging situations, often compromising their values and personal authority in order to maintain relationships. When girls import the mores of their social lives into formative learning experiences, they cross a Rubicon: what begins as a private, social phenomenon comes to define public pursuits and potential.

For instance, the social belief that conflict is personal and destructive is stifling vigorous self-expression in school. Many girls feel anxious about engaging in classroom debates or having the wrong answer because of possible relational consequences. Second, the fear of appearing conceited or "all that," a socially dangerous and punishable infraction, has seamlessly entered girls' nonsocial lives. To avoid coming on too strong, girls adopt self-defeating postures and phrases when they express ideas. They are also unable or unwilling to articulate their strengths. Finally, the rumors and indirect aggression that dominate girls' social conflicts are regularly used to address problems on sports teams. Although girls' indirect aggression of course occurs in other extracurricular settings, such as clubs and associations, I focus in this chapter on girls' athletic experiences.

The terms of success in middle and high school make it easy to overlook these developing proclivities. For example, class participation may be part of most grading rubrics, but debate rarely is. Nor is the ability to resolve conflict directly or speak with confidence about one's talents. Excellence can be had by Good Girls who study late into the night for exams, raise their hands when they know the right answer, and play their corner of the field with aplomb. But a Good Girl performance, while earning top marks, does not build the muscles for skills that will be required for distinction later on.

At present, too many girls fly beneath the radar by pulling straight A's without ever learning how to speak with authority, own their gifts, or resolve conflicts in healthy ways. As accomplished as middle- and high-school girls may appear, their performance is often Good masquerading as Great.

This migration of habits is a warning, smoke rising from the horizon of girls' futures. The Good Girl pressure that undermines girls' strength in personal relationships will continue its destructive sprawl in adulthood. Sports teams and classrooms are the closest girls get to "professional" environments, making them training grounds for developing leadership skills. Yet they can just as easily become places where girls learn habits that limit them as adults. It is here that the glass ceiling may begin taking shape and where the Curse of the Good Girl can become a way of life. To help girls go from Good Girls to Real Girls, we must redefine the measure of success.

## CONFLICT IS ALWAYS PERSONAL

At well-manicured public high schools teeming with college-bound young women, girls told me about the high cost of speaking their minds in class. They portrayed self-expression as risky, if not dangerous. If what they said was wrong, hurt someone's feelings, or led to disagreement, there could be personal consequences. As a result, girls were censoring themselves and their ideas.

The personalization of classroom conflict is testament to the overarching importance of relationship in girls' lives. The disruption of interpersonal connection can bring a girl's life to an abrupt halt, disabling her ability to concentrate on school and to function generally. The fear of losing relationship drives many girls' social decisions, leading them to suppress their strongest beliefs in favor of preserving connection. The same seems to be true in the classroom: the fear of loss is defining some girls' academic decisions, causing them to withhold their opinions in favor of keeping the waters calm. "It really matters," an eighth-grader said,

> when you're arguing against a popular person, because then you don't want to hurt their feelings or you don't want to look like you're trying to compete against them to get . . . to, like, make yourself look better. But you sort of want to get your point across. But you have to make sure, like, you get it across without trying to hurt anyone else.

Speaking was less about making a point than a carefully considered negotiation. Opinions were potentially aggressive, waves in the waters that girls worked so hard to keep still.

Strong ideas, whether personal or academic, signal difference, poison to girls desperate to fit in. Stand out in class, one seventh-grader said, and you worry "that everyone would talk about me, that everyone would not want to be with me." As girls come to believe that ideas have relational consequences, their fear can harden into silence. "If you say something and you know your friends are not going to like it, you don't want to say it, even though you think it's, like, really important to you," an eighth-grader confided.

High-school girls spoke less dramatically about conflict in the classroom but were clear to show how it limited their participation. Heated debates could mean more than a lively exchange of ideas. A junior explained,

> Like, if [someone is] talking about something and I say something, I would be afraid that other people would have, like, a whole opinion of me, and that's why they won't want to talk to me, because of one thing I said. That's why I'm very careful of what I say, because I don't want people to get the wrong impression.

You could be on perfectly good terms with someone, she told me, but a disagreement could cause a person to say, "Oh, well, you're a horrible person for saying that, and I can't believe you said that, and I hate you now." In this student's mind, if people disagreed with her ideas, it would mean they did not like her. Disagreement over an issue was tantamount to a broken relationship. This student was not learning to develop her ideas for the sake of intellectual growth and exchange. Her lessons in public self-expression were occurring through the filter of who might be watching and what others might say.

Girls are renowned team players who excel at group work. Less often discussed is their tendency to pick up others' slack silently, choosing to shoulder most of a group's workload rather than challenge an idle peer. "You don't want to hurt their feelings by saying something. I don't know, you don't want to tell them what to do," one sophomore told me. "Because I just think in friendship you want to make it as equal as possible." According to this rather warped Good Girl logic, equality could be achieved if no one told anyone what to do—even as one person did all the work.

When girls apply the rules of friendship to their work experiences, delegation becomes impossible, even as they carry the loads of entire groups. By automatically labeling peers "friends," conflict immediately defaults to a personal problem. The chain of command required for effective task execution is shunned, and personal authority is subordinated to relationship. As one middle-schooler put it, "I'd rather do the work than have a fight."

Silent workhorses rationalize their sacrifice with the belief that they can do the job better than everyone else. One freshman said that "I do everything, and it's, like, really awful sometimes, because I don't even give people a chance, but I feel like you're going to mess it up." Many of these girls reported being paired with less-talented students by their teachers, who seemed to intuit the girls' willingness to do the work of two.

It is hardly a coincidence that corporate women typically suffer the same pair of problems: Known to stay late at the office, they finish up the work of others long gone, too "nice" to tell their colleagues that a late night is required. They soothe themselves by believing that perfect work done alone is better than the decent work of an imperfect group. As business experts have noted, these women usually neglect other responsibilities, such as informal networking at restaurants and parties, to get their late-night work done. They stagnate in middle management. They are Good but never Great.

Traditional hierarchy is certainly not the only or even the most effective way to accomplish a goal. Many women and girls prefer balanced distributions of power in which there is no fixed leader, every opinion is considered, and control is shared. The findings on such ventures are mixed, with efficiency often frustrated in "leaderless" groups. Regardless of their merits, and despite what females may prefer, fluency in both leadership styles will be crucial for girls to reach their potential.

AT THEIR BEST, CLASSROOMS HUM WITH INVIGORATING VOL- leys of questions, answers, and debate. Participation is not about just getting it right, but about thinking on your feet, taking a risk, and throw- ing your idea into the mix. For many girls, raising a hand may not be a quick-thinking response, but rather the end of an invisible process of mulling, wondering, strategizing, and worrying. A junior named Melissa explained,

> I'll overanalyze my point in my head, and then I just won't say anything, because I'll be so worried that what I'm going to say people are going to attack and attack my opinion. . . . Sometimes I get so wrapped up in, you know, like if there's someone in the class whose opinion I don't want to disagree with, then I just won't talk.

Melissa frequently lost pace with her class. The obstacles she overcame to speak made her class participation rehearsed and unspontaneous. Good Girl pressure led her to weigh the value of her own voice against those of her peers; for Melissa, speaking up was like running a race with a heavy backpack, while others, who participated freely, ran ahead unburdened. As she imported her social fear of conflict into classroom discussion, Melissa was not acquiring the skills to think on her feet. Instead she was learning to ruminate, deferring to the voice in her head, articulating her ideas too late, if at all.

Melissa also worried that her answer might be wrong, a common anx- iety among girls and women. Being right is being Good: it means follow- ing the rules and fitting in. On the surface, the fear of being wrong seems to be the discrete, personal worry of a driven individual. Yet as we saw in the last chapter, girls' quest for perfection is as much about their need to appear that way to others. Being wrong is making a mess someone else has to clean up, and that makes girls feel exposed and selfish. As with being involved in a social conflict, girls believe that a wrong answer can make you different or less liked in someone else's mind.

Girls' obsession with flawlessness is therefore almost beside the point; the real issue is how they displace concern for their own performance with what others might be thinking of it. Emma, a self-identified "recovering perfectionist," said, "I had a conversation with my friends over this. If you, like, answer the question in class, you will, like, think about that comment, like, two days after that. You will keep on replaying it in your head, pick apart what parts you thought were incorrect. Did I sound stupid? Did I say a word too much, was I too loud?" Emma was less concerned with the content of her answer than with the superficial style of her presentation. Her attention was consumed by the Good Girl rules she might or might not have broken.

Vanessa, a Division I college soccer player, recalled how the need to be right manifested on the playing field in high school. Two of her teammates were talented, but "they never opened their mouths, because they didn't want to make a mistake. They always played it safe. They never yelled at anyone, because they didn't want to be yelled back at. They wanted to be an all-around good person. . . ." The measure of success—of being an "all-around good person"—was the uninterrupted quiet of others' approval.

The fear of error sandbags girls to the firmest ground of their thinking. Determined to be right, they shy away from risks and play it safe. Psychologist Roni Cohen-Sandler describes such girls as inhibited "from experimenting, trying out ideas, and making discoveries," and as people who did not "get to test out their skills or courage." Ironically, as the horizon of their thinking shrinks, failure grows even more ominous, mostly because it has become so unfamiliar. A high-school senior told me,

"You're so used to not asking stupid questions or always knowing the right answer, . . . when you fail it's a lot more pressure, it's a lot more upsetting."

When the muscles to speak atrophy, the muscles to think may follow. Thirteen-year-old Kayleigh returned to GLI for a second year and was unaccountably quiet. The summer before, she had been effervescent in workshops. Seventh grade had changed her, and I took her aside. "I've gotten in the habit of not thinking about things as much," she said calmly. "I know I should say more, but I'm worried people will judge me. I'm not thinking in workshop as much as I could be. If I was thinking more, I would actually have more ideas." Good Girl pressure was diverting Kayleigh's thoughts from reflection about ideas to worry about others. Watching herself through others' eyes, she underwent a troubling reversal of cognitive flow: instead of meditating on her internal experience, she had become fixated on the people around her.

Psychologists Carol Gilligan and Lyn Mikel Brown observed similar patterns as they heard "I don't know" creeping into adolescent girls' answers to their interview questions. The fear of losing relationship had led to what a colleague called an intentional "repression of knowledge." In fact, Kayleigh's concern for others did not sit alongside her actual thoughts. It had eclipsed them.

## IT'S NOT WHAT YOU SAY, IT'S HOW YOU SAY IT

When they do speak in class, girls lean on an assemblage of self-defeating behaviors to lessen the power of their words. These patterns of speech and gesture cluster unconsciously in girls' sentences like a virus, sanding the edges off convictions. They dumb down or invalidate whatever is said, not to mention the speaker herself.

For ten years I have watched girls turn statements into questions by inflecting up with their voices: "I think Martin Luther King was nonviolent? Because he believed in civil disobedience?" This makes the speaker appear uncertain and even afraid, ready to abandon her idea at a moment's notice. The volume of girls' comments is frequently unstable, peaking at the beginning of a sentence and sliding into whispery nothingness near an idea's end.

Girls regularly open their statements with apologies and disclaimers like, "I'm not sure if this is right," questioning their opinions before even expressing them. "Kind of," "sort of," and "like" gather like dust in girls' statements, including the ones in this book, obscuring their true force. Even the seemingly innocuous "I was just going to say that . . ." makes girls appear less entitled to participate, as though sneaking in sentences through a side door.

Then there is the body language: I frequently observe girls twisting hair coquettishly, covering mouths, lowering heads, and holding themselves in poses that resemble those of reedy girls in magazines: tiny, nonthreatening, cute. All this while answering a question in class discussion, reading aloud, or giving a presentation.

These behaviors seem ornamental but are central to girls' self-expression. Verbal genuflection ensures that girls know their place and do not take up too much of it. It weaves a cloak of Good Girl modesty around speakers, allowing them to participate without coming off as too smart or too self-accepting. Appearing to like yourself, after all, is an eight ball in girls' social universe. Demeaning yourself among friends (*I'm so ugly, I'm so stupid*) is de rigueur, but self-confidence is a punishable offense.

This rule of social conduct has now crossed over into the classroom. Diana, a sophomore, summed up the comments of many girls I met. "With girls, you can't be confident in an idea, because other girls will think, 'Oh, she's so proud of herself, she thinks she's amazing.'" Jenny, also a sophomore and a vigorous class participant, self-monitored constantly

Self-Defeating Statements include introductory phrases such as:

- Disclaimers ("I'm not sure if this is right, but . . . ," or "This is probably totally wrong, but . . .")
- Apologies ("I just wanted to say that . . .")
- Declarations of uncertainty ("I guess I . . .")

Sprinkling speech with:

- Diminishers ("kind of . . ." "I mean . . ." "like . . ." "sort of . . ." "you know . . .")

. . . and ending speech with:

- Inflections that make statements sound like questions ("Holden Caulfield was really depressed? And he was a rebellious teenager?")
- Attempts to find agreement (". . . do you know what I mean?" . . . "don't you think?" . . . "you know?" . . . "okay?" . . . "right?")
- Sentences that lose volume and become inaudible

. . . and putting yourself or abilities down:

- "I'm so stupid."
- "I failed that test" or "I'm going to fail that test."

Self-Defeating Gestures include:

- Playing with hair
- Hands hovering around the mouth
- Slouching (admittedly universal in young people, but it suppresses the voice)

when she spoke. "I'll be, like, did I sound too pushy with [my answer]? Like, am I trying? I meant to just say it, but people might think I'm trying to persuade it, like your ideas are wrong. Yeah, like snobby, like you're wrong and I'm right." These niggling anxieties pressure girls to turn passionate, distinctive opinions into run-of-the-mill, indifferent remarks.

It is often suggested that boys cause this withering of strength, but I rarely teach boys, and I still see it. That's worth noting, since girls' struggles in school are mostly taken out of boys' hides. When present, boys do have an effect. Girls spoke bitterly about the spectacle of a peer acting ditzy for male attention. It's harder, a sophomore told me, "to stick by what you feel if other people are playing dumb and getting a positive response." The attention cut both ways. A junior said she was labeled a feminist by boys when she took a "strong stance." "Feminist," of course, was cutting code for unfemale, lesbian, or loser.

Women with indirect speaking styles may still be confident, effective, and well liked. However, when girls habitually lace their speech with disclaimers, they are not learning to take a stand. They always seem on the fence, neither believable nor confident. And even if girls are internally intact, the importance of appearances can hardly be overlooked.

Typically, it's not how you say it but what you say that is the measure of success at school; similarly, on the average sports team, it's what you do but not how you do it that makes a Most Valuable Player. This is, simply put, a mistake. Especially where girls are concerned, the delivery of an idea should be evaluated along with the idea itself. As girls become women, being right will only get them so far. Far more likely that it will be about timing: where, when, and how an idea is proposed. In the daily mix of a workplace, the right answer becomes less clear-cut, and opinions carry more weight. If your delivery fails to instill the trust and confidence of your peers, all the right answers in the world will get you only so far.

It follows that if you're not allowed to sound smart, you're not allowed to *say* you're smart either. Girls habitually demean their own abilities in self-put-downs, the most common of which are "I'm so stupid" and some variation on "I just totally bombed (or am going to bomb) this exam." These comments provide insurance for the sticky circumstances of success. "If you don't bomb it, people are happy for you," my sixteen-year-old intern explained, "and if you do, you get sympathy."

Like the self-put-downs of girls' social universe, these comments can be indirect pleas for compliments. In the classroom or on the playing field, however, they become pronouncements of weakness.

A middle-school English teacher at an elite all-girls school assigned her class an essay in which each student would outline her talents and best qualities. Uproar ensued. "I have never had such a chorus of rebellion and resistance to a topic," the teacher told me. "They felt like they were bragging. They felt like they were being snobby. They felt like they were showing off." She told the students the paper would be private; no one would have to read it aloud. They refused. "They still could not do a 'celebration of me.'" The girls were so distraught that the teacher never did the exercise again.

When I first began asking girls and women to say what they liked about themselves, I often heard responses such as "I like my hair" or "I like my eyes." I wised up, telling them they couldn't answer the question with a body part. On a hot day at the Girls Leadership Institute, twelve middle-school girls answered the question, and a curious thing happened.

"I like that I am a good friend."

"I like that I care about other people's problems."

"I like that I am loyal to others."

"I like that I can read others' emotions well."

"I like that I am open to others."

One girl said she liked that she was a good soccer player. Another girl said she liked that she was fun. Most of these girls, however, spoke their strengths in terms of their relationships.

This was no coincidence. Being a friend and taking care of others were the safest strengths the girls could claim. To say they excelled at being liked, or liking others, stationed them squarely in Good Girl territory. That these girls were overwhelmingly unable to say, "I'm a great singer" or "I am an honest person"—that they could describe their worth only in terms of relationship but not of self—suggested they were consciously avoiding owning their assets as individuals.

There is, of course, nothing wrong with claiming caregiving as a skill. The problem comes when that's all that girls can claim and when they don't feel permission, or know how, to say anything else. The ability to talk about your skills is vital to professional success, beginning as early as the college interview process. Later, when you are being interviewed for a job, the person hiring you wants to know why she should pick you over someone else. What makes you special? Why should you have this job? According to Peggy Klaus, author of *Brag! The Art of Tooting Your Own Horn Without Blowing It,* professional women who did *not* toot their own horns got fewer plum assignments and promotions. They saw setbacks in referrals, work schedules, and salary.

The inability to own one's strengths is, paradoxically, partly responsible for girls' dramatic responses to criticism. It's simple: if you can't say what's good about yourself, it's that much harder to cope with your failures. Challenges, after all, are best faced with positive self-talk. Make a mistake and you can tell yourself, "I'll try again, I'm smart, hardworking, and determined. I can do this." But if you cannot speak highly of yourself, it will be harder to encourage yourself internally or to cushion the blow of bad news. With no balance of positive and negative in your head, the negative easily drowns out the positive, and it's that much harder to pull yourself out of the mud.

At almost every workshop I have ever taught on this subject, at least one girl takes umbrage. "I know what I'm good at," she usually says. "I just don't need to tell other people. I am confident quietly." In a way, she is telling me that she can be herself *inside* and that she doesn't much care if she has to be careful around others. What she feels is what counts.

Which seems to beg the question, is a self truly authentic if it cannot be itself in the presence of others?

What troubles me about this girl's complaint is her hope that she might comfortably splinter her self. That is, her desire to be "confident quietly" is actually a subtle wish to keep her true self private while showing a safer, dimmed version to the world. She also assumes that this careful negotiation of real and fake, public and private, will keep her in control of how others view her. The hope that others will see her for who she really is, no matter what she actually reveals, is a naïve and utterly Good Girl prayer.

In reality, the person we show to the world inevitably influences others' perceptions of us. We are always dynamically connected to the people around us, whether we want to be or not. The first impressions of our actions and comments tell people plainly how we want to be treated, who we are, and what we are capable of. Even if girls frequently dwell in assumption and second-guessing, this does not mean that the rest of the world does. It is precisely the belief that people will "see the real me" that fuels the silence of adult women who do not advocate for themselves in the workplace and who wait—and keep waiting—for others to do it for them.

## ODD GIRL OUT ON THE FIELD

I was a four-sport-a-year jock, a veritable poster child for Title IX. Most afternoons you could find me slinging a fastball or a foul shot. Sports were my daily inoculation against Ophelia. I learned to take risks, deal with failure, and use my voice.

But something happened on my teams that we never discussed. We went to an away game, there was an incident—say, a player thought a teammate was being condescending on the field—and everyone got back on the bus. It was dark as midnight by five-thirty, and the usually male coach rode up front, dozing and clueless. Five rows back, all hell quietly broke loose, girl style.

As it happened, the story did not belong only to me. The girls I interviewed described settling their athletic conflicts the same way they handled hallway and online flare-ups: with the indirect, painful aggression I documented in *Odd Girl Out*. By now this should hardly be surprising: if girls apply the rules of friendship to their public lives, the darker habits of female intimacy will likely follow.

Sports teams present the closest facsimile of a workplace girls will get: you are not there (primarily) to socialize, you have to go every day (or almost), you have a job to do, and you are not friends with everyone. When girls import "mean girl" behavior into sports, they are essentially learning to use these tactics to resolve work-related conflicts. When tactics become habits, they will form the basis for girls' approach to a wide range of nonsocial problems.

Sometimes it can be as simple as refusing to pass someone the ball. A high-school sophomore explained how it worked on her soccer team. When one girl becomes the target of a teammate's anger,

> they can intentionally make her look bad on the field by, like, we'll pass her the soccer ball and it's a perfectly good pass, but somehow they'll make it so she'll mess up. They'll bump her or they'll trip her, like, they'll make it spin so that when she touches it, it flies off, and then they'll be, like, "God, why'd you do that? You had a perfect shot!"

Thus exposed in front of the coach, these girls lost playing time as a result.

Some girls use the sports field to settle social scores that begin at school. A high-school lacrosse player sought revenge on behalf of her sister, who was in conflict with another player. The angry player tried to get her teammates to hate the other girl, refused to pass her the ball, and pegged the ball at her head. "The practice got nowhere," an observing teammate told me. "It just ruined it."

That road can run both ways. "If you confront someone or if you get in a fight with someone [on the field], they have friends—that person will go talk to her friends and say, 'Don't talk to her, she's a bitch, because her and I got in a fight on the field. Her and I got in a fight during dance class.' So that way it will turn into something more than just the two of you." Conflicts move freely between classrooms and locker rooms.

The cost of importing social tactics into athletic life can be steep. Some middle-school coaches said they believed that girls compromised wins, as one put it, "to make their point." These coaches spent as much time helping teammates find common ground as they did running plays. Peace was a prerequisite for performance; in its absence, trust was a casualty. "It'll make it hard for us to, like, become a team, become one, because there's always someone they're putting down or taking out of the group," a cheerleader explained. Vanessa, the Division I soccer player, said trust was the most important thing in women's sports. "If you can't trust your team, you can't play with each other."

Despite the party line that sports are a panacea for adolescent female ills, athletics are actually fertile territory for girl conflict. Sports teams do not just challenge Good Girl norms, they turn them on their heads. The best players assert themselves in high-pressure situations, yelling for balls, asking for help, and telling others where to go and what to do. In the heat of the moment, players leave Good Girl airspace.

Vanessa has spent most of her life struggling to negotiate the friction between the pressure to be Good and her mission to become a great athlete. She has been punished by teammates in subtle and profound ways. "It's completely different for guys," she explained. "Once they're on the field, they yell at each other, they get pissed off, and off the field they're friends again." With girls, she told me, "it's always carried on and off the field. . . . If someone yells at them to get into a certain position, they take it personally and are like, 'Stop yelling at me.' They're upset."

For this reason, Linda, a middle-school coach, actually urged her players to think of themselves as having two identities: girl and athlete. "When I pick my team," she told me, "I would say to them, very forthright, 'You're not a girl, you're an athlete. And I expect you to be an athlete. I expect you to come out here, I expect you to play the game, I expect you to do things a certain way.'" Focused not just on what her team did but on how they did it, Linda created a crucial second set of expectations for players, accounting for the intangible Good Girl pressure that was keeping them from becoming great. Although it may seem as if she believed that "girl" and "athlete" were mutually exclusive, I do not think she meant it that way. She was trying to expose the places where "girl" and "athlete" diverged and demarcate a different set of norms for the girls' athletic experiences.

THE RULES OF GIRL WORLD FOLLOW GIRLS FROM THE CLASS-room and sports field into their public lives at work. In her bestselling book *Play Like a Man, Win Like a Woman: What Men Know About Success That Women Need to Learn*, Gail Evans observed intense anxiety in corporate women who made mistakes. Playing it safe, they spoke only when certain they had the right answer. Evans also heard women diminishing their strength verbally, speaking "softly," "timidly," and "without authority or power." When it came to arguments among male colleagues, it was "a good fight, something strong, dignified, something that has rules." Conflicts among women were verboten. When they did happen, she writes, "the rules [went] out the window." These gender-specific habits, Evans writes, prevented women from winning at the corporate game.[1]

What ails professional women hardly materializes out of thin air on the first day of work. Visit any middle or high school in America and you can observe these phenomena in girls right now. Girls' reputation for academic excellence belies the accumulation of troubling habits of self-expression. Left unchecked, these habits will harden into glass ceilings later on.

The synchronicity between girls and women is both a part of the problem and its solution. That is, if girls learn these habits from women teaching them how to be female, our strategy for girls' empowerment demands a focus not just on the lessons being learned but on who is teaching them.

# Six

# MY DAUGHTER, MYSELF

In the search for answers about girls' plummeting self-esteem, talk typically turns to the culture: a cabal of anonymous forces churning out deplorable marketing strategies, television shows, and celebrity "role models." But many of the people who care most about girls inadvertently teach them the rules of Goodness. Research has linked a child's temperament to the culturally based gender-role attitudes of her parents. When mothers act like Good Girls, they can teach daughters lessons in disempowerment. In other words, girls may lose their voices, but sometimes adult women lose girls.

If you think I'm tossing my hat into the already overcrowded mom-bashing ring, know that my intent is just the opposite. Mothers are constrained by rules similar to the ones that bind their daughters. Just as the terms of being a Good Girl undermine a girl's potential, the pressure to be a Good Mother can limit a woman's ability to set the right example for her daughter.

Mary was Shirley Temple as mother: petite with a cap of ash blond curls, and saucer-size blue eyes. She wore bright, youthful clothing and a generous smile. Patricia, her daughter, had just turned ten. Like a Russian nesting doll, she was a miniature of her mother: button cute, blond ringlets, baby fat. Unlike her mother, she had some rough edges: At the mother-daughter workshop, Patricia's attention drifted roguishly. She whispered with the other girls when she thought I wasn't looking. I watched Mary watch her daughter, then size up the other mothers and girls.

Patricia's silence during discussion didn't bother me—she was the workshop's youngest participant—but after about an hour Mary noticed. Her gaze reached out to hold Patricia's. Mary's mouth pursed, and her chin thrust forward: *Participate!* she seemed to say.

Patricia came to life during the games we played. Racing impishly around the room, she plowed into the other women and girls, finally knocking over a chair.

"Patricia!" Mary whisper-yelled. She glanced at the other mothers, then led her daughter to the corner of the room. I watched as she spoke to Patricia, both of their backs to me. Patricia listened intently. When they rejoined the group, Mary smiled widely, Patricia motionless at her side.

For our next game, each mother-daughter pair announced its own name and accompanying sound effect. We met the Queen Bees (*zzzzzz!*), the Fighting Tigers (*mrowr!*), and the Simbas (*roar!*). When we arrived at Mary and Patricia's team, Mary smiled.

"We are," she announced proudly, "the Happy Faces." She framed her face with her hands and smiled widely.

Later, as we explored how the pressure to be perfect can make it hard for girls to accept their mistakes, we decided to go around the room and share a recent mistake we each had made. Soon Patricia was cowering in the corner, whispering and crying to her mother, who murmured back urgently. Eventually I approached them.

"Is everything okay?" I asked quietly.

"Well, Patricia here is upset because she sees now how she treats me when she's angry. She thinks she's a bad girl."

"That's okay," I said, trying to sound reassuring. "We've all made mistakes. That's important to tell girls."

"I don't think so," Mary said, shaking her head. "Patricia is afraid the others are going to find out she's a bad girl. She refuses to tell anyone. Poor little thing doesn't want anyone to know she's been a bad girl." She smiled firmly—approvingly. The conversation was over.

In their book *The Mommy Myth*, Susan Douglas and Meredith Michaels argue that mothers are under increasing "surveillance" by a culture bent on a "new momism": pressure on a woman to, among other things, "devote her entire physical, psychological, emotional, and intellectual being, 24/7, to her children." Through a tidal wave of parenting books, politicized research, and media images, the new momism defines impossible standards of who is "good" and punishing terms for who is "bad," policing mothers into guilty exhaustion. On television, they wrote,

> good mothers rough-housed with their kids, they tickled them, marched in indoor parades with them, took them to the zoo, handmade their kids' Halloween costumes. . . . Good mothers were always in a good mood and ready to play. Bad mothers wore fancy business suits. . . . Bad mothers kept a messy house. Bad mothers resorted to store-bought Halloween costumes. Bad mothers did not listen to their kids, yelled at them, and were not adequately empathetic. . . . Bad mothers got home too late and didn't have dinner on the table in time.

Television's Good Mother was little more than a vessel for her children's needs, a woman whose opinions and thoughts barely extended beyond the pale of their well-being. She was a household's CEO of nurturing, the executive in charge of caregiving and self-sacrifice. In biting contrast, a Bad Mother dared to have a life and identity beyond parenting.

The specter of the new momism hovered over my interviews with mothers. I was told that a Good Mother would "do anything for her children." Some women confessed their belief that only a Good Mother would give up her career to stay at home with her children, and one confided, "When I choose something other than my children, I feel guilty." So much nurturing, one woman told me, made her feel as if "we give so much that we lose ourselves. I never had a chance to be me." These women described a loss of authentic self to mothering that bore a chilling likeness to the loss of self sustained by many of their daughters.

Indeed, Good Mothers appear to be dead ringers for Good Girls. More from Douglas and Michaels:

> The best mothers always put their kids' needs before their own, period. . . .
> For the best mothers, their kids are the center of the universe. The best
> mothers always smile. They always understand. They are never tired. They
> never lose their temper. . . . Their love for their children is boundless,
> unflagging, flawless, total.[1]

Substitute the word "girls" for "mothers" and "friends" for "kids" and you're looking at a Good Girl. The culture's expectations of Good Mothers thus demand that moms model a Good Girl all grown up: a way of being in the home defined by sacrificing or repressing a full range of feelings, thoughts, and needs. Daughters watch and learn, absorbing an intergenerational transfer of messages about how a woman should look, be, and act.

In a well-appointed dining room in Phoenix, elbows conspicuously absent from a glittering table, women gathered to talk about the challenge of raising strong daughters. They described a daily struggle to negotiate their identities as professionals, mothers, and wives, and they voiced concern about the selves they put on display for their daughters.

More than one of these mothers said they switched between different personas at home and at work. As they crossed the threshold into their home, the mothers seemed to closet their voices along with their briefcases and blazers. Maureen, a corporate executive, said,

I feel like at work I have a lot of high standards and I'm pretty rigid with our people. I expect all these things. And at home I'm pretty soft, you know, I walk into the house, and I'm like [*her voice softens*], "Oh, well, if you don't want to do these dishes, I'll do 'em." "Oh, you made a mess today." "Oh, I'll clean the kitchen. . . ."

Yasmin was a manager in a male-dominated profession. "I go home from being in charge at work to doing all of the traditional things, all of the cooking, all of the cleaning, all of the role-playing," she told me. And Holly, a midlevel manager, said,

I'm totally different [at work]. I know the minute I go, I have that shield up. I'm ready to take on. I'll take on conflict anywhere. In fact, I'll deal with it directly, it's not a big deal, it's not emotional. It's just, do it. . . . [At home I am] much more vulnerable. No . . . [*lowers her voice*] just let me get it done, don't worry about it, because I really don't want to have that nag-you-one-more-time. If I hear myself nag one more time, I think I'll shoot myself. I tend to get a little bit martyrish.

Each woman was quick to explain the switch in voice. Said Maureen, "I don't enforce [doing chores], because then you'll have conflict, and you don't want to have conflict." Yasmin's role-play was a way not to "have anyone become angry. . . . I will perform my role in ways that no one will get mad." And Holly: "I just want everyone to get along."

According to these women, and others I spoke with around the country, keeping a home neat was not just about running a vacuum but avoiding emotional mess. One woman told me that locking anger out of her house was "the driving force" in her parenting. When I asked another mother what conflict in her home meant to her, she replied, "We're not good, we're not doing it right. At least to me. If there's dissent and yelling and unhappiness and conflict, then I'm doing something wrong as a mother. My children don't love each other enough because I have failed somehow." Like so many of their daughters, these mothers seemed to believe that conflict was "bad," inimical to what a Good Mother should create in her home.

Many also said the terms of being a Good Wife meant keeping the home peaceful as a husband returned from a day's work. Too much fighting and incomplete housework irked one woman's husband, leaving her as an "intermediary" between him and her children. Sounding like the girls from chapter 5 who would rather complete an entire group's work than ask for help, she said it was simply "easier to go ahead and take care of this problem before it's even a problem."

Being a Good Wife could occasionally come at the expense of what was right for a daughter. "Your husband comes home, your girls are fighting, they're loud, they're yelling at each other," one mother told me. "He doesn't like the noise, so you tell them, 'Oh, Dad's coming home, you need to be quiet.' You just taught them, 'Boys don't like loud noise, they don't like arguments, you can't get angry.'"

Most of these mothers were neither quiet nor passive. They were often garrulous and silly, bringing our group interviews to a halt with gusts of laughter. Yet they described adopting withered personas at home that were shells of the women they were outside it. And they were teaching their daughters troubling lessons: *Conflict is a threat to the security of the home and your most precious relationships. I will sacrifice my needs if it means we don't have to fight and can keep our relationships intact.*

Douglas and Michaels traced this personality switch to confusing cultural messages about women and power. If women are free to embrace the competitiveness, ambition, and determination of their male peers at work, home is another story entirely. Mothers, they wrote, "are pulled between two rather powerful and contradictory cultural riptides: Be more doting and self-sacrificing at home than Bambi's mother, yet more achievement-oriented at work than Madeleine Albright." The result, they write, is that "the competitive go-getter at work had to walk through the door at the end of the day and, poof, turn into Carol Brady: selfless doormat at home." In this way mothers are victims of a cruel cultural setup: in order to succeed as mothers, they must model the destructive, self-effacing behavior that compromises their daughters' development.

These women seemed capable of shedding Good Girl norms at work, yet somehow unable to bring more empowering norms home. In *The Beauty Myth*, Naomi Wolf argued that media images of women became more feeble, underfed, and oversexualized just as women's liberation seemed to be taking off. This was hardly a coincidence; the burgeoning power of women was met with a compensatory blow in another area of their lives. The same is true here: as Good Girl pressure loosens in workplaces, Good Mother expectations grow more rigid, ensuring that women will be consistently exhausted and self-critical—and unable to bring stronger selves home at day's end.

As my conversations with mothers deepened, I learned that it was not simply Good Wife or Good Mother pressure that influenced these women's attitudes toward conflict. There was a Good Girl still living inside many of them, a semi-dormant self their daughters seemed to reawaken. The mothers' reactions to their daughters were grounded in the lessons about anger and conflict they had learned as girls—and were now transmitting to their daughters.

Barbara had two teenage daughters, and her "hot button" was when they argued. I asked her what she told them. "You'll never be friends when you're older, so you've gotta get along now, because if you don't get along now, who's going to ever like you?" she said. Barbara thus taught her daughters two Good Girl lessons: conflict terminates relationships ("You'll never be friends when you're older"), and girls who fight (or are angry) will not be liked by others. As a mother, Barbara knew that the girls were testing their relationship, using the security of the sibling bond to experiment with anger and conflict. But as a Good Girl, she couldn't stop herself. "I know it's a really bad message I'm sending out," she told me. The Good Girl inside her had eclipsed her as a mother.

When it came to fighting with their daughters, some mothers confided being unable to tolerate discord. Their comments about conflict with their daughters sounded eerily like girls talking about conflict with each other. At the dining-room table in Arizona, Kristie told the group that when her daughter was angry with her, she could not rest until the storm had passed.

"I have to resolve it," she told me. "It makes me . . ." She searched. "It churns my stomach."

"I feel cut off," her friend agreed.

"Anxious," another mother said.

One mother described her thoughts during a conflict with her daughter, and it was hard to distinguish them from thoughts she might have about a friend: "Why would she be mad at me? What did I do wrong, what did I do wrong? Why?" One mother told me that, in general, conflicts cripple her ability to function. "I have to fix it, because I'm not okay if I have a problem with you until you let me know I'm okay. Otherwise I'm just not going to be. So until I heal whatever that conflict is, I'm not going to be okay. . . ."

All of this surprised me. Before I began interviewing mothers, I assumed they would use the unconditional bond with their daughters to resist the Good Girl limits on conflict in relationship. Certainly, plenty do. Yet many mothers said their need to repair conflict with their daughters was just as powerful as, if not more unbearable than, the urgency they felt with other intimates. An angry daughter evoked fear and isolation. Several located their anxiety in the fear that their daughters didn't "like" them. The sense of disconnection and separation was overwhelming. "I can see myself knocking on the door and opening the door," one mother told me. "She just . . . her back is to me."

Not surprisingly, it was their daughters who wanted to be angry, who pleaded with their mothers to leave them be. Melanie described running down the hallway after her daughter and facing a locked door. "Mom, please, just leave me alone," she recalled her daughter saying.

"I want to get it—because I feel so badly, that I want to get it done as quickly as possible. . . . I feel sick, I feel internally sick." she told me. "I just want to make it right." When I asked her if she feared losing her daughter, she said no. "It's just because she means so much to me."

"What I worry about," her friend offered, "is they're in that room and somehow I've damaged them emotionally, and they'll come out when they're twenty-five." Again, isolation and separation hinted quietly in these sentences. A moment later another mother admitted, "Sometimes I know I need to stand my ground, but I don't want them not to like me. I don't want there to be disharmony."

The girls were communicating a need to be angry and in conflict, and their mothers could not fulfill the request. Good Mother pressure likely played a supporting role in the women's feelings about conflict: increasingly, mothers feel compelled to be all things to their daughters, including a best friend. In girl terms, this means a loving, unbroken, conflict-free relationship. Indeed, one mother told me that her angry daughter makes her feel "inadequate, I feel like I failed."

But the need to repair conflict before it has had a moment to breathe; the sense that conflict is an emergency, a fire to be put out; and the fear of separation and anxiety of not being "liked"—these come straight from the Good Girl playbook. By allowing Good Girl instincts to define their relationships to their daughters, these mothers were teaching their girls that conflict was intolerable within a relationship and that negative emotions must be snuffed out.

In *You're Wearing That? Understanding Mothers and Daughters in Conversation*, Deborah Tannen argues that in mother-daughter relationships "all the rewards and pitfalls that characterize girls' and women's conversations are amplified."[2] That is, if conflict is hard for females generally, it's exponentially loaded for mothers and daughters. Women told Tannen that their "saddest disappointments" in relationships with their mothers and daughters revolved around distance.

Mothers and daughters are so deeply enmeshed, Tannen writes, that difference and disconnection present huge challenges. Female relationships are grounded in sameness (for example, Tannen describes how a woman who says, "I'm always misplacing things" is often met with a friend's response that "I'm the same way") and connection. Attention is constantly paid among females to closeness and alliances. For girls and women, she writes, "emphasizing sameness is a way of reinforcing connection."

Tannen writes that sameness between mothers and daughters also sends a "metamessage," or hidden meaning, that "you're a right sort of person and all's well with the world." That's why too much difference between mothers and daughters can create deep treads of anxiety between them. In the case of daughters deviating from mothers—say, in their approach to conflict and anger—mothers may interpret difference as an implicit criticism or an attempt to disconnect. And when daughters pull away from mothers, the distance can be overwhelmingly painful.

The problem is that mothers appear to be the prime targets of children's anger. Tannen cites a study that found children disproportionately sought out conflicts with mothers rather than fathers. "It is," Tannen writes, "as if mothers are emotional lightning rods, absorbing and grounding the emotions—both negative and positive—that are swirling around the family." If girls are experimenting with conflict largely on their mothers, it may be that women bear a special responsibility to reflect carefully on their behavior in conflict with their daughters. As I show later, it is mothers who teach their daughters the ABCs of conflict.

## TAMING THE GOOD MOTHER

When my brother and I were growing up, our mother occasionally caved in to our begging and took us to Roy Rogers after school. As the smell of fried snacks intoxicated our little nostrils, there always lingered the fear that our mother would say something again. That she would complain about the fries.

When the fries weren't hot enough for my mother's liking, she made sure to say something to the fry cook as we passed through the line. This, I felt, was humiliating beyond reason. "Please, Mom," I begged, eyes bugging, "just leave it. They're fine." She ignored me.

The worst was when she figured out that the fries were cold after we were already seated. I sat, helpless witness to the extended scene of her pushing herself up from the table, bristling and frustrated, the day's wear on her face. I gazed out the window and imagined throwing myself under the next passing bus.

She was never mean, always respectful. She was just saying she wanted the hot fries she had paid for. Back then I couldn't see that. All I saw was a massive Good Girl violation: my mother was speaking up, asking for something, saying she didn't like or agree with something. She wasn't being *nice*. The day I effortlessly asked for a waiter to reheat my cold dinner was the day I realized the lesson she had taught me with those then-embarrassing acts.

Karen was just beginning to grasp the powerful lessons she might teach her daughters. She and her family lived a halcyon life in a northeastern suburb. Carrie, her youngest, was a thirteen-year-old spitfire, charging like a bull through the house when she was angry, smothering her mother with hugs when the emotions ran their course. It was fifteen-year-old Elizabeth who worried her. In her quiet older daughter, Karen saw someone quick to sacrifice her needs for others and blame herself for things not her fault. She saw a girl who, she told me, was "afraid to speak her mind for fear of what might happen." In her older daughter, Karen realized suddenly, she saw herself.

The thought materialized a few years back. Karen had just turned forty and decided, once and for all, that she would end her marriage to a "strong-willed, pushy kind of man" who "has just mowed me over all these years." She had stayed in it for the kids, as so many women do, but began to see the impact of her decision on her daughter. The girl Elizabeth had become, Karen realized in horror, was an echo, a shadow of her mother: it was

Karen, not her daughter, who had been first in the family not to speak her mind, who took the blame to end a tirade, who put everyone's needs ahead of her own.

Karen believed that her choice to stick out a tough marriage was right for her daughter. A Good Mother kept the home whole. Not surprisingly, she invoked her identity as a mother to explain her behavior. "As a mother and an adult in the world we live in, there are times you need to do things to be supportive to the people around you. You may not want to do it. I think I've done that so much that Elizabeth has learned to put her needs second." Karen went on, taking an inventory of the messages she had unwittingly sent her daughter. "I gave up my job so I could be home with the kids. She knows I love to work. . . . If I'm angry with someone, I try not to say anything. . . . If you go back five years, I would just get angry and suck it up and then get over it. I have a hard time expressing my disappointment."

What if, she asked me, Elizabeth becomes a doormat? What if she doesn't express herself or take risks? "I'm afraid for her," she told me. "I don't want her to wait until she's forty-something and realizes." So Karen decided to change her life, as much for her daughter as for herself. She went back to school so she that when she left her husband, she would be able to support the girls. She became keenly aware of the example she set in her day-to-day interactions, finding little moments to model assertiveness. "On the highway," she told me, "there was a truck that wouldn't move over. I said, 'Write down his license number.' I said, 'Give me a paper and a pen.' Elizabeth said, 'Don't do that!'"

Karen talked with Elizabeth about Elizabeth's tendency to blame herself all the time. She told her daughter she was tough and persevered to help Elizabeth communicate her needs. Karen also understood she was growing more transparent to her maturing daughter. "I think [Elizabeth] sees that I don't want to be married. I think she sees right through me," she told me. "I don't think I'm fooling anybody, especially her." It was a ruse unlikely to continue for long. Where Karen used to allow Good Mother and

Good Wife pressure to define her parenting, she began placing her daughters' interests squarely at the center of her decisions. Her newfound awareness meant that big change was on all their horizons.

## WAKE-UP CALL

The Good Mother anticipates needs before they even arise, and in this area forty-four-year-old Michelle excelled. She knew how to run a home. Michelle had left her career to unleash her talents on parenting two girls. Motherhood became what Michelle did, who she was. She was good at it. But the summer her daughter Taylor attended the Girls Leadership Institute, Michelle learned the dark side of her painstaking vigilance.

Michelle had always worried about her daughter, and she knew that fifteen-year-old Taylor would demand her best efforts as a mother. Taylor was sensitive, she wore her heart on her sleeve, and even the little things were hard on her. When she was upset, Taylor could be inconsolable, awash in dark, intensifying emotions. Michelle wanted to protect her. When Taylor struggled with adults or peers, Michelle told her it wasn't her fault.

> I think I would sort of just try and steer her away from it instead of just let her go for it. If a teacher didn't like her, it just broke her heart. I just made excuses. . . . Instead of saying, "Taylor, you're being oversensitive, this is not that big a deal."

She took Taylor's side at every turn in the road, even if it meant ignoring Taylor's own troubling role in a situation. "I didn't challenge her," she told me.

"As a mother, I thought I was doing the right thing by protecting my kid from all this other crap and the realities of the world," she added. If Michelle defended a person who upset Taylor, or tried to explain a teacher's upsetting decision, it would undo Taylor even more. So Michelle learned to withhold painful truths. "I overprotected her from things so that she didn't have to feel those things," Michelle told me.

Mother-daughter conflicts took one of two paths: Taylor became inconsolable or enraged. When Taylor was upset, her mother backed off, defaulting to her usual protective posture. She figured that by leaving Taylor alone, she would not deepen her daughter's wound. It was Taylor's anger that triggered a wholly different response. Deborah Tannen found that many women criticized their daughters out of fear that they were bad mothers. Michelle's anger followed a similar vein; she told me that Taylor's anger was a threat to her control over the house, a sign she was failing to be a Good Mother. She would not tolerate it.

> It was so important to me to be a good mom and to raise good girls, I would think, "Oh my God, I'm totally screwing up, and I don't even know it. You do not have your act together on this mothering thing at all." I would get panicked about fooling myself that I am doing a good job, and I would get insecure. . . . [I would engage in] really bad behavior. . . . I didn't want to lose my image in my own mind.

Michelle's parenting traveled a course of extremes directed by her vision of what a Good Mother was: she either cowered in the face of Taylor's pain in order to protect her or pounced on Taylor's anger in order to assert her own authority in the home.

Taylor, whose story I told in chapter 1, arrived at the Girls Leadership Institute furious at her mother for divorcing her father. Convinced that their relationship would not survive if she spoke up about the divorce, Taylor refused to share her feelings. To cope, she lashed out at her father, remained silent around her mother, and stopped eating.

Reached by phone, Michelle stood on the dock of a Minnesota lake and listened to me say—with Taylor's permission—all the things her daughter couldn't tell her. It was, she later told me, as if "a volcano went off." She had walked on eggshells with Taylor, tiptoeing around her daughter when she was in distress, leaving her alone altogether when she was upset. Michelle had clamped down on Taylor's anger. When Taylor was upset, she realized,

> she either said nothing or came out really angry and mean. And that's when I would say, "You have no right, blah, blah, blah." But if she holed up and I could see the pain, then I didn't say anything at all. Anytime that girl tried to communicate with me, I just shut her down.

In Michelle's mind being a Good Mother meant protecting Taylor from the bleak realities of life. From where she stood, Taylor saw a mother who did not want to talk about—who could not abide—painful things. Taylor learned that negative emotions and experiences needed to be smoothed over, put somewhere else in order for relationships to survive. Taylor had watched her mother avoid her dark feelings, and now Taylor tried to avoid her own.

Michelle realized that her refusal to engage with Taylor's full range of emotions had communicated the opposite of what she'd intended. "I believed that my behavior up until that moment proved to her how much I loved her, . . . [but] she thought my love came with conditions, and . . . she was working to meet those conditions, and it was hard as hell for her." When mother and daughter finally talked, they resolved to share and respect all the emotions in their relationship, no matter how painful or challenging. Taylor told me recently, "We are closer than we ever were when we were pretending to be happy."

NEARLY EVERY MOTHER I MEET WANTS TO KNOW WHAT SHE can do to empower her daughter. Almost all expect suggestions for their girls: join a team, volunteer, pursue a cause. But the best thing a mother can do for her daughter is to be herself, with all the challenges that being real entails. Being real means taking up space and having needs; it means drawing the line and saying no. Being real means walking into every room as the same woman, whether you're in a conference room or a family room. And being real means not just tolerating the messiness of relationship but embracing it as the raw material of a family's growth and development.

Any kind of authenticity begins with self-awareness: to be yourself you have to know who that is. At the end of the day, the best gift a mother can give is to take—that is, take the time to find herself, set a new example, and shatter the vise grip of the Good Wife/Bad Wife and Good Mother/Bad Mother labels. When a mother's behavior breaks the rules, she gives her daughter the authority to live by her own.

# PART II

......................................

# BREAKING THE CURSE

# INTRODUCTION TO PART II: FROM GOOD GIRLS TO REAL GIRLS

This section of the book offers concrete strategies to guide your daughter from Good Girl to Real Girl. With scripts and tools from the Girls Leadership Institute, you will empower your daughter to become a young woman who says what she feels and thinks, embraces her limits, and presents an authentic self to the world.

The good news is that she already has what it takes to break the Curse of the Good Girl. Your job is not to add new ingredients to create a brand-new girl. You will, in partnership with your daughter, bring forward the Real Girl who has always existed within her. Your job is to act as a guide and escort your daughter back to herself: to what she really thinks and feels, what she wants, who she is in relationships, and what she doesn't want to do and be.

You will raise her Good Girl consciousness, exposing a set of restrictive rules that circumscribe her development as an individual. Most girls are well aware of media pressure to be thin and popular. Good Girl consciousness goes deeper, and girls grasp the difference quickly. Dana, from chapter 1, realized that the most dangerous cultural pressure for girls was "not about being popular or having a boyfriend, . . . it's about making people happy and seeing people's reactions when I do something in class. I didn't realize before that I was a people pleaser."

Every year I help parents and daughters discover the impact of the Good Girl curse across the most important areas of their lives. This is where the journey to a strong inner core begins, allowing them to name and control the forces undermining authentic self-expression. Parents and daughters reflect about who they are and make new choices in their relationships.

To begin this process, consider this question: How are Good Girls supposed to look and act in our society? Work with your daughter, using the format of the list on pages 1–2. You also might enjoy making a collage of Good Girl images from magazines and using the images as a guide to naming the Good Girl qualities.

Here are some questions you can discuss together or answer yourself.

1. In what ways are you a Good Girl?
2. Where do Good Girl messages come from? Who are the Good Girls on TV and in movies? What do they look like in magazines? Who are the people in our lives who tell girls to be Good?
3. Who are the Good Girls in your class? What makes them that way?
4. What are the advantages of being a Good Girl? How might being a Good Girl limit you?

Don't expect your daughter to have all the answers. Nor should you plan to agree with her assessments. Judge or disagree too strongly and you'll lose her. Avoid demonizing the Good Girl; remember, after all, that you are exposing rules she has been expected to aspire to and live by for her entire life. Don't shake the earth; the point is to stimulate her thinking about cultural messages, introduce the Good Girl concept, and encourage self-reflection. This is hard work, and it's an ongoing process of self-discovery.

Now make your own Bad Girl List. On a piece of paper, write down the answer to this question: How are Bad Girls supposed to look and act in our society? Make a list as you did for the Good Girl or use magazine images (although it may be harder to find those).

Here are some questions you can discuss or answer yourself.

1. Are there any Bad Girl qualities that it might be good to have?
2. Which Bad Girl qualities do you think you have?
3. Which Bad Girl qualities do you want to have?
4. Think of some women who have changed the course of history. For instance, when Rosa Parks refused to move her seat on the bus, what Bad Girl qualities did she display?
5. What might be limiting about being a Bad Girl? What are the advantages?

As I showed in chapter 1, stereotypical Bad Girls are superficially aimless, destructive, and irresponsible. Yet the decision to be Bad is equally a sign of courage, the willingness to resist convention and be who you want to be. Bad Girls take up space with their bodies and voices; they are immodest, tough, and proud. They don't care what other people think.

The point, of course, is not to tell your daughter to be "Bad" but to expose the fallacy of the Good and Bad Girl stereotypes. "Good" and "Bad" drain girls of their authenticity by telling them who and how to be. The labels are there to pressure and scare her: Bad Girls get punished, and Good Girls get asked to the prom.

This is a chance to tell your daughter that you don't want her to be either of these girls. A Real Girl has both Good and Bad in her and available to her. She chooses who she wants to be, and her internal architecture is by her own design.

A final note: some of the exercises in part II come with suggested answers that can be found in the Appendix. Keep in mind that these are only suggestions. There are no "right" answers to these questions.

*Seven*

# I FEEL, THEREFORE I AM: BUILDING EMOTIONAL INTELLIGENCE

The field of emotional intelligence provides important tools to restore girls' connection to their emotions and facilitate genuine self-expression. In this chapter I will introduce you to building blocks that will help girls access, express, and accept a full range of thoughts and feelings.

## THE SCHOOL FOR EMOTIONAL LEARNING

Flight attendants tell us to don oxygen masks before helping a child, and with good reason. If you're not okay, you can't help the person who needs you. The same is true of parenting, and especially of building emotional intelligence. EI isn't inherited like a gene; it's built within the family, which Daniel Goleman calls the "first school for emotional learning."

Your daughter's empowerment begins with you. Assessing your own relationship to emotions will illuminate the school for emotional learning your daughter has been attending. It will also increase your self-awareness as a parent and as a person, maximizing your consciousness of the messages you send or don't send.

Reflect on these questions, taking special care to consider how your experiences might affect your daughter's attitudes toward feelings.

1. Were there certain emotions that were discouraged or considered off-limits in your childhood home?
2. When you were growing up, what was your family's attitude toward vulnerable emotions like sadness, embarrassment, guilt, or fear? Was toughness or keeping a "stiff upper lip" a coping mechanism for pain?
3. What was your childhood family's attitude toward the emotions associated with conflict? For instance, was anger freely expressed?
4. How often do you share your feelings, especially the most challenging ones? If you tend to keep your feelings to yourself, why? Where did you learn how to do that?
5. [For women] How does the pressure on women to be caregivers (selfless, kind, etc.) influence the range of emotions you express?
6. Do you question, minimize, or degrade your emotions? Like the girls in chapter 2, do you advise yourself not to "make a big deal" out of things or to be "too sensitive?"

As noted in chapter 1, all parents impose a set of "display rules" on their children, putting unspoken pressure about which emotions should be shown and when, which feelings cause discomfort in others, and which ones parents support most. Display rules are the basis for emotional instruction, and they are a critical part of a child's socialization. Some rules, however, can be limiting. Casual family axioms can create restrictive frameworks for emotional expression. When a parent warns a girl, "If you have nothing nice to say, don't say anything at all," the daughter learns that negative feelings may not be tolerated. Over time the "muscles" required to express those feelings may atrophy, leaving her ill prepared to negotiate them at home and in the world. As an alternative consider, "It's not what you say, it's how you say it," a framework that allows for a full range of emotions respectfully expressed.

To raise a socially acceptable daughter, parents may inadvertently reinforce the emotions that support the Good Girl profile, while discouraging other feelings. The terms of social success for girls favor display rules that can limit a full range of emotional expression. One mother I worked with caught herself urging her daughter to be "nicer" to her soccer teammates. "She wasn't very warm," the woman recalled. "Kind of standoffish, just wanting to play. But then I thought, 'How cool! She doesn't feel the need to be everyone's friend. It's me who wants to be like that, not her.'" This woman's self-awareness illuminated her display rules and enabled her to change them for her daughter.

Consider your own display rules. Are there certain emotions you may invite from your daughter? Are you less hospitable to others? For instance, in chapter 6 I explore how mothers' fear of conflict with their daughters can limit the healthy expression of anger in girls. Think about which of your daughter's emotions create anger, anxiety, frustration, or fear in you. How might your reaction affect her emotional self-expression?

## MODEL USING "EMOTION WORDS"

You can enrich your daughter's emotional intelligence by using more emotion words yourself.

Think of these words as a kind of language you're introducing into your home. An emotional vocabulary is best used across a variety of situations throughout the daily life of a family: moments that are exciting, happy, and challenging. Try to be casual and not hokey; slip the words into your sentences, but don't force them. For example, if you're going to say something like, "It's great that we're going to have dinner as a family tonight," you might say, "I'm really happy we're going to have dinner tonight." Or if you find yourself saying, "I don't want to hear another word," see if you can add something like, "because I'm feeling really overwhelmed."

You can also observe others' emotions. For example, "Your sister seems very excited about going to camp," or "Grandma looks pretty irritated with Grandpa."

Use emotion words with care. Remember that as the parent you are both rule maker and caregiver. Do not invoke emotions as a way to compel your daughter to do something. Saying "It will make Daddy feel hurt and sad if you don't do this" is manipulative. It also sends the message that your daughter should act primarily to please you and repair your emotional state, rather than acting from her own sense of obligation. When girls prioritize pleasing others, they can disconnect from their own needs, leading to relationships in which they are unable to state their needs and resist abusive peers. When your daughter disappoints you, make sure she understands first which rules or values have been violated.

## TALKING ABOUT FEELINGS

Ask your daughter how she is feeling. The more she talks freely with you about her feelings, the less dangerous or "weird" it will seem to express herself in other areas of her life.

Try not to limit conversations about feelings to times of distress. Although many parents say they regularly ask their children how they are feeling, kids are most commonly asked, "How was school?" or "What did you do today?" Although the answers provide windows into emotion, the questions do not prompt a child to develop her emotional vocabulary.

If you ask her how she's feeling and she says "fine," Dr. Maurice Elias recommends replying with something like, "Fine-happy? Fine-bored?

Fine-angry?" If she refuses, don't push it. Try again at another time. Be as casual as possible. If you sit down opposite her, fingers interlocked, with a concerned look boring out of your eyes, you may scare her off. Try it while you're driving, cleaning up, or watching TV. Finally, use this tool family-wide. If your daughter perceives she is the only one being asked, she may grow suspicious and feel isolated or punished.

When she is upset, avoid posing yes-or-no questions like "Are you okay?" or "Are you upset?" Try open-ended questions such as "How are you feeling?" and firm observations: "You seem upset about something."

## AFFIRM YOUR DAUGHTER'S EMOTIONS

Good Girl pressure to be kind and selfless erodes comfort with feelings that deviate from being Good. Emotions like anger, hurt, and jealousy can feel wrong or inappropriate, leading girls to question their most powerful internal experiences.

When a girl challenges her feelings, she second-guesses herself. Dwelling internally on the question of whether she has the right to feel, a girl is delayed from making vital decisions in her relationships. Her confidence in her version of events is also undermined. For instance, thirteen-year-old Tara didn't want to be angry at a friend's mean jokes, so she told herself that the joke wasn't as bad as she had first thought. Tara told herself that she was just being sensitive that day. Tara's discomfort with anger distorted her version of events and allowed her friend to take advantage of her. This loss of personal strength compromised Tara in her relationship but, most crucially, pulled her away from what she really knew to be true.

Helping a girl accept her feelings is thus an essential part of raising a strong girl. A parent's impact is powerful in this area.

Psychologist Robin Stern has written that when adults don't validate children's emotions, children learn "not to trust their inner emotional information." In *How to Talk So Kids Will Listen & Listen So Kids Will Talk,* Adele Faber and Elaine Mazlish show how parents diminish children's emotional experience by denying feelings, philosophizing about them, giving advice, and defending the person who has upset the child. Imagine, for instance, that your daughter came home and told you her friend made fun of her cell phone, then said she was just kidding.

1. *Denial of feelings.* "It's not that big a deal. Maybe you're being a little sensitive about this."
2. *Philosophical response.* "That's how girls are: mean, catty, exclusive. You may as well get used to it."
3. *Advice.* "Why don't you just call her and find out if she's mad at you?"
4. *Defense of the other person.* "Are you sure you're not taking it the wrong way? That's just how she is. Spunky, you know? She likes to make jokes."

To these I would add one more:

5. *Attribution of intent.* "She's just jealous of you."

The best way to build a girl's emotional self-confidence is to empathize with her distress. Empathy may appear to be the simplest response, but I have found in my work with families that it is also the most challenging for a parent to practice. When we empathize, we recognize and accept someone else's emotions. When a child is in pain, a parent wants to repair that emotional state, not wallow in it. For many parents, taking the time to recognize their child's pain can leave them feeling helpless, anguished, or responsible.

It may be useful to remember that when you empathize, you do more than just help your daughter through a rough spot. Your response to your daughter's feelings conveys two levels of meaning. On the first level, the specific situation unfolds: you talk with your daughter about what she's going through. On the second level, you give your daughter permission and support to have the emotional experience itself. If you challenge, deny, or ignore her emotions, you may communicate that her feelings are unacceptable. Empathy is thus an important opportunity to validate a girl's emerging sense of self.

When your daughter expresses an emotion, try to affirm, sympathize, or empathize with her experience. For example:

YOUR DAUGHTER: "Mom, she made fun of my cell phone and then said, 'Just kidding.' But everyone was laughing."

WHAT YOU CAN SAY: "You must feel really betrayed by her." OR "I can see why you would feel hurt. That sounds embarrassing." OR "I'm really sorry this happened."

Keep a few things in mind: First, empathy is a starting point. Other interventions are usually called for, and I explore these in more detail in chapter 10. Second, do not confuse affirming her emotions with mirroring them. If your daughter is extremely upset, you do not need to mimic her to affirm her experience. In fact, overreacting will send the message that it's you who needs to be cared for, not her. It will also ramp up the intensity of the experience. Keep in mind the weaving toddler who fell on her face and looked to you as a barometer for how to react. Finally, your daughter's emotional experience may not always jibe with reality. Avoid using empathy to resist the truth of a situation. If your daughter overreacts to an incident, strike a careful balance between affirming her feelings (*"I can see how you would be feeling hurt"*) and sharing your perception of events.

# HELP GIRLS ACCEPT
# THEIR EMOTIONS

At the root of their discomfort with feelings are often unconscious assumptions girls make about whether it's valid to have and express emotions at all. Dr. Marsha Linehan's Myths About Emotions illustrate the ways adults commonly trivialize their feelings. They are especially relevant to girls.[1]

I encourage you to talk about these myths with your daughter. You are likely to hear your daughter verbalize at least one of them, but if you don't, you can initiate a conversation by saying something like, "A lot of people think there's a right way to feel in every situation," or "When I was growing up, I thought negative feelings made me a bad person." Below are ways the myths might emerge in everyday conversation with your daughter and talking points to help you respond.

**MYTH:** THERE IS A RIGHT WAY TO
FEEL IN EVERY SITUATION.

*Might sound like:* "I'm making too big a deal out of this." "I'm just being a drama queen." "I shouldn't be angry." "I'm too sensitive." "It doesn't matter."

*Response:* There's no wrong or right when it comes to feelings. You have the right to feel any way you want—you just don't have the right to *act* any way you want. We're all unique individuals, and that means we each have different feelings and situations that upset or thrill us. Your emotions are a big part of what makes you who you are. Your feelings are part of you, just like your arms and your legs. You may not love every part of yourself, but it's who you are, for better or for worse.

In life you will find yourself in many situations when your feelings aren't shared by someone else. That's normal, but when someone doesn't respect your emotions or makes you feel as if there's a "right" way to feel, that's a sign that person is not respecting *you.*

## MYTH: LETTING OTHERS KNOW THAT I AM FEELING BAD IS WEAKNESS.

*Might sound like:* "If I tell them I'm sad, they'll think I am a killjoy and go to the party without me."

*Response:* Feeling bad is a natural, normal part of being human. No one is immune to it. Some people think that being a best friend means being happy and supportive all the time. But people who never open up and share their bad feelings often look to others as if they're perfect or have no problems. If someone thinks you're perfect, she may feel nervous or embarrassed to share her own true feelings, and then your relationship may not be very real, honest, or deep. The closest, most satisfying relationships are ones in which two people can openly address and resolve the feelings that most challenge them.

Remember, too, that if you don't tell someone what's bothering you, she can't support you through a rough time. If she is the one who made you feel bad in the first place, she can't help fix the problem. The more we hold in our feelings, the more we become like pots of water over a fire—eventually we boil over, exploding or losing control of our behavior. That can truly make us and our relationships weak.

## MYTH: NEGATIVE FEELINGS ARE BAD AND DESTRUCTIVE.

*Might sound like:* "I'll hurt her feelings." "She won't be my friend anymore if I tell her what I really think." "She'll turn everyone against me if I tell her the truth." "They'll make fun of me."

*Response:* Negative feelings are only "bad and destructive" if they are followed by destructive actions. Everyone has negative feelings, and there's no getting around them. It's what we do with our feelings that counts. You can't make those bad feelings go away. The more you try, the bigger the feelings will get, until you lose control and do something you regret. It is far more destructive to hold your feelings in than to express them respectfully and calmly. Let's talk about how you can do that.

**MYTH:** SOME EMOTIONS
ARE REALLY STUPID.

*Might sound like:* *"I don't know why I care." "It's no big deal." "This is stupid."*

*Response:* There are no stupid emotions. Sometimes we label our emotions stupid because they make us feel stuck or unproductive. We might also feel annoyed at our emotions and wonder, "Why do I care so much?" When you spend time being upset with yourself rather than facing your feelings, it's that much harder to resolve them. Judging yourself will only create more negative feelings, distracting you from the real problem.

**MYTH:** ALL PAINFUL EMOTIONS ARE THE RESULT
OF A BAD ATTITUDE.

*Might sound like:* *"What's wrong with me?" "I should be more positive." "This wouldn't be happening if I were (or weren't). . . ."*

*Response:* It's true that the way we think about situations can affect how strongly we feel. If you don't get invited to a party and you think, "I guess I'm a total loser," you'll probably feel strong waves of sadness and humiliation. If instead you think, "That's a bummer, but I guess I can't be friends with everyone," you might feel a bit better. But you're still going to feel rejected. No one is above a bad day. No matter how good your attitude, you can't talk your way out of your feelings. Part of being human is feeling good *and* bad.

**MYTH:** IF OTHERS DON'T APPROVE OF MY FEELINGS, I OBVIOUSLY SHOULDN'T FEEL THE WAY I DO.

*Might sound like:* "My friend says I overreact to stuff, so I'm not going to tell her what I'm feeling."

*Response:* Your feelings form the basis of who you are and what you need. If you look to others to approve of your feelings, you will lose yourself. You'll try to feel and think the way other people want you to. That can make you vulnerable to having people take advantage of you.

Our society tells girls that if they want to be "normal" and accepted by others, they have to be nice all the time and have lots of friends. As a result many girls worry that if someone doesn't approve of their upset feelings, they will lose the relationship with the person. The fear of disapproval leads some girls to "change" their feelings by pretending not to be upset when they really are, apologizing when they don't mean it, or accepting someone's apology before they're ready. Changing your feelings to earn others' approval won't only affect you, it will harm your relationships. For instance, if you apologize to end a fight but don't really mean it, you show someone a false version of yourself. Your friend may think she is forgiven when she hasn't been at all, and you will hold a grudge. Your friendship will pay the price.

When you tell yourself you shouldn't feel a certain way, you're likely to feel guilty and even ashamed. As your feelings intensify, they will become overwhelming, sabotaging other areas of your life.

**MYTH:** PAINFUL EMOTIONS ARE NOT REALLY IMPORTANT AND SHOULD BE IGNORED.

*Might sound like:* "No one else has a problem with this." "What's wrong with me?" "I don't know how I feel."

*Response:* The more painful the emotions, the more urgently they should be addressed. Try thinking about your emotions like a body part that's hurting. If you got a bad cut, you would clean and cover it. If you ignored it, it might fester into an infection that spread all over your body. The same is true of painful emotions: when we don't deal with them, they take over our lives in destructive ways.

WHEN YOU FLIP THE MYTHS ABOUT EMOTIONS ON THEIR heads, a series of affirmations emerge. Ideally, every girl should believe the following about her feelings:

1. There is no right or wrong way to feel about what happens in my life or relationships.
2. In safe situations it's okay to tell others how I'm feeling, even if my feelings make me appear vulnerable.
3. Upset feelings are healthy and normal.
4. Good people can have bad feelings.
5. I am the only person who can say how I'm feeling.
6. It doesn't matter whether others approve of my emotions, because they are mine.
7. Negative emotions are important and must be acknowledged.

If you are not sure how your daughter feels about her emotions, try some of the following questions or lead-ins:

- "It seems like you think you shouldn't be upset about this."
- "Do you think feeling this way is your fault?"
- "It sounds like you think your feelings are not important."
- "You seem to think your feelings are wrong."

# DEFINE INSIDE
# AND OUTSIDE FEELINGS

Limited emotional intelligence curbs the range of emotions girls can express in conflict. Their confrontations become reactive or tearful—in other words, stalemates. When asked to express their feelings, most girls can say only that they are "angry," "annoyed," "frustrated," or "pissed off." They are often willing to say little else.

To expand their emotional range, I began teaching girls to differentiate between two types of feelings: *Inside Feelings* and *Outside Feelings*. Imagine you are watching an angry, face-to-face conflict between two people. What are the emotions you can physically observe each person having, just by looking at them? Most people say they see anger, frustration, annoyance, hatred, rage, or irritation. These are Outside Feelings, the emotions you can usually *see* someone having during a conflict.

Now imagine the emotions those two fighting people might have but not show: hurt, disappointment, embarrassment, guilt, anxiety, and fear, among many others. These are Inside Feelings, what we feel but don't often show during conflict.

Girls mostly express Outside Feelings when they are upset ("I'm so annoyed," "I'm really mad"). Expressing Outside Feelings suggests you are spoiling for a fight. The feelings almost always trigger anger or defensiveness in the other person. They turn cheeks red and pump adrenaline through veins. They may also be expressed nonverbally, through heavy sighing, eye-rolling, "ach"-ing, or the continuous, mind-numbing use of the word "whatever."

It's not illogical: after all, it's far safer to tell someone you are angry than it is to let down your guard and say you're hurt. Anger, however, is known as a "secondary emotion"; we always feel it on the heels of another emotion. We usually feel embarrassed, offended, or disrespected first, then revert to prickly anger to protect more tender feelings. But Inside Feelings are almost

# INSIDE/OUTSIDE FEELINGS

## OUTSIDE FEELINGS

Frustrated

Angry

Irritated

Annoyed

Enraged

Disgusted

## OUTSIDE BODY LANGUAGE

Rolling eyes

Shifting weight

Turning away

Slouching

Hand on hip

No eye contact

"Whatever"

### INSIDE FEELINGS

Insecure    Disappointed

Sad    Afraid

Excited    Confused    Betrayed

Vulnerable    Self-conscious    Jealous

Guilty    Humilated    Used

Embarassed    Hurt    Anxious

Put down    Shamed

Inferior    Regretful

Panicked

always at the heart of what really bothers us, bringing the truth to the surface. For girls, whose most important conversations often skirt the heart of what really bothers them, Inside Feelings become a vital truth-telling device.

Inside Feelings are also more likely to hose off a fuming person and defuse a conflict. When you say you're feeling hurt, anxious, or worried, people are more likely to listen. As a wise fifth-grader once told me, feelings are like mirrors: Give an Outside Feeling, get an Outside Feeling reflected back. Give an Inside Feeling, and maybe you'll get one in return.

Teaching girls to identify and express Inside and Outside Feelings can transform their behavior in conflict. Seventeen-year-old Gina, in a conflict with Liz, was able to distinguish between being "just frigging angry" and feeling "hurt" and "embarrassed." No longer hell-bent on defending herself, Liz became more willing to listen.

Inside Feelings are not a panacea for conflict. There are no guarantees, and you can get burned when you open up. Why, parents ask me, should I tell my daughter to make herself vulnerable with someone who has not been good to her? Imagine that sharing Inside Feelings is like taking off a heavy winter coat without knowing whether the air will be cold or mild. For example, let's say Gina told Liz she was hurt or embarrassed, and Liz laughed or rolled her eyes. Liz would have been blasting Gina with cold air, and Gina would have put her coat back on. That is, she would have gotten tougher in the conversation and reverted to safer territory. But Liz did listen to Gina's Inside Feelings with respect, so Gina left her coat off. From that position the girls had a peaceful, open conversation.

Like honesty, vulnerability is a practice, and it is a dying art for girls who think toughness is the new girl power. Vulnerability must be understood as an important form of self-expression. When toughness is poured like cement over girls' most tender feelings, their authentic emotional expression is eclipsed. They are unable to articulate precisely what bothers them and are likely to resort to aggressive strategies instead.

When girls do not make themselves vulnerable in relationship, they fail to acquire crucial lessons about intimacy and respect. If Liz had degraded Gina when she shared her Inside Feelings, Gina would have learned that Liz didn't respect her. It might have been an important turning point for Gina, helping her improve her standards for relationship. Letting down your guard, when carefully considered, is an act of great courage and power.

This does not mean Outside Feelings are "wrong." Anger and frustration are vital for girls to feel. When it is time to confront someone, however, acting on anger without reflection is unproductive. Without a wider range of emotions to consider, it is hard to address problems with a clear head. Inside Feelings are important when trying to reflect on a problem or resolve it, but they are certainly not the only feelings girls should express.

This is especially important to keep in mind during a bullying situation. When someone victimizes your daughter, sharing Inside Feelings is dangerous. The perpetrator doesn't deserve the gesture of vulnerability that sharing Inside Feelings involves. Expressing Inside Feelings is best reserved for day-to-day interpersonal conflicts, in relationships marked but not defined by conflict.

## BRING INSIDE AND OUTSIDE FEELINGS HOME

I spend several weekends a year with parents and daughters around the country, leading workshops designed to improve communication and empower girls in peer relationships. I ask parent-daughter pairs to write scripts of their most difficult conversations: the ones that play out repeatedly, that are yelled in cars, up and down stairs, and on either side of slammed doors. Then each pair performs. Their only rule: no whitewashing the truth. If they scream at home, they have to scream for the group. No "Whatever" will go unmuttered, no "You don't appreciate anything I do for you" will go unshouted.

Meet Gwen and Claudia. By fourteen, Claudia had clearly inherited the spunk and verbal prowess of her lawyer mother. This made for some intense arguments. Lately it was all about Claudia's cell phone. Here's the script they wrote:

GWEN: Claudia, do you have your cell phone with you?
CLAUDIA: Yeah.
GWEN: Did you charge it?

CLAUDIA: I forgot.

GWEN: But we talked about this. You're going out with your friends today. What if your cell phone runs out of power and you can't reach me? What if I can't reach you?

CLAUDIA: Stop freaking out, Mom, I have almost two bars. It's not a big deal.

GWEN: (*Sighs with annoyance*) This is the last time. You just don't listen.

CLAUDIA: No, I just forget. Why are you being so ridiculous? Anyway, I read an article that said that if you charge your phone every night, you do damage to it.

GWEN: You're just making excuses. I'm telling you right now, you are going to charge that cell phone.

CLAUDIA: I *do* charge it, just not every night. You're so paranoid! Why don't you trust me?

When asked to share their feelings, the only emotions they revealed were Outside Feelings: the anger of an exasperated mother, the annoyance of a daughter wanting to be left alone. Gwen and Claudia wanted to change the conversation. They went back over their script and identified the Inside Feelings they had during each line of their performed conflict.

GWEN: Claudia, do you have your cell phone with you? *I feel anxious.*

CLAUDIA: Yeah. *I feel nervous.*

GWEN: Did you charge it? *I feel worried.*

CLAUDIA: I forgot. *I feel guilty.*

GWEN: But we talked about this. You're going out with your friends today. What if your cell phone runs out of power and you can't reach me? What if I can't reach you? *I feel afraid.*

CLAUDIA: Stop freaking out, Mom, I have almost two bars. It's not a big deal. *I feel embarrassed.*

GWEN: *(Sighs with annoyance)* This is the last time. You just don't listen. *I feel disappointed.*

CLAUDIA: No, I just forget. Why are you being so ridiculous? Anyway,
I read an article that said that if you charge your phone every night,
you do damage to it. *I feel guilty.*

GWEN: You're just making excuses. I'm telling you right now, you are
going to charge that cell phone. *I feel anxious.*

CLAUDIA: I *do* charge it, just not every night. You're so paranoid! Why
don't you trust me? *I feel ashamed.*

Identifying their Inside Feelings gave mother and daughter a different
way to understand a conversation that had dug deep treads in their relationship. As they explored the emotions underpinning the conflict, the
truth rose to the surface. Gwen was angry, but she was also nervous and
afraid. Claudia was not only annoyed but guilty and disappointed.

Practice identifying Inside Feelings in the next exercise. Begin by reading the scene between two middle-school girls.

JESSICA: Brit, can we talk for a second?

BRITNEY: Uh, sure. . . .

JESSICA: So you know how Stacy and I have been managing the basketball team this year?

BRITNEY: Of course I do. What about it?

JESSICA: Well, nothing. I mean, it's just that . . . I . . . I think I might
go on vacation with her family this year.

BRITNEY: Oh. . . really?

JESSICA: Yeah. They have this amazing vacation house and a boat.

BRITNEY: Oh . . . okay. . . . but you've always gone away with my
family for New Year's since third grade.

JESSICA: Well, I know! I know. But your grandma is going with you
guys this year. Right?

BRITNEY: I guess. . . .

JESSICA: So, like, I really wanted to check with you before I got tickets to go with Stacy. I mean, I know you didn't buy tickets yet, and
I figured you'd be totally cool with it, but I just wanted to double-
check, right?

BRITNEY: Uh . . . yeah.

JESSICA: Cool! Because my parents are talking with Stacy's parents
tonight, and . . . well, I just wanted to make sure you were cool with
everything.

BRITNEY: Sure.

JESSICA: Okay. I gotta go. Bye, babe!

In this scene Jessica tells Britney she is going on vacation with a new
family this year but makes it seem as if she is asking Britney's permission.
When girls read this scene, they usually demonize Jessica, who appears
thoughtless and insensitive. Asked to speculate about what will happen the
next day, girls predict that Jessica and Britney will give each other the silent
treatment and avoid each other indefinitely.

Read the scene again. This time name the Inside Feeling each girl might
be having. The chart on page 144 can guide you.

JESSICA: Brit, can we talk for a second?

Jessica's Inside Feeling: ———————————————————————

BRITNEY: Uh, sure. . . .

Britney's Inside Feeling: ———————————————————————

JESSICA: So, you know how Stacy and I have been managing the basketball team this year?

Jessica's Inside Feeling: ———————————————————————

BRITNEY: Of course I do. What about it?

Britney's Inside Feeling: _____

JESSICA: Well, nothing. I mean, it's just that . . . I . . . I think I might go on vacation with her family this year.

Jessica's Inside Feeling: _____

BRITNEY: Oh . . . really?

Britney's Inside Feeling: _____

JESSICA: Yeah. They have this amazing vacation house and a boat.

Jessica's Inside Feeling: _____

BRITNEY: Oh . . . okay . . . but you've always gone away with my family for New Year's since third grade.

Britney's Inside Feeling: _____

JESSICA: Well, I know! I know. But your grandma is going with you guys this year. Right?

Jessica's Inside Feeling: _____

BRITNEY: I guess. . . .

Britney's Inside Feeling: _____

JESSICA: So, like, I really wanted to check with you before I got tickets to go with Stacy. I mean, I know you didn't buy tickets yet, and I figured you'd be totally cool with it, but I just wanted to double-check, right?

Jessica's Inside Feeling: _____

BRITNEY: Uh . . . yeah.

Britney's Inside Feeling: _____

JESSICA: Cool! Because my parents are talking with Stacy's parents tonight, and . . . well, I just wanted to make sure you were cool with everything.

Jessica's Inside Feeling: _____

BRITNEY: Sure.

Britney's Inside Feeling: _____

JESSICA: Okay. I gotta go. Bye, babe!

Jessica's Inside Feeling: _____

*(See Appendix for suggested answers.)*

In my experience, girls who complete this exercise often write that Jessica feels guilty and anxious, while Britney feels hurt and betrayed. When they consider both girls' Inside Feelings, they become more aware of Jessica's conflicted situation.

I ask girls to imagine what the conversation would be like if Jessica and Britney shared their Inside Feelings. Some predict they would get into a fight, and that others would get involved and take sides. "Maybe they could have worked it out," others suggest. "Britney would have told Jessica how she felt," "Britney would have seen that Jessica felt guilty," or "Jessica could have seen how she hurt Britney." Girls begin to feel some empathy for Jessica. In Girl World, where so little is spoken directly, truth is often silenced, withheld, or misinterpreted. By infusing emotions into the conversation, the truth begins to emerge.

Try writing a script of a challenging conversation you have with your daughter. Write the dialogue exactly as it happens. After each line identify the Inside Feelings you both might be having. See how the meaning of the conversation changes. The next time you fight with your daughter, consider departing from your usual script. Share an Inside Feeling to defuse the anger and illuminate what is really happening between you.

To introduce the concept of Inside and Outside Feelings to your daughter, consider the following questions:

- Would you react differently to someone if she said "I feel hurt" instead of "I feel angry?"
- Is there a difference between how people act when they know they feel hurt and how they act when they feel angry?
- Sometimes when I get angry, it's because I have other feelings inside that make me even more upset, and getting angrier seems easier and safer. Does that ever happen to you? What feelings might be underneath your anger?

## HOW TO SAY IT

Every conflict, no matter how big or small, is about getting something you want from another person: a concession, a confession, a commitment to stop or start doing something. This is crucial for girls to understand: conflicts are opportunities for gain, not loss; they allow you to get the things you need to feel better and have more fulfilling relationships. In this section you learn how to leverage your emotional self-awareness to get what you want from difficult conversations.

Every summer at the Girls Leadership Institute, we put girls into pairs and have them face each other, with each person's palms touching the other's. Then we ask one girl to push her palms against her partner's. The same thing happens every time: the other girl instinctively pushes back.[2]

The same is true in conflict. If you "push" on someone verbally, the other person will automatically push back, either by defending herself or by launching her own offensive. Pushing dooms conversations, and girls do a lot of it.

The three most common ways girls push are these:

- *The "You Statement"*: These are sentences that begin with *You* and contain accusations. "*You've* been ignoring me." "*You* don't know what you're talking about." "*You said* things about me behind my back." Most people automatically begin defending themselves: "No I haven't." "Yes I do." "No I didn't." Conflicts flame up from there.
- *Always and never*: "You *always* make me late for class." "You *never* listen to me." Tell someone she never does something and she will immediately try to tell you about the times when she did.
- *The Character Attack*: Saying something about someone's personality or self. "You're *rude . . . mean . . . a bitch*," and so on. When you attack who a person is, rather than what she did to upset you, she will immediately try to defend her character.

Keep in mind that pushing is not necessarily verbal. Using the "death stare," rolling your eyes, or making noises during a conversation will also escalate a conflict.

Nothing good comes from pushing conversations. Voices get raised, hips are thrust out, and accusations pile up. You can't get what you want from a conversation like that. The "I Statement" is a promising alternative. Simple and clear, it is the least "pushy" way to express a problem and set the stage for getting what you want.

# I STATEMENTS

"I felt [emotion] when you [specific action]."

"I felt *hurt* when you *laughed at me at lunch today when I said* Sponge-Bob *was my favorite show.*"

Warning: girls of a certain age—usually the ones who have learned to control their eye-rolling muscles—are known to bristle at I Statements. Be prepared. Your daughter may inform you that "no one talks like that." You can take two approaches: First, when you learn something new, it takes a while to get comfortable with it. Whether it's riding a bike or learning a new word, most things feels weird at first. Second, you can actually make I Statements sound more like the way you talk (more on that later). But don't give up: you are teaching them the crucial mechanics of communication. Trust me, no matter what they say, girls are desperate for ways to navigate their relationships. They are listening.

The I Statement is effective for several reasons. It puts your feelings first, asking the other person to consider the impact of her behavior on you. Second, someone can easily defend herself against an accusing You Statement, but it is harder to challenge what you feel. Third, when you describe what someone did, like "I felt hurt when you laughed at me," you avoid attacking who someone is, like "I felt hurt when *you were rude* to me."

I advise girls to use Inside Feelings in their I Statements when possible. Inside Feelings clarify our perspective with a mix of power and vulnerability, taking the listener to the heart of what bothers us. Outside Feelings are powerful but provocative. They often trigger defensiveness in the listener, distracting her from attention to your feelings and needs.

Consider the difference in how you might react to these two I Statements:

"I feel *hurt* when you make fun of my clothes."

"I feel *angry* when you make fun of my clothes."

Girls say they would respond more positively to the Inside Feelings sentence; if someone said she was hurt, they would be more likely to show concern or at least inquisitiveness. If someone said she was angry, girls say they would generally prepare to defend themselves.

# COMMON I-STATEMENT MISTAKES

## Being Vague

Girls' first I Statements tend to be vague. This is hardly surprising; after all, the more detail they include, the harder it is to take back what they say. The trouble is that vague I Statements are easy for others to deny or ignore.

Consider Hope: A sixteen-year-old supergirl, she got straight A's, held down a part-time job, was class president, and did dance squad four times a week. But she couldn't make a specific I Statement to save her life. When her two friends, Star and Courtney, started leaving her out of mall trips, movie nights, and sleepovers, Hope ran through the Good Girl justifications. She tried pretending it was okay. She told herself not to overreact. She figured she was too busy to hang out anyway. Finally, rolling her eyes at her own tears and running her knuckles angrily across her cheeks, she asked me if we could work on it. It took a while to access her Inside Feelings, but Hope found them eventually.

"I feel hurt and put down when you leave me out," she began.

I spontaneously decided to play the part of Star.

"What do you mean?" I squealed. "We love you, sweetie! We call you, but you're always busy, you know? Come on, don't be upset!" Hope stared at me helplessly.

My impromptu performance came from a tattered old script: Good Girl pressure to avoid conflict trains girls to minimize or deny conflicts altogether. Hope had to know how her vague I Statement might be answered. We went back to the drawing board. I asked Hope to identify the *who, what, where, when,* and *why* of what bothered her. With a little prodding, Hope began listing the activities she felt excluded from, along with the days the events took place.

You can help your daughter become a more powerful speaker by prompting her to include specific details in her I Statements. Below are vague I Statements that girls commonly make, along with strategies to help speakers be more specific. Even if you do not teach your daughter I Statements, you can still empower her to articulate her problems effectively. The point is to develop her ability to be specific, so she can successfully communicate and get what she wants. If you can persuade her to practice with you, or if she expresses her feelings but doesn't quite hit the mark, try these teaching prompts.

---

**I feel nervous when you get mad at me online.**

PROMPT: When and where did this person get mad at you? Can you give one example of what she wrote or did?

**I feel hurt when you leave me out.**

PROMPT: When and where did the person leave you out?

**I felt embarrassed when you made fun of me.**

PROMPT: What did he say when he made fun of you? When and where did it happen?

---

Be on the lookout for these other common I Statement mistakes:

OMITTING YOUR EMOTION.
"I feel like you are leaving me out."

*What you can say:* "Can you use an emotion word to describe what you feel?"
*Why:* "I feel like . . ." is not an emotion; it's the start of a thought.

## REVERTING TO AN OUTSIDE FEELING.
"I feel angry when you exclude me."

*What you can say:* "Can you use an Inside Feeling to describe what you feel?" Or, "Are there any other feelings you have underneath the anger?"

*Why:* Anger tends to cover over Inside Feelings such as hurt, put down, or betrayed, and that's what is really bothering you. When you express Outside Feelings, people may react defensively and escalate the conflict.

## HIDING A YOU STATEMENT INSIDE AN I STATEMENT.
"I feel disappointed because you are being mean."

*What you can say:* "I'm glad you're telling me how you feel, but you were attacking *me* rather than *the thing* that I've done to upset you. Can you focus on the specific thing I am doing that you think is mean, rather than on who I am as a person?"

*Why:* "You are being mean" is a You Statement and contains a character attack, a negative remark about who someone is as a person. Most people respond by defending themselves and will stop listening to you. It's much more effective to talk about the *thing* someone has done, rather than *who someone is.*

Remind your daughter that she can make I Statements her own. They sound stiff at first, but they don't have to be in practice. An example of a more colloquial-sounding I Statement might be, "I feel really insecure when you don't return my calls. The last two times I called, it took you three days to call back," or "Yesterday when you said I was too demanding at the mall, I was really embarrassed."

ROLE-PLAY IS AN EXCELLENT WAY TO PRACTICE CONFLICT skills with your daughter. Choose an interpersonal problem she is having

*Practice turning these You Statements into I Statements. Remember to be specific: Where did it happen? When? Who was there? You will need to create your own details to build the most effective I Statement.*

|  | YOU STATEMENT | I STATEMENT |
|---|---|---|
| EXAMPLE | You always ignore me. | I felt hurt when you ignored me yesterday after school. I tried talking with you when you were with Ilana. |
| Something a parent might say to a daughter | You never clean up your room. | |
| Something a daughter might say to a parent | You are the strictest parent out of all the parents I know. | |
| Something a friend might say to you | Why are you always asking me to tell you secrets about other people? | |
| Something you might say to a friend | You never ask me what I want to do. | |

*(See Appendix for suggested answers.)*

and playact a conflict. Play the role of the person your daughter is confronting. If she is too vague about her problem, deny it, just as I did with Hope. You can go in and out of character, prompting her for detail with some of the questions above.

Confronting another person is never easy, and there are no guarantees.

I Statements are not magical fairy dust, and girls should not be led to believe otherwise. Difficult conversations are always unpredictable. I Statements are channels for truth-telling; they are a best bet, not a silver bullet. But when girls avoid conversations altogether, the truth can only be guessed.

*Eight*

# FROM ASSUMING TO KNOWING

When girls sequester their real thoughts and feelings, relationships become mysteries. Unanswered questions proliferate: *Is she mad at me? Did she mean that?* Anxiety mounts. In the absence of knowing, girls begin assuming: this is what she must think, feel, and mean. These often-snap decisions are tinged with panic and fear, and they beget destructive responses. This chapter will teach you to help your daughter to understand and resist assumption-making.

Girls are astute observers of their social world. It's not that they aren't watching what is happening, it's that they don't ask about what they see. Assumptions are Good Girl maneuvers that give girls a way around the tough questions that could lead to conflict. They are fundamentally symptoms of passivity in relationship, enabling girls to conduct their relationships in their own heads.

Teaching girls to recognize assumptions is the first step.

**Define an assumption.**

An assumption is when you make a decision about something without having all the details. It's always best to use an example to explain, so describe the Anna and Reena story from chapter 2: Anna and Reena pass each other in the hall. Anna says hi, and Reena doesn't respond. What might Anna think? Most girls will say, "Anna thinks Reena is mad at her." Ask your daughter how Anna knows that Reena is angry. She'll probably say, "Because she ignored her."

Is being angry at Anna the only possible reason that Reena might not have responded to Anna? Girls tend to point out at least two other possibilities: Reena might have not heard Anna, or Reena might be having a really bad day. If you're not totally sure why someone has done something, or how that person feels, but you decide you know anyway, that's making an assumption. If Anna decides that Reena is mad at her, she has made a decision without having all the details. The bottom line is that you can't infer; you must *know*. No guessing allowed!

Practice identifying common assumptions girls make by underlining the assumption in each of these girls' thoughts.

*Example:* I can't believe she didn't say hi to me in the hallway. <u>She must be mad at me.</u>

1. We were just having this huge conversation online, and she signed off. I must have said something to offend her.

2. She told me she had no plans this morning, but I just heard she was going to the movies with my friends. I guess she didn't want me there.

3. Those girls are talking about me. They keep looking at me while they're talking.

4. Mrs. Sales doesn't like me. She says I'm not working up to my potential.

*(See Appendix for suggested answers.)*

**Talk about the consequences of assumptions.**

An assumption is a thought, and thoughts do not always just happen and go away. Thoughts are seeds that take root in our minds, spawning shoots of feelings and more thoughts. To illustrate the power of thoughts, have your daughter list the emotions, thoughts, and actions that are likely to result from the underlined assumptions below.

*Example:* I can't believe she didn't say hi to me in the hallway. She must be ignoring me.

EMOTION(s): shocked, hurt, angry
THOUGHT(s): What did I do? What's her problem?
ACTION(s): Find out from others what's going on. Give her the silent treatment.

1. She told me she had no plans this morning, but I just heard she was going to the movies with my friends. *I guess she didn't want me there.*

EMOTION(s):
THOUGHT(s):
ACTION(s):

2. We were just having this huge conversation online, and she signed off. *I must have said something to offend her.*

Emotion(s):
Thought(s):
Action(s):

3. *Those girls are talking about me.* They keep looking at me while they're talking.

Emotion(s):
Thought(s):
Action(s):

4. *Mrs. Sales doesn't like me.* She says I'm not working up to my potential.

Emotion(s):
Thought(s):
Action(s):

5. Tess is talking to Mike, the guy I have a crush on. *She's trying to take him away from me.*

Emotion(s):
Thought(s):
Action(s):

*(See Appendix for suggested answers.)*

**Question assumptions.**

Once you know what assumptions are, you can catch yourself making them in the moment (instead of when it's too late). When you feel it happening, there is one simple thing to do: ask if there are any other reasons the person might be feeling or acting this way.

For example, if you find yourself thinking, *She didn't save me a seat at lunch, so I guess she'd rather sit with other people,* you have to be 100 percent certain there are no other reasons she didn't save that seat. Or if you're fuming that *she tells me where to stand at practice because she thinks she's better than me,* you must be sure that's the reason.

Author and educator Lisa Sjostrom suggests encouraging girls to *wonder* about their assumptions. Wondering is the experience of curiosity and doubt; it opens the mind up, allowing you to look around and consider other possibilities. Try some "wondering" exercises below.

> *Example:* I can't believe she didn't say hi to me in the hallway. *She must be mad at me.*
>
> I WONDER: *I wonder if she is angry at me, or if she is having a bad day, or if she didn't hear me.*

1. My best friend is hanging out with the popular girls and spends less and less time with me. She must think I'm not cool enough.

   I WONDER:

2. My friends say that shirt looks good on me, but they're probably lying.

   I WONDER:

3. I can tell by the way that girl is talking to Joe that she wants to steal him away from me.

I WONDER:

Assumptions are not limited to peer interactions. Last year Caroline became convinced her teacher thought she was stupid. The teacher complimented other students but seemed to question everything Caroline said. Caroline's older brother had been a student a few years before, so Caroline decided her brother had been smarter. "She can't believe that I'm not as good as Daniel, so I should just not even try," she told me. Then she decided to wonder. She realized she had no idea what kind of student Daniel had been in class. "Then I started feeling more confident for some reason, and now . . . I take it as a huge compliment that she thinks I can come back with an educated retort."

**The answer is to observe and then ask.**

The antidote to assumptions is information. In other words, the only way to know something for sure is to ask. "*Are* you mad at me?" "*Why* did you get up from the lunch table without saying good-bye?" Sometimes, you may not need to ask. If you are patient, time may bring an answer. If Anna had waited to see Reena again later that day and Reena had acted normally, Anna would have known that Reena wasn't angry. The self-control required for such a discovery is worth the effort. Remember that incessant "Are you mad at me?" questioning can become irritating and should be used carefully.

I Statements (see chapter 7) can also yield an explanation of why someone acts a certain way. In chapter 2, Ruby assumed that Candace had talked about her plans with Jess to one-up Ruby. When Ruby told Candace, "I feel inferior when you talk about your plans with Jess," Candace opened up and explained the real reason she talked so much.

**Assumptions are small betrayals.**

When we assume the worst of someone's intentions and emotions, we assume the worst possible version of who she is. It was fourteen-year-old CJ who described her assumption about a close friend as a minor betrayal. She was in a computer lab at school watching from two rows back as her friend read an old Instant Messenger transcript. Suddenly CJ felt sure the friend was reading something mean about her, and, as she puts it, "my mind went off."

CJ calmed herself down and asked her friend directly. The transcript had nothing to do with her. CJ told me she was left feeling "like I hurt her, because I assumed she was doing something mean and that [meant] I didn't trust her." CJ had learned that assumptions were built on distorted versions of other people. Before girls assume, they should consider whether the person has earned the feelings and intentions they are attributing to her.

## THE END OF HINTS

The belief that a true friend should be able to read your mind is deeply ingrained in girls' expectations of relationship. The tendency to drop hints and become angry at someone unable to guess your internal state has troubling implications. Hint-dropping is a Good Girl gesture that affirms one's genteelness at the expense of full self-expression. It allows girls to avoid owning their most difficult thoughts and feelings.

It's among peers that girls learn the relational tools they will use in other contexts. As girls learn to share their strongest feelings indirectly, they are likely to import those habits into intimate or professional settings. Below I list a few ways to encourage girls to become more active participants in their relationships.

**Emphasize the responsibilities of friendship.**

We spend a lot of time telling girls what a good friend should be, but we focus mostly on what girls should be *getting* from friendship. Girls need to be reminded what they are obligated to *give* to a relationship; in particular, they are responsible for communicating their thoughts and feelings directly. You are not being betrayed if adults and peers don't know how you feel—you just haven't told them how you feel.

**Look out for hints.**

When your daughter is upset, does she drop hints by becoming sullen or silent, slamming doors or rolling her eyes? If you respond to her hints by asking, "What's wrong?" and cajoling her to talk, you are rewarding the indirect behavior. Try asking, "Is there something you're trying to tell me? I would really appreciate it if you could be direct." If she refuses, try not to pursue it. Explain that you would like to talk, but only if she can have a conversation. If she still refuses, consider how you may affect her discomfort with self-expression. For example, do *you* drop hints when you are upset?

**Explore the big picture.**

Explain the link between self-expression and getting something you want or need. For example, CJ went to a Billy Joel concert with her family. She figured they would stay until the last song. When her parents wanted to beat the traffic and leave early, she fell quiet. She hoped they would realize how much she wanted to stay, even as she agreed to leave. They didn't take the hint. "I think that was a turning point," she told me. "I'm not going to get what I want if I don't ask for it."

That day CJ's hint-dropping cost her a few songs. If she does not learn an alternative, her indirectness may be the only tool she can access as an adult in the workplace, and it will limit her potential. Remember the woman in chapter 2 whose hints about wanting an assignment in Paris cost her the job. Talk with your daughter about the link between precise speech and getting the things you want, whether it's a job, an apology, or a change in a friend's behavior. Remember, assertive self-expression is a skill that requires practice. The more you can model and encourage the behavior at home, the better.

*Nine*

# COMING CLEAN: TELLING AND HEARING THE TRUTH

It's old news that girls need help initiating tough conversations, and many worthy organizations teach girls the skills to speak up. We have directed far less time and attention to teaching girls how to respond. Girls' lack of practice with direct conflict leads them to minimize, deny, or become overwhelmed when confronted. The honest conversations crucial to authentic relationship cannot occur.

The importance of understanding girls' conflict-resolution behavior cannot be overstated. What they learn in their relationships often becomes the template for their public or professional habits. If we want girls to become women who can negotiate conflict with confidence, the time to intervene is now.

At the Girls Leadership Institute, we impose "Rules of Engagement" that guide girls' behavior in face-to-face confrontation. Structure provides a familiar, predictable framework that gives each girl a fair hearing. Below I list the rules, along with the messages girls send in relationship when they do not hew to basic fairness in conflict.

**Rule #1: Leave the Past in the Past.**

Lila was upset that Rosie got a ride home from the mall with another friend. Lila thought Rosie was going home with her.

"Chill," Rosie told Lila. "You ditched me last spring at the dance—remember—and there was no one to take me home. At least you got a ride this time."

THE RULE: Rosie should respond directly to Lila's complaint without mentioning the past. It is not appropriate to bring up a time Lila did the same thing to her, or any other mistake Lila has made.

GIRLS WHO BRING UP PAST CONFLICTS TEACH THEIR FRIENDS:
- "I hold grudges and never really forgive my friends. I'm keeping a file on your bad behavior that I'll pull out anytime you tell me I did something wrong."
- "Don't bother trying to tell me if you have a problem with me, because I will always have an answer that makes what you say meaningless."

**Rule #2: Keep the Conflict One-on-One.**

Lila and Rosie kept talking, and Lila refused to give up. "You shouldn't have left," Lila said.

"I couldn't find you," Rosie retorted, "and Grace agreed. She said that if you weren't there, it probably meant you forgot or were just doing something else."

THE RULE: Rosie should not bring anyone else into this conversation. The conflict is now unfair: it's "two" against one. Mentioning Grace is almost like having her stand next to Rosie and gang up on Lila. Lila is likely to get nervous and defensive, wondering if Grace and Rosie have been talking about her behind her back.

GIRLS WHO BRING UP OTHER GIRLS IN A ONE-ON-ONE CONFLICT TEACH THEIR FRIENDS:

- "I can't have a conflict with you without someone else to back me up. I can't really be trusted to keep things private between us."
- "Whenever you fight with me, you might be fighting with all my friends. Since I'm mentioning them in this conversation, I've probably already talked to them about you, so watch out: you might get in trouble with them, too."

**Rule #3: Curb the Impulse to Overreact.**

Rosie started to cry. Lila tried to comfort her, but Rosie stormed away and sat on the floor near a bay of lockers. Within minutes two girls were tending to her.

THE RULE: When Rosie cried, she ended the conversation, forcing Lila to comfort Rosie and table her own grievance. Rosie's public tears signaled that a drama was under way and immediately drew other girls into the situation. Rosie thus escalated the conflict. Lila was unable to talk through her problem with Rosie, all but ensuring that Lila would hold a grudge. If she was unable to continue talking, Rosie should have sought the comfort of an adult, or a single girl in private, but not several girls in a public space.

GIRLS WHO CRY IN PUBLIC WHEN CONFRONTED TEACH THEIR FRIENDS:

- "Don't criticize me, because I can't take it. I fall apart and get other people to take my side. Then you might really be in trouble."
- "You're better off not saying anything at all."

## CONTROLLING OVERREACTIONS

Getting upset during a conflict sometimes seems like a sincere expression of how bad you feel: the harder you take it, the sorrier you must be. Girls often react this way because they unfairly expect themselves to be perfect friends. But overreactions allow a single problem to call one's entire self-worth into question, undermining girls' ability to resolve interpersonal problems.

Have your daughter try the exercise below:

- List three qualities you have that absolutely define who you are. Do not list physical characteristics. Write something about your character or personality.
  1.
  2.
  3.

- List one time you didn't show each of those qualities.
  1.
  2.
  3.

When the authors of *Difficult Conversations: How to Discuss What Matters Most* asked me to do this, I was shocked. I had written:

1. Funny
2. Generous
3. Loving

*Easy,* I thought. *I am absolutely those three things.*

Except, of course, when I'm not, like the time when I made a joke that offended someone, or felt bitterly toward a friend who had something I wanted, or did any other number of things that made me unfunny, ungenerous, and unloving.

The lesson, of course, is that you can't be one thing all the time. No one is perfect.

Girls love this exercise because they realize how much pressure they put on themselves to be that one thing all the time, whether it's being nice, funny, or a good friend. When you try to be one thing all the time, and when you expect yourself to be that flawless, you tend to freak out when you do mess up. Likewise, the more comfortable you are with accepting your own imperfections, the less they will shatter you.

If your daughter tends to overreact when someone is upset with her, remind her of this exercise. Then ask her what she would tell her best friend if her friend got upset about a confrontation. Your daughter will probably say, "I'd tell her that everyone makes mistakes. Nobody's perfect. It's not the end of the world. Let's talk about what you can do to fix this." Encourage your daughter to talk to herself the way she would comfort her best friend. Promote the use of a mantra she can employ to talk herself down from an overreaction. Levelheaded thinking will help steady her in the face of confrontation.

When girls minimize or overreact to conflict, they are seeking ways to avoid looking directly at the truth. Our goal is to help them understand that having a friend brave enough to tell the truth is a blessing; that the alternative is a relationship rife with grudges and unspoken, festering emotion; and that honesty is far more than telling the truth. It is the courage to hear it.

## "JUST KIDDING" AND "NO OFFENSE"

"Just kidding" and "no offense" have become troubling staples of the Good Girl vocabulary. Girls use these phrases to avoid responsibility for mean or uncomfortable remarks. The logic is this: If I'm just kidding, you can't get upset. If I say "no offense," you can't take offense. In other words, if I didn't mean it, it didn't happen. The phrases normalize duplicity in girls, stunting the development of straightforward communication.

If we do not challenge these verbal quirks, we indirectly give girls permission to continue using them. The ability to say something difficult but true is a critical life skill that will serve your daughter in every area of her life. The last thing any parent wants is for his grown daughter to remark to a colleague, "No offense, but I thought your presentation could use some work." Below I suggest ways to help end your daughter's dependence on these habits.

**Expose the "just kidding" logic.**

Use a concrete analogy to illustrate the hidden message of "just kidding" and "no offense": *If I didn't mean it, it didn't happen.* Ask your daughter to imagine accidentally knocking a vase off a shelf and breaking it. If she came to you and said, "I didn't mean to do that," would that mean it didn't happen?

Similarly, whether or not you meant a joke has nothing to do with whether or not it happened. You may not have meant it, but, like the vase, that person may still feel "broken."

**Label the behavior aggressive.**

Seemingly unintentional meanness is also known as indirect aggression. Affirm that you find "just kidding" and "no offense" inappropriate. Compare the behavior to a type of aggression she already takes seriously: overt insults or hitting, for example. Remember that children are less likely to behave aggressively when they have a reason not to, so set a cost for violating the rules, like the loss of Internet or cell phone for a brief period.

**Create a No-Joke Zone (NJZ) in your home.**

We all have a No-Joke Zone, or things we do not find funny but that other people might. For example, by the time I was thirteen, I had huge feet. I was mortified by any attention south of my ankles, especially jokes ("Flipper," "Bigfoot," etc.). My best friend's feet were petite, and she had no problem if someone cracked a joke about them. Her bushy hair, however, was another story. "Feet" were my NJZ, and hair was hers. Girls have told me their NJZ is weight, braces, family structure, or complexion. The list of possibilities is endless.

I have taught the NJZ to girls, guys, and families as a code they can use to draw the line on an offensive joke. When someone makes a joke that crosses the line, you say, "That's an NJZ" or simply "NJZ." When an NJZ is called, the other person must apologize sincerely. Then you change the subject. Move on and talk about something else.

Telling someone to "chill out" or wondering why she can't "take a joke" denies responsibility for hurting the other person. When you respect the NJZ, you own your mistake and acknowledge the other person's feelings. The NJZ creates a new script to replace the old "Can't you take a joke?" retort. It puts the premium on honesty, teaching girls that what is important is not whether you made a mistake but how you deal with it.

### Eliminate "no offense" from your family's vocabulary.

Comments that begin with the phrase "no offense" almost always wind up being disrespectful. There are two uses of "no offense": you use it either to be genuinely mean or to justify saying something hard to hear. Either way it's used as a Get Out of Jail Free card. You can always retort, "I said 'no offense,' okay?" If you cannot say something without saying "no offense," you are better off finding another way to say it.

### Explain the cost of "no offense" and "just kidding" to relationships.

It's an open secret among girls that "no offense" and "just kidding" let you get away with saying hurtful things. In other words, most girls assume that the speaker was not really joking, did mean it, and is now lying about it. As a result, "no offense" and "just kidding" corrode trust in relationships. When you use these phrases, the message you send to others is, *I'm not totally honest about what I really feel and think.*

**Ask her what's really bothering her.**

People who follow up mean remarks with "just kidding" may be sitting on something deeper that they are struggling to express. Tell your daughter, "It's not what you say, it's how you say it. It's okay to say what you really feel, but there are more respectful ways to express yourself."

**Brainstorm alternatives.**

Suggest different ways she can express herself. Instead of saying, "No offense, but . . . " she might try, "I'm worried that what I'm about to say might hurt your feelings." Remember, it's not appropriate to say, "I don't mean to hurt your feelings, but . . . " because we fall into the trap of valuing intent over impact.

Girls often use "no offense" to ask for something, as in, "No offense, but could you leave us alone?" I recommend substituting, "It would be great if you could . . . " or "I would really appreciate it if you . . . " or "Would you mind . . . " Talk together about respectful ways she can ask for what she needs. Think about how you can model them yourself.

**Check yourself.**

Do you use humor as a way to take swipes? Your daughter is always watching and listening. She will follow the example you set.

## HELPING GIRLS OWN UP

Sheila Heen, Douglas Stone, and Bruce Patton, the authors of *Difficult Conversations,* have written that conflicts are largely about assessing blame.

When we fight, we are really seeking the answers to questions like "Who is the bad person in this relationship?" "Who made the mistake?" "Who should apologize?" "Who gets to be righteously indignant?" The need to pigeonhole one person steers the conversation away from the search for a solution.

Heen, Stone, and Patton propose a tool called *contribution* as an alternative to blame, and I have used it to great success with girls. Contribution asks different questions: "How did we *each* make this situation bigger or worse?" and "What did we *each* do or not do to get ourselves into this mess?"

Blame is a dead end. It labels one person as "wrong" and the other as "right." Contribution proceeds on the assumption that we all could have done something differently. It works because, when you think about it, it's rare that both parties to a conflict have not added to the problem in some way. If conflict is a kind of partnership, so is responsibility. Contribution says that everyone who makes a mess has to clean up the room.

Contribution fits the idiosyncrasies of Girl World to a tee. Girl conflicts typically spin a lot of yarn before anyone actually deals with them. By that time whole casts of characters have become players in some way. Sit down with a girl (or five) to listen to her tell the story of a conflict and your head will spin within seconds: it's quickly apparent that there are few innocent bystanders.

With its premise that no single person is responsible, contribution can prevent the feelings of excessive self-blame that shame girls. Contribution also provides much-needed structure to girls' chaotic conflicts.

There is one scenario in which contribution does not apply: bullying. If a girl lashes out at another girl randomly and without provocation, it is not the responsibility of the victim to name her contribution.

---

THE RULE:

In almost all arguments, both sides have somehow contributed to the conflict.

WHAT IT SOUNDS LIKE:

I'm sorry that I . . .

    told Brianne about your birthday party.

    agreed to go out with Jeff.

    ate all your fries.

I realize that I should not have . . .

    told Brianne about your birthday party.

    agreed to go out with Jeff.

    eaten all your fries.

Delivery is key. Use a sincere tone of voice and make eye contact.

---

When I mediate conflicts between girls, they know they will be expected to identify their contribution to the problem. You can teach the concept in your own home and school and make it a part of your conflict-resolution protocol.

Now practice finding the contributions in the following scenarios.

    **Example:** *Dahlia is friends with Molly and Crystal. Molly and Crystal don't like each other, and each of them gets annoyed when Dahlia hangs out with the other girl. Lately Crystal has been saying things like, "I'm just not sure how we are going to keep being friends, the way things are going." Last night Crystal asked Dahlia if she wanted to hang out, but Dahlia already had plans with Molly. Dahlia told Crystal her mother said she couldn't go out. When*

*Dahlia was at Molly's, they told someone over Facebook they were together, and somehow it got back to Crystal. Crystal is really angry with Dahlia.*

DAHLIA'S CONTRIBUTION: She lied to Crystal about her plans.

CRYSTAL'S CONTRIBUTION: She threatened to end her friendship with Dahlia if she kept hanging out with Molly. This is relational aggression, a kind of social holdup where the weapon is your friendship: "Do this or I won't be your friend anymore."

1. Kendra and Elise are best friends. On Tuesday, Elise told Kendra she had a crush on Jared. Kendra had a crush on Jared, too, but she didn't bother saying anything, because Elise is the type of girl the guys always like. On Friday, at the movies, Jared sat next to Kendra and tried to hold her hand. Kendra didn't pull away, because she was too freaked out not to. Elise was sitting on the other side of Jared and left in the middle of the movie. On Monday, Elise didn't speak to Kendra and told two of their mutual friends about what was going on. On Tuesday, when Kendra passed Elise with some people, Elise looked at Kendra and then went back to talking with her friends.

KENDRA'S CONTRIBUTION:

ELISE'S CONTRIBUTION:

2. Lauren is upset because her father, John, often leaves the house to drive her to school just a few minutes before school starts. This makes Lauren anxious and frustrated, because she absolutely hates to be late. John thinks Lauren is overreacting. Yesterday Lauren asked her dad if he would set his alarm a little earlier, because she had a presentation at school the next day. John said he would. Today, the day of the presen-

tation, Lauren's alarm didn't go off, because she forgot to set it. John usually wakes Lauren up, but he didn't today, because he was running around trying to be ready in time. Lauren ran downstairs and yelled at her father that he was ruining her life and that she would now clearly fail the presentation.

LAUREN'S CONTRIBUTION:

JOHN'S CONTRIBUTION:

3. Nicole is an extremely social person, and she has a hard time with the fact that her daughter, Danielle, is very, very shy. When they are in public together with Nicole's friends, Danielle barely says a word. This embarrasses Nicole. Nicole has spoken to Danielle several times about the need to respond to others politely. This weekend Nicole and Danielle were coming out of a store when they bumped into someone from Nicole's job. When the person said hello to Danielle, she looked at the ground. On the way home, Nicole barely spoke to her. Danielle asked her mom what was wrong, and Nicole said, "Nothing." But later Nicole told Danielle she had to find another way to get to her friend's house.

NICOLE'S CONTRIBUTION:

DANIELLE'S CONTRIBUTION:

4. RachelJS74: wassup!
   Whit9999: nm
   RachelJS74: how r u??
   Whit9999: ok
   RachelJS74: r u mad at me!?
   Whit9999: kind of ;)
   RachelJS74: what's wrong!???

Whit9999 has signed off.

[Whit9999 is Whitney. She is angry with Rachel because she thinks Rachel ignored her today at lunch.]

RachelJS74: r u there
Sharynnn333: yes
RachelJS74: has whit talked 2 u
Sharynnn333: yes
RachelJS74: r u mad at me too!!!!!?????
Sharynnn333: no.
RachelJS74: good. u can't get mad at me whit has been ragging on u behind yr back again this year and i have so defended u
Sharynnn333: what??????
RachelJS74: i know, right? she is such a snob

WHITNEY'S CONTRIBUTION:
RACHEL'S CONTRIBUTION:

*(See Appendix for suggested answers.)*

## COMMON CONTRIBUTION MISTAKES

When we apologize or take responsibility, we often want to explain our mistakes. If you need to explain your contribution, make sure it does not sound like an excuse. The difference between an excuse and an explanation is that an excuse makes it seem as if your behavior was justified or that you were not at fault. It may refer to the other person as the reason you did something.

**EXCUSE:** *I'm sorry I told Brianne about your birthday party. Somebody had to. It was getting embarrassing for her. She was 99 percent sure of it anyway!*

An explanation, on the other hand, clarifies your behavior. It gives the other person some insight into your feelings or experience. It may also make you somewhat vulnerable. Sometimes it helps to explain your behavior with the language of emotions.

EXPLANATION: *I'm sorry I told Brianne about your birthday party. I was feeling embarrassed that she was not invited and pressured because she kept asking me about it.*

Notice the difference between an excuse and an explanation in these examples:

1. EXCUSE: *I'm sorry I agreed to go out with Jeff, but you went out with my boyfriend a week after I broke up with him.*

   EXPLANATION: *I'm sorry I agreed to go out with Jeff. I really like him, and I have been upset that I haven't been asked out in months.*

2. EXCUSE: *I'm sorry I ate all your fries. You got up from the table to use your cell phone.*

   EXPLANATION: *I'm sorry I ate all your fries. When you got up from the table, I thought you were done eating.*

## EASY-TO-MISS CONTRIBUTIONS IN GIRLS

The most common contribution I see in girls' conflicts is the one easiest to miss: not telling someone you had a problem at the time and stewing instead. Let's revisit the scene with Britney and Jessica.

JESSICA: Brit, can we talk for a second?
BRITNEY: Uh, sure. . . .

JESSICA: So you know how Stacy and I have been managing the basketball team this year?

BRITNEY: Of course I do. What about it?

JESSICA: Well, nothing. I mean, it's just that . . . I . . . I think I might go on vacation with her family this year.

BRITNEY: Oh . . . really?

JESSICA: Yeah. They have this amazing vacation house and a boat.

BRITNEY: Oh . . . okay . . . but you've always gone away with my family for New Year's since third grade.

JESSICA: Well, I know! I know. But your grandma is going with you guys this year. Right?

BRITNEY: I guess . . .

JESSICA: So, like, I really wanted to check with you before I got tickets to go with Stacy. I mean, I know you didn't buy tickets yet, and I figured you'd be totally cool with it, but I just wanted to double-check, right?

BRITNEY: Uh . . . yeah.

JESSICA: Cool! Because my parents are talking with Stacy's parents tonight, and . . . well, I just wanted to make sure you were cool with everything.

BRITNEY: Sure.

JESSICA: Okay. I gotta go. Bye, babe!

The attractive candidate to blame is Jessica, who only pretends to ask Britney for permission to go on vacation with a new friend. Now cut to Monday at school: Britney ignores Jessica. Jessica is confused; Britney had acted as if she had no problem during their phone call. In mediation Britney will have to own her contribution, which is smaller than Jessica's but no less significant: she should have told Jessica how she felt in the moment. When Britney gave Jessica the silent treatment on Monday, she escalated the conflict.

# THE ART OF THE APOLOGY

The Curse of the Good Girl has also influenced how conflict is resolved. The word "sorry" has lost its meaning in the culture at large, in part because "sorry" has become slang for "excuse me" and "oops." The number of public apologies has mushroomed, while the apologies themselves have become hollow and insincere. This "apology phenomenon" has diluted what a true apology looks like and sets a bleak example for young people.

Girls are habitual overapologizers, often misusing "I'm sorry" as a Good Girl tool to repair relationship, avoid conflict, or salvage a reputation. Talk with your daughter about the message that overapologizing sends to others, reminding her that others may not share her perception of apology. For example, say your daughter is in a fight with a friend who never apologizes. She doesn't know why, but she is getting the cold shoulder and will continue to get it until she gives in. Your daughter is convinced she has to apologize to save the friendship. To her, apology represents resolution: she repairs the relationship, and the friendship continues. Yet there is much more at stake when she apologizes for the wrong reason.

You can illustrate the larger cost by encouraging your daughter to differentiate between the short- and long-term consequences of her choices. Explain that her decisions communicate things to people about how she wants to be treated, how others can (or can't) treat her, and what she stands for as a person.

If you apologize, what will happen? *We'll make up and be friends again. I won't lose her.*

If you apologize, what will you teach this friend about yourself in the long run? *That I'll always apologize and she doesn't have to. She can do whatever she wants to me, because she knows I'll apologize, even if I'm not at fault.*

If you don't apologize, what will happen? *She probably won't talk to me, and our friendship will end.*

If you don't apologize, what will you teach this friend about yourself in the long run? *That I will not be taken advantage of, and that I don't want to be friends with people who act that way.*

This exercise also illuminates the difference between a sure thing and the unknown in a friendship. This girl knows what will happen if she apologizes; it's what she's always done. But it's not clear where standing her ground will lead. When girls say things like, "She won't be my friend anymore if I don't apologize, I just know it," they are attempting to foreclose against the anxiety of actually doing it. It is important to point out that this uncertainty is where the potential for change in relationship lies.

The tendency to overapologize affects young women's workplace habits. According to Deborah Tannen, some women use apologies as acts of generosity at work, but male colleagues often interpret them as admissions of fault. This can affect a woman's image and her potential to succeed professionally.

If you have a daughter who rarely apologizes, ask what her choices communicate. If she is in a fight with a friend or sibling and refuses to give in, talk about what her actions teach others about her.

If you don't apologize, what will happen? *She'll apologize to me, and we'll be friends again.*

If you don't apologize, what will you teach this friend about yourself in the long run? *That I think she is always the one who does something wrong. Unless she apologizes, I won't be her friend anymore.*

Then ask two more:

If you do apologize, what will happen? *She might apologize back. But she might not.*

If you do apologize, what will you teach this friend about yourself in the long run? *That I'm weaker than she is. But also that I respect her opinion and am big enough of a person to admit when I'm wrong.*

**Avoid Saying "That's Okay."**

Girls tend to respond to apologies by automatically replying, "That's okay," "Don't worry about it," or "No problem." These comments are intended to make the other person feel better and smooth over the relationship. But responding to apology by saying that "it's okay" sends the message that what the person apologized for *was* okay. Of course, sometimes it was okay, but many times it wasn't.

Encourage your daughter to say thank you instead. It's much harder—sort of like saying thanks for a compliment about your shirt instead of humbly saying, "Oh, this old thing?"—but it communicates strength and confidence. A thank-you acknowledges the truth of the situation without revisiting it.

**Know Why You Are Apologizing.**

When your daughter decides to apologize to someone, make sure she knows why she is doing it. Apology is called for only when you genuinely believe you have wronged someone and regret it, not because you are afraid to lose the person, be confronted by others, or damage your reputation. Remorse should be the guiding motivation. You don't apologize to save relationship or save face. You don't do it because you want a response. You do it to make amends with the other person and, in a way, with yourself.

**Know What to Expect.**

Apologies can effectively conclude conflicts, but some girls struggle with the transition between apology and a relationship's getting "back to normal." Conversations can be strained at first, and the friend your daughter apologized to might adjust more slowly than she would like. Remember that apologies are not erasers. Sometimes the aftermath of an apology can be as important as the apology itself, a time when the other person is gingerly stepping back into the friendship, making sure she really can trust again. Try not to rush it.

It helps to return to the metaphor of the body. A friendship is like a body part. Both are vulnerable to scrapes, bruises, and breaks. Conflicts wound friendships, and wounds need time to heal. If you run on a sprained ankle, you may damage it permanently. The same goes for an injured friendship: push it too hard, too fast, and you may do it more harm.

**Define a Sincere Apology.**

"I'm sorry you feel that way" is not an authentic apology. A genuine apology is given in a sincere tone of voice and with respectful eye contact. It takes responsibility for a specific act and expresses regret.

"I'm sorry this is so hard for you," "I'm sorry, but . . ." and "I'm sorry if . . ." are not up to snuff. These can be expressions of sympathy, but do not confuse them with apologies.

**Model Genuine Apologies.**

Children who grow up in homes where adults do not apologize usually learn to apologize because they are ordered to do it. In this context saying "sorry" is not unlike doing a household chore, part of the price of living under your parents' roof. When children witness the vulnerability and emotion of a parent apologizing, the lesson is visceral. Remember Daniel Goleman: the family is the "Primary school for emotional learning." This kind of modeling takes courage but is singularly powerful.

# PUTTING IT ALL TOGETHER: THE FOUR STEPS OF HEALTHY CONFLICT

I've had countless conversations with girls seeking advice about their relationships. Every story, no matter how complicated or outrageous, converges at a single point: the need to confront someone else. When I tell girls that this is the answer, that they must find the courage to speak the truth, their eyes begin to wander. Their bright, hopeful faces dim. They think I have a magic wand, something that will let them bypass the stress of conflict.

Magic wand, no. Map, yes. This section takes the tools you have learned and introduces Four Steps girls can use for difficult conversations. The Four Steps teach girls vital conflict-resolution skills. By affirming the relationship in Step One, girls practice peaceful outreach. In Step Two, the I Statement, they articulate a problem in detail and demonstrate emotional self-awareness. By owning their contribution in Step Three, girls show transparency and authenticity. In the final step, girls define a goal and provide a specific solution to achieve it. Like any conflict-resolution strategy, the Four Steps are most effective when used one-on-one and in person. A note of caution before beginning: The Four Steps help girls address conflict with friends and acquaintances. They should not be used with a bully or with anyone who threatens your daughter's emotional or physical safety.

**Step One: Affirm the Relationship.**

Say something positive about the relationship (it does not have to be a friendship). This step is important because many girls think that conflict will terminate their relationships. Use this step to assure the person that there is a future beyond the conversation.

- *"You are really important to me."*
- *"I really like working with you on this project."*
- *"You are a great friend."*
- *"I care about you a lot."*

***Avoid using the word "but" to move between steps. Try "and" instead. For example, "You are really important to me, and . . ."**

**Step Two: Use an I Statement.**

Define the specific problem and how you feel about it. Try using an Inside Feeling and articulating the who, what, where, when, and why of what's bothering you.

- *"I felt hurt when you ignored me in the hall between second and third periods. I said hi and you didn't say anything back."*
- *"I felt embarrassed when you made a comment about my clothes in front of my friends on Sunday morning in the kitchen."*

**Step Three: Say Your Contribution.**

Explain what you did you to make the problem bigger or worse.

- *"I realize I forgot that you made plans for us last Saturday."*
- *"I'm sorry that I checked my phone when you were talking."*

**Step Four: Ask How You Can Solve This Together.**

This is the part where you say what you need from the other person. That's not easy for a lot of girls, because it involves asking for something. Good Girls are givers above all, and asking feels dangerous. That's why Step Four allows for a little bit of both: You can say what you need and also offer to do something yourself.

- *"I can look at my calendar before I make plans. Can you be more clear about what time of day you want to hang out?"*

Be specific with your solutions. As with I Statements, girls tend to get vague here. Avoid asking for someone to "be nice to me," "spend more time with me," or "include me more." Instead make suggestions that include where, when, and how your solution can happen. The same applies for saying what you plan to do differently: to stay specific, revisit your contribution and make it your promise to change. That is, if your contribution to a conflict was forgetting plans with a friend, your solution going forward should be to check your calendar more carefully.

## PRACTICE

*Practice the Four Steps by reading the following two scenarios.*

Marissa and Julia are eighth-graders and close friends. Marissa stomps over to Julia's locker.

"I cannot believe this, but Lucy is actually angry that I asked her to reschedule our plans on Saturday," Marissa said breathlessly.

"Wow . . . sorry. . . ." Julia stuttered. *Uh-oh*, she thought, eyes searching over her friend's shoulder.

"I mean, what is wrong with her?" Marissa sighed. "She is so hyper-sensitive."

*What am I supposed to say?* Julia thought. Marissa knew that Julia and Lucy were friends.

"Uh-huh," she said.

"What were you saying about her last year?" Marissa wasn't taking the hint. "About how she was, like, unreliable?"

Julia had no choice. "Well, yeah, I mean, we had a fight about who I was inviting to my birthday party."

Marissa thrust her chin out. "See? I knew it. She hasn't changed at all! Are you guys really tight?"

"Sort of . . . I mean, we worked stuff out. . . . " Julia looked away.

"Anyhow, will you have lunch with me today? I totally don't want to have to deal with Lucy at all."

"Okay . . ." Julia agreed, chewing on her lip.

*Julia must use the Four Steps to tell Marissa that she doesn't want to be in the middle of Marissa's fight with Lucy.*

*Example:*

FOUR STEPS FOR JULIA

1. *Affirm the Relationship:* I really care about you, Marissa, *and*
2. *I Statement:* I felt pressured and anxious when you asked me about my fight with Lucy. I felt like you wanted me to take sides.
3. *Contribution:* I'm sorry I didn't say anything about how I felt at the time.
4. *How Can We Solve This Together?:* I can be more honest about my feelings in the moment. Can you please not talk to me about your problems with Lucy?

TRY THIS ONE ON YOUR OWN.

Rebecca and Jewel were best friends. After vacation, Jewel started spending more time with Annaluz. Jewel still saw Rebecca, but not nearly as much, and Rebecca felt left out. Sometimes, when Jewel was around Annaluz, she didn't act the same way she used to. Rebecca felt very anxious and worried.

Jewel asked Rebecca to give her and Annaluz some private time. When Jewel and Annaluz tried to have lunch by themselves, Rebecca came over with other girls and then acted as if it wasn't her idea to join Jewel and Annaluz.

*Rebecca must use the Four Steps to talk to Jewel.*

Affirm the Relationship: _____.

I Statement: I felt_____ when you_____.

Contribution: I'm sorry I_____.

How Can We Solve This Together?:

I can_____. Can you_____?

*(See Appendix for suggested answers.)*

## BRINGING THE FOUR STEPS HOME

By practicing the Four Steps in their own homes, girls become more comfortable taking them to their peer relationships.

Gwen and Claudia, whose pushing scripts I shared in chapter 7, used the Four Steps to try a new way of communicating. Their fight over Claudia's uncharged cell phone repeated every few days, and as the You Statements multiplied—"You're paranoid," "You're ridiculous," "You never listen"—so did their frustration.

Gwen and Claudia sat down to work through their Four Steps, with two rules: First, both knew that this would not be a discussion between peers. As the parent, Gwen had the upper hand, and there were some obligations Claudia would have to fulfill simply because she was the child. Second, both had to come up with solutions they could realistically make happen. Their Four Steps are below:

| GWEN | CLAUDIA |
|---|---|
| 1. I love you, Claudia, and<br>2. I feel *anxious* and *afraid* when you leave the house without your cell phone fully charged. I'm *worried* that we won't be able to reach each other in an emergency if your phone has no power.<br>3. I realize I yell at you about this.<br>4. I can change my tone if you can charge your phone every night. | 1. Mom, I care about you a lot, and<br>2. I feel *anxious* and *guilty* when you yell at me about charging my phone.<br>3. I'm sorry for not charging my phone when I say I will.<br>4. I can charge my phone at night if it gets down to three bars. Will you stop yelling at me about it? |

Mother and daughter came up with different solutions: Claudia still didn't want to charge her phone every night. Gwen thought about it. She knew that Claudia didn't use her phone that much at school, so three bars was something she could offer.

"Okay," she told Claudia. "But I still want to check your phone every day before we go to school." Claudia, happy to have won her concession, agreed.

I am not suggesting that every conflict with your daughter should become a negotiation. As the parent, you make the rules. But presumably you're not a dictator, and some conflicts leave room for negotiation. These are opportunities to teach your daughter conflict skills and for her to practice in a safe environment. Even if the conflicts repeat—and they invariably will, especially where teenagers are involved—it is the practice, and the habits being learned, that count.

Try writing your own script of a typical pushing conversation you have with your daughter (it doesn't matter who initiates the pushing). You can use the template below. Then try rewriting the conversation using the next page.

## Pushing Script

Pick a tough conversation you regularly have with your daughter. Write the dialogue *exactly as it usually happens.*

CHARACTER 1:

CHARACTER 2:

CHARACTER 1:

CHARACTER 2:

CHARACTER 1:

CHARACTER 2:

CHARACTER 1:

CHARACTER 2:

CHARACTER 1:

CHARACTER 2:

*Your Four Steps*
Affirm the Relationship: _____.
I Statement: I feel _____ when you _____.
Contribution: I am sorry that I _____, or I realize I _____.
How Can You Solve This Together?
I can _____. Can you _____?

**Practice Makes Perfect**

When your daughter is ready to confront a peer in person, remember that conflict resolution is a skill that requires practice. As with anything else, the more you do it, the more comfortable and able you become. I ask girls to "rehearse" their Four Steps before actually using them with anyone. To do this, each girl writes out her Four Steps and trains a partner to act like the person she plans to confront. Then they "perform" the conflict a few times, improvising different reactions and endings.

Try the same thing with your daughter. Have her write out her Four Steps and coach you to act like the peer she plans to approach. It's best to role-play different versions—for example, one where the peer denies what your daughter says, one where she gets angry and defensive, and another where the peer listens affirmatively. In these role-plays, your daughter should strive to maintain a respectful tone, a firm voice, and strong eye contact throughout.

Keep your feedback light and courteous. Avoid predictive comments like, "There's no way she'll listen to you if . . ." When you suggest she try something else, call your alternative a "different" way instead of a "better" one. Most important, remember your differences. She may not yet have learned what you know. Meet her where she is, not where you wish she would be. Notice her strengths and limitations in equal parts. Keeping the journey in mind, remember that even a simple rehearsal with your daughter is a victory, even if she never uses the Four Steps in real life.

# PREPARING YOUR DAUGHTER FOR PEER CONFLICT: IT'S NOT WHETHER YOU WIN OR LOSE, IT'S HOW YOU PLAY THE GAME

For the last seven years, I have traveled around the country answering questions from girls, parents, and teachers about peer conflict. I generally hear the same questions wherever I go: "How can I get this to stop?" or "How can I get these girls to be nice to my daughter?" or "How can I get my daughter away from these girls?" The questions are fair and important, but what they are really asking is, "How do I fix this problem?"

This approach concerns me. A single-minded focus on the endpoint of a conflict naturally removes our attention from the journey. It can lead us to view conflicts in terms of success or failure, rather than what might have been learned in the process. In fact, girls' potential to develop conflict-resolution skills is located in the little victories and bumps along the way, even when the Emerald City still lies in the distance.

Consider one such victory: the moment Vicky, one of my students, made an excuse and got off the phone instead of letting her friend provoke her into a fight. Did Vicky challenge the friend's behavior? No. Did she do something gutsy and significant? Absolutely.

Likewise this bump: When Hope asked Star and Courtney to make more of an effort to include her, they seemed receptive. The girls hung out together, but a week later it was more of the same exclusion for Hope. It took her six months of rejection, sorrow, and anxiety to figure out that she had lost her close friends. Did she succeed in her confrontation? No. Did she learn important lessons about betrayal and disappointment in relationship, the futility of her best efforts, and knowing when to give up? Without question.

As you guide your daughter through peer conflict, temper your quest to "fix" the situation with attention to what she has the opportunity to learn. Consider some of the skills or experiences your daughter will begin to realize in the course of her conflicts, even when they are unresolved:

- Risk-Taking
  - Approaching someone and initiating a conversation
  - Expressing yourself under pressure
  - Asking for what you need
  - Telling someone how you feel
  - Refusing to continue an unsafe conversation (walking away, hanging up, signing off)
  - Being the first to apologize
- Self-Awareness
  - Affirming your values (refusing to go along with the group, calling out behavior that bothers you)
  - Defining your standards of relationship
  - Knowing your strengths and limitations
- Resilience
  - Accepting that things don't always go your way—and that you can survive it
  - Accepting that people disappoint you but knowing that it doesn't change who you are or your value to others

Celebrate the little victories. Explore what she learned from her moments of failure: when she confronted that girl about spreading rumors, and the girl denied it and told her to chill out; when she tried making peace with an angry friend and was rebuffed; when she agreed to talk something over online and found out that her friend had shared the transcript with other girls.

It's often the anguish of watching your daughter hurt that inspires a fix-it mentality. Approaching her struggle as a learning experience will challenge you to not only accept but value situations that are messy, uncertain, and unresolved. Remember that the stakes already feel daunting to her. She is probably putting more than enough pressure on herself. If you can redefine success and failure when it comes to your daughter's growth, and privilege a learning experience over a winning one, you will teach your daughter that we are as enriched by our failures as we are by our triumphs.

*Ten*

# FACING CRITICISM WITH CLEAR HEADS

This chapter will help you improve your daughter's response to feedback by modifying the way she thinks about it. Girls' overreactions are driven by two destructive thoughts: criticism means that someone is upset with me personally, and the mistake defines me as an individual. These thoughts consign girls to an endless mental chorus of self-reproach, frustrating their potential. By teaching girls to recognize and correct distorted thinking, we can help them to "reinterpret failure."[1]

Cognitive psychologists believe that our thoughts about events, or how we interpret them, determine how we feel and act. If our thoughts become distorted or unreasonable, extreme emotions and actions follow. Girls' most inflammatory thoughts are generated by unfounded assumptions about themselves and others. When a girl looks at a test grade and thinks, *I'm stupid,* she uses a single event to make a mental leap about who she is as a person. When she decides *The whole team is mad at me because I missed that basket,* she simply guesses at what others think and feel. By ignoring what's real and true, girls fall down the rabbit hole into warped views of themselves and the world around them. They become distracted and distraught.

When girls overreact to criticism, they are usually admonished not to "be silly" or are simply told they are overreacting. This is a well-intentioned attempt to change a girl's perspective about failure, but your daughter will benefit most from learning how to change her perspective herself. When a girl jumps to the conclusion that criticism means someone is angry with her or that it defines her as a person, it suggests that her focus lies with what others think, rather than what she knows to be true of herself. The strategies in this chapter will anchor your daughter to what is real about herself and her life, providing her with the tools to resist self-destructive thoughts.

This chapter will also ask you to consider your own relationship to limits. The way you respond to your daughter's challenges provides vital cues to her about how to interpret failure. The example you set is crucial.

## THE POWER OF THOUGHTS

Our most powerful thoughts are like pebbles falling into water: just as the ripples extend outward and swell, so do our thoughts reverberate, giving rise to feelings that intensify as we muse. Carmen's thoughts came quickly when she picked up her English paper before study hall. Upon viewing the sea of red marks, she thought, *I'm an idiot. I'm never going to get into college.*

A high-school junior, she made a significant formatting error. The teacher had warned Carmen about it before, so she was penalized accordingly. As she walked down the hall, Carmen began feeling hopeless. She cried in the bathroom. She did not want to talk to the teacher to get help, as she might usually do, but instead thought about transferring out of the class. She felt embarrassed, ashamed, and sad.

It wasn't the criticism per se that launched Carmen. It was her interpretation of the situation—her thought that she was an idiot who would never get into college—that set in motion an extreme, self-punishing reaction. Psychologist Aaron Beck called these mental triggers *automatic thoughts*, cognitions that occur on a barely conscious level but which set off chain reactions of intense feelings, thoughts, and actions.

| EVENT | AUTOMATIC THOUGHT ⟹ | EMOTIONS ⟹ | THOUGHTS ⟹ | ACTION ⟹ | THOUGHTS |
|---|---|---|---|---|---|
| Feedback on paper | I'm an idiot. I'm never going to get into college. | Shame Sadness Embarrass-ment | I want to quit. I want to be alone. | I'm not talking to the teacher. | Maybe I can transfer to a less-challenging class. |

Two assumptions drove Carmen's distorted thoughts. First, when she called herself an idiot, she allowed a single incident to pronounce who she was as a person. Psychiatrist David Burns calls this *labeling*, or merging your identity with your mistake. You tell yourself *you* are stupid instead of thinking that you did a stupid *thing*. You become your mistake, as though nothing else existed besides.

Carmen's second assumption, that she would not get into college, was another fantasy. Burns calls this *fortune-telling*, predicting the worst without the evidence to support it. For instance, you make one mistake as a writer for the yearbook and decide you will never be chosen to become an editor.

These thoughts were hardly rational, but Carmen truly believed them. People in the grips of distorted thinking have, in a sense, lost touch with reality and facts. Even if you are Carmen's parents and you know that not only is she not stupid, but she is absolutely going to college, your well-intentioned, logical reassurances will likely amount to a hill of beans.

Instead cognitive psychologists suggest engaging a distorted thinker in a careful evaluation of her beliefs. By being asked calm questions that encourage girls to state facts, girls can have their distorted thoughts contract into more realistic proportions. The basic steps include:

1. *Identifying the Distorted Thoughts.* In Carmen's case these were "I'm an idiot" and "I'm never going to get into college."
2. *Checking the Evidence.* Determine the accuracy of the thoughts by looking at both sides.
   a. *"I'm an idiot."* Is Carmen an idiot? On the one hand, she made a careless mistake. But Carmen also has a 3.0 GPA.
   b. *"I'm never going to get into college."* Carmen's GPA guarantees her a spot at a four-year college. She may not go to Harvard, but she will go somewhere.
3. *Redirecting.* Set goals *with* Carmen (not *for* her) to help her focus on ways she can improve her performance: what can she do to avoid repeating the error? For instance, could she set up a meeting with her teacher or write herself a note on the wall next to the computer?

If Carmen considers the evidence, her sweeping pronouncements may lose steam, making a distorted thought like *I'm so stupid* begin to look more like *I made a careless mistake,* a much less intense interpretation.

Obviously, this will not erase Carmen's mistake, nor should it. At their best these techniques lower the intensity of the thoughts associated with failure. They are more likely to steady Carmen, clear her head, and free her up to find a solution. In the next section, I use these techniques in conversation.

# TAKING IT PERSONALLY: SHE HATES ME

There are two ways girls commonly personalize criticism. The first is the decision that the evaluator actually dislikes her. Girls typically make this assumption following a direct interaction with someone, usually an adult.

Burns calls this *mind-reading*. Mind-readers decide what someone thinks or feels without knowing the truth.

Emily came home convinced her teacher hated her. She told her mother, Amy, that she was stupid.

Consider this sample dialogue, with intervention techniques in italics:

EMILY: I'm stupid, okay?

AMY: I can see why you'd feel that way, but *the reality is you made the honor roll last year.* Plus, we had a really interesting conversation last night about the industrial revolution. Those are hardly the marks of someone stupid. *So are you stupid, or could you use a little improvement in this particular area?*

EMILY: Maybe I was smart up until this year. I peaked at twelve.

AMY: *What about the A on your science-fair project?*

By gently providing evidence that Emily isn't stupid, Amy tries to pry Emily away from identifying with stupidity itself. She avoids the appearance of a lecture by asking questions, prompting Emily to assert the facts that may bring her thinking more in line with reality. Notice how Amy tries to reframe Emily's response: "Are you stupid, or could you use a little improvement in this particular area?"

Amy neither judges nor dismisses her daughter. Telling Emily something like, "You're not stupid! Don't be so dramatic, you were valedictorian last year," would invalidate Emily's position and make her defensive. Instead Amy affirms her daughter's emotional experience. Even though Emily's reaction to criticism may seem "hormonal" or melodramatic, she truly believes what she thinks about herself and the teacher. Amy takes her seriously, walking a line between challenge and empathy, increasing the likelihood that her daughter will listen.

AMY: *Why not go see Ms. Blum tomorrow and set up a time to go over your work?*

EMILY: No way. She hates me.

AMY: *How do you know she hates you?*

EMILY: Because she picks on me nonstop?

AMY: *So she's never been nice to you, not once?* No sign of liking you whatsoever?

EMILY: Obviously she was really nice to me when I was out for Nana's funeral.

AMY: She was. And *she was awfully nice about you in her written comments.*

EMILY: Well, maybe she changed her mind.

AMY: She might be frustrated by the fact that you're talking to your friends in class, but I'm not sure that translates into her hating you. Let's be fair: You've always struggled with organization, and you're not exactly a wallflower in class. Sometimes you go too far. I know it's hard to hear you're not doing well. But that's something you can fix with a little extra work and commitment. So why don't we try to sit down right now and figure out a strategy to help you resist the temptation to talk to Megan and get your homework better organized?

Amy counters Emily's belief that the teacher hates her with evidence to the contrary. She also asks Emily to produce her own proof to back up her assertions. Yet she doesn't lie to her daughter about the situation: Ms. Blum is upset, and there is no point in denying it. Emily made some mistakes. She needs to accept the consequences of her actions. Undistorting Emily's thinking should not mean revising what has happened. The point is not to say, "You're perfect, don't change," but to steer the conversation toward an accurate explanation and a solution.

Sometimes empathy and evidence only go so far. You may need to take a harder line. When your daughter becomes convinced that an evaluating adult dislikes her, talk about the tendency of women and girls to let critiques of their skills become statements about their relationships. Be firm: just because someone criticizes your performance, that does not automatically mean the person doesn't like you. Have your daughter remember a time when she was evaluated but did not take it personally. For example, if she didn't think her soccer coach was upset with her when he told her to hustle more, why not?

Your daughter may respond that she likes her coach more: he's *nice* to her, he *likes* her, and the team is fun. Pay attention when she uses words like "nice" and "cool" to describe adults. This is a sign that she may be applying the rules of friendship to professional relationships. These are her first nonfamilial or social relationships, and she should understand the difference. Your daughter needs to know that no matter how much she likes certain teachers or coaches, they are not her friends. She will have many relationships in life where being liked is not the point, including those with a colleague, a doctor or lawyer, a boss or subordinate. Personal connections with teachers are wonderful, but a teacher's first priority is to teach, and your daughter's goal is to learn. A "nice" relationship with someone is not a precondition for working with or listening to her.

This can feel like the opposite of empathy. It isn't. By showing your daughter the difference between legitimate criticism and an attack, you are teaching her a social skill that will serve her throughout life. You are socializing her into the etiquette of professional relationships. When you support an adult's constructive feedback, you set a crucial example for your daughter, endorsing truth-telling and honesty in relationship, even when it hurts. These critical moments of modeling and skill-building may sting in the moment but will reap huge rewards over time. Your daughter will thicken her skin and learn to follow Real World rules instead of Good Girl rules. She'll do it now, instead of ten or twenty years down the road.

# THE INVISIBLE
# EVALUATOR

Girls can personalize their mistakes without ever being criticized directly. The thought goes something like this: *If I make a mistake, I have let someone down, and she will be mad at me.* Because girls often believe conflict terminates relationship, what they are really thinking is, *If I disappoint someone, she won't like me anymore.*

When your daughter believes that a person is upset with her for a mistake, work directly with her assumption about what others feel by looking for the evidence. The intervention techniques are in italics.

GIRL: The whole team is so pissed at me because I fouled out of the game.

ADULT: *Has anyone said anything about being mad at you?*

GIRL: No, but I can tell they are.

ADULT: *How?*

GIRL: You know . . . you can just tell. Everyone was listening to music on the bus on the way home, it was like they were all so upset.

ADULT: *Well, I agree that you did make a mistake, and you may have let someone down, but it doesn't automatically follow that the person is upset with you. The only way to know that for sure is to ask directly. What can you do to know for sure?*

GIRL: Ask, I guess.

Of course, in girls' communication underground, the teammates on the bus may really be angry but refuse to express it directly. In response to being asked if they are upset, they may offer an icy, "I'm fine" that says they are anything but. Still, even an indirect sign of anger is at least some evidence of reality, rather than the assumptions involved in watching people listen to music on the bus.

When a girl is too overwhelmed to share her thoughts, you may need to do a little digging. Psychologists Dennis Greenberger and Christine Padesky suggest asking several directed questions to get to the heart of distorted thinking.

- What was going through your mind just before you started to feel this way?
- What does this say about you if it's true?
- What does it mean about you, your life, and your future?
- What are you afraid might happen?
- What's the worst thing that could happen if it's true?
- What does this mean about how the other person(s) feel(s)/ think(s) about you?
- What does this mean about the other person(s) or people in general?[2]

I have found these questions invaluable with distraught girls. I used these techniques in a conversation with fourteen-year-old Alicia.

RACHEL: I know it's tough to be criticized—I have a hard time with it, too—and I'm really sorry you're hurting. But why do you think you're taking this so hard? *Do you think this says something about you as a person?*

ALICIA: Why should anyone trust me now? I've blown it.

Alicia immediately revealed her distorted thought: *no one will ever trust me again.* With her fortune-telling thought exposed, I engaged it, giving Alicia examples of times people had successfully relied on her in the past. The intervention techniques are in italics.

RACHEL: But you have a much bigger track record than this one incident. You were great at leading your team at the ropes course, and you emceed the talent show. This is not the only thing people know about you.

ALICIA: Nobody's going to remember that now.

RACHEL: *What's the worst that could happen here?*

ALICIA: People will see that I screwed up.

RACHEL: *What does people seeing you screw up have to do with how they feel about you?*

ALICIA: They might be mad. Or not like me as much.

Asking Alicia to consider the worst that could happen teased out her real fear: people will see she screwed up. The next question (What does this have to do with how others will feel about you?) focused on the perceived impact to her relationships. This is a critical question for girls, who are endlessly preoccupied with how their actions affect others' opinions of them. Remember: these conversation techniques are not intended to erase the experience of failure. The questions provide answers about why we are so upset, clearing the fog around our most powerful emotions and thoughts. When we know why we feel something, it often lowers the intensity of our response.

# DENIAL

A girl in denial is not exactly eager to share her thoughts or feelings. She would probably prefer not to talk with you at all. Forget her thoughts for the time being and take a more circuitous route. Ask some of the following questions:

- What do you think the intention is of the person giving you this criticism? What do you think s/he is thinking?
- How might your reaction to the feedback affect your relationship

with the person giving it? What does your reaction teach this person about you?

- How will your response improve your ability to repair the problem?
- Even if you don't agree with the criticism, is there any part of it that makes sense to you?
- What can you do to move forward in a positive way, even if you don't agree with the feedback?

Coaches and teachers are like our first "bosses." Throughout your daughter's life, she will find herself in situations where people evaluate her performance. Refusing to listen conveys apathy about her work and disrespect to her superiors. Staying open to feedback is also important for successful group work with peers. If she consistently resists, your daughter's peers may stop communicating with her, putting her at a disadvantage. If all else fails, the bottom line is this: she may not always agree with the feedback, but she will have to find a way to respect it.

IF NOTHING ELSE, SHOW YOUR DAUGHTER HOW LEARNING TO accept criticism can help her live a happier life. Make the connection between accepting feedback from friends and the quality of her friendships. When she cannot face a friend's criticism, it pushes her away, making the friend think she can't be honest with your daughter. The same is true for other kinds of feedback; when you overreact, your productivity is shot.

As you try these techniques with your daughter, keep in mind that whether you succeed is not as important as consistently using them. Even if your daughter does not recover each time, she is listening and participating in the conversation. Your empathic questions model a specific approach to failure, one that, over time, she will learn to use herself.

# TALKING TO YOUR DAUGHTER
# ABOUT DISTORTED THINKING

I have taught girls to recognize and challenge their distorted thinking, and in this section I suggest how you can introduce the concept to your daughter.

Explain to your daughter that overreactions to criticism and failure often occur because of how we think. The way she interprets her mistakes will affect the way she feels and acts. To demonstrate this, ask her to imagine making an error in a performance of her favorite activity and thinking, *I'm such a loser.* How would her thought influence her feelings and behavior? She would probably feel worthless and continue to flounder, if not give up altogether.

Caroline called thoughts like these the "crazy freak-out voice" (CFOV) in her head. The CFOV makes negative assumptions about ourselves and other people's beliefs about us, without any proof to support it. It makes us feel worse and do things we may regret. The thought *I'm such a loser* is a CFOV, because a single mistake does not define you as a person.

Caroline's CFOV said untrue things about herself and others. When she made even a small mistake, the voice piped up, "How could I have been so stupid to do that?" When she tripped, the voice said, "How can everyone forgive me for tripping?" When she made a joke that people found only a little bit funny, the voice said, "They hate me, they think I'm, like, the weirdest person ever." When Caroline's CFOV made noise in her head, she would feel anxious, depressed, and sad. She would want to be alone or snap at family and friends.

When girls are criticized, their most common CFOVs are labeling ("I'm stupid/a loser/ugly/etc."), mind-reading ("She hates me"), and fortune-telling ("I'll never make the team"). When we're in the grips of our CFOV, the thoughts *feel* true, yet they almost never are. These are powerful assumptions that have little grounding in reality. Your daughter can practice identifying the CFOV below. (See Appendix for answers.)

**Example:** *I can't believe coach got mad at me. He totally hates me.*

CRAZY FREAK-OUT VOICE: *He totally hates me.*
WHY: This is mind reading. The girl has no idea what the coach thinks of her.

1. *Dad said I needed to come home before midnight. He doesn't trust me. I can take care of myself.*

CRAZY FREAK-OUT VOICE:
WHY:

2. *I got a ninety-two on the test. Danielle got a ninety-three, and we had the exact same answers. I don't even know why I bother. Ms. Nakra wants me to fail.*

CRAZY FREAK-OUT VOICE:
WHY:

3. *I'm an idiot. The yearbook editor said I forgot to write the names of the people on the backs of my photographs. Now I can't remember who they are.*

CRAZY FREAK-OUT VOICE:
WHY:

4. *I forgot to ask the car pool to stop at the store on the way home so I could get my mom an ingredient she needed for her dinner party. The party is going to be ruined.*

CRAZY FREAK-OUT VOICE:
WHY:


5. *My friend just told me I talk about myself too much, and that she feels like she can't really talk to me when she has a problem. I am a horrible friend.*

CRAZY FREAK-OUT VOICE:
WHY:

*(See Appendix for suggested answers.)*


Ask your daughter to write two Crazy Freak-Out Voices she has heard in her head.

THOUGHT 1:
THOUGHT 2:


## BE YOUR OWN BEST FRIEND

Now that your daughter can recognize her CFOV, the next step is to teach her to confront it. Caroline learned to cope with her CFOV by identifying a "Smart Voice" in her head. The Smart Voice would talk back to the CFOV and provide perspective: "Dude, you're being crazy. That's not true and you know it. Chill out." The Smart Voice was reasonable and knew the facts. It argued with her CFOV. The problem, Caroline told me, was that when she got criticized, the CFOV often drowned out her Smart Voice. "When someone calls me out on something," she said, "it completely tunes out the Smart Voice. It trumps the Smart Voice. It adds to my Crazy Freak-Out Voice."

To find her Smart Voice, Caroline tried to put her best friend in her head. In other words, if Caroline's best friend happened to live inside her brain and heard her saying mean things to herself, what would she tell Caroline? Her best friend's "voice" would support and calm her, becoming Caroline's Smart Voice.

Encourage your daughter to practice the same technique: Ask her to imagine that she applied to be the editor of the school newspaper, did not get the job, and began thinking, *I never win anything. If I wasn't so lazy, I would have gotten my application in on time.* Now ask her what her best friend would say if she were inside your daughter's head and heard this. (If your daughter does not have a best friend, ask her what a close friend would say, even a hypothetical one.)

Her best friend would probably do some version of the following:

1. Show your daughter *proof* she was wrong about being lazy or not winning anything. For example, the best friend might say, "That's not true. You get amazing grades! You can't be lazy and do that."

2. Suggest a *realistic reason* for her situation. For example, she might say, "The reason you didn't get the job isn't that you're lazy. Maybe you don't have enough experience yet. Maybe there's someone more qualified for the position."

3. Suggest *what to do* next. Perhaps her best friend would suggest another job to apply for or some things your daughter could do to bulk up her résumé.

By learning to "be your own best friend," girls can talk themselves through an overreaction. They can develop mantras to sustain them in times of distress.

Emphasize that these techniques are not a panacea for failure. As one girl told me, "None of this changes the fact that I bombed my test, or got benched for half a game, or whatever." She's right. You may have confronted your CFOV, but that does not mean the mistake went away. Of course it didn't. The point is to learn how to avoid going into Code Red when something goes wrong and to deal with yourself when you do start to freak out. Knowing how to cope will make it easier to take future risks.

By being her own best friend, Caroline has learned how to cope with her CFOV. "I learned to differentiate between the two voices," she said. "I feel like now I can be like, 'That's my crazy response,' and now I have to come back with a logical response." She is quick to point out that it doesn't work every time. Merely knowing your CFOV doesn't mean you can totally eliminate it. It just means knowing it, but that can be half the battle. As Caroline says, "I can't always do it, but I try a lot harder now."

## NURTURING RESILIENCE

Some parents are easily provoked to challenge teachers or coaches on their distraught daughters' behalf. Students are paying the price; a spike in parental aggression has led some beleaguered professionals to censor honest evaluations, depriving girls of the chance to improve their skills and comfort with feedback. Like it or not, your relationship with the adults in your child's life is inherently political. Before you pick up the phone, think carefully.

Remember that kids are famous for "hearing" things that adults never said. Girls are likely to hear two in particular:

**"She yelled at me."**

I hear this an awful lot from girls who were spoken to in a firm, un-raised voice. They seem to play back, in their heads, what they heard at the highest possible volume. This aural disconnect is a by-product of the Good Girl curse, in which there is no middle ground between a girl who is nice all the time and a girl who is a bitch. The same is true of vocal tones: girls are unusually sensitive to tone, and may hear hostility where there isn't any. Remind your daughter of the difference between speaking and shouting. A tone that does not sound "nice" does not automatically become "mean."

**"He was mean to me."**

Did your daughter tell you the adult attacked her character? Try to get an accurate rendering of what was said. It is perfectly reasonable to ask your daughter, "Did the coach say *you* were a brat or that your refusal to run laps for warm-up was bratty? What were the exact words?" Again, empathy and inquiry can coexist. If you are still not sure about her account, keep reading.

# PROCEED WITH CAUTION

Your conversations with the adults in your daughter's life set the tone for her approach to failure. They also send messages to adults about how they can relate to her. Self-reflection is vital. Before you talk to a teacher or coach, consider these questions:

- How much of my strong emotions is related to my daughter's being upset, and how much is related to my daughter's specific complaint?
- How much of my feelings is about my own wish for my daughter

to be a better player (student, etc.), and how much is about her specific complaint?

- Does my knowledge of this adult (coach, teacher, etc.) come mostly through my daughter's descriptions or directly through my own acquaintance? If I know the adult personally, is this how s/he has acted in the past? If I don't know him/her, do I need more information before I act?

- If I approach this adult, what will my actions teach my daughter about dealing with criticism?

Ideally, your daughter should confront the adults who disappoint her on her own. Learning to speak with adults is crucial practice for conversations with superiors later in life. It's a skill girls practice less and less, especially when they can e-mail the teacher or coach instead. If your daughter is willing to talk with the adult, discourage the use of e-mail; it allows girls to remain in their comfort zone of avoiding face-to-face conversations.

# KNOW THYSELF

In more peaceable times, consider your own relationship to evaluation. Girls look to their parents' approach to failure as a cue to their own. For instance, I had a friend whose father lost his temper when she failed to do something he wanted to teach her. Basketball, stick shift, chemistry— whatever it was, when she couldn't understand it, he exploded. Her father's loss of temper taught her that failure was highly emotional, a disaster of sorts. Failure also meant disconnection from someone she loved.

Ask yourself if, when you encounter a setback, you consistently:

- Blame your *self* instead of your actions. For example, "I'm so naïve" instead of "What I did was really naïve."

- Fortune-tell. For example, "I'm never going to get another chance to be considered for this promotion" instead of "Maybe the opportunity will come again soon; if not, I may have to think about trying for another position."
- Deny responsibility and get defensive. For example, "She's not in a position to say these things to me."
- Personalize. For example, "My boss has it in for me."

There isn't a person among us who doesn't struggle with criticism. The point is not to be perfect around your daughter but to be conscious of what your responses teach her. It's okay if she sees you overreacting; just don't forget to share your thoughts when you feel calmer later on.

# DIFFERENTIATE BETWEEN A CRITIQUE OF WORK AND A CRITIQUE OF THE SELF

The way an adult gives criticism will affect how girls receive it. If a girl loses her cell phone twice in six weeks and her mother tells her she is ungrateful and careless, the mother has attacked her daughter's sense of self. In other words, her mother is criticizing *who she is* instead of *what she did.* When you make a defining statement about a girl's character, she is much more likely to be overwhelmed by feelings of shame and embarrassment. Labels like "ungrateful" and "careless" trigger destructive thought distortions. After all, it is much easier to recover from doing a wrong *thing* than from feeling as if you're a wrong *person.* Instead, explain that cell phones are expensive and not easily replaced. Talk about the obligations that come with the privilege of having a phone. Listen to the way you criticize your children. Make sure you are focusing on what they do, not who they are.

# BECOME A PARTNER TO YOUR CHILD'S TEACHER OR COACH

Ask your child's teachers and coaches about her relationship to feedback. How would they describe her ability to take constructive criticism? Does negative feedback affect her participation? What kind of response does the adult observe? Has the coach or teacher addressed your daughter directly about it? Identify specific goals for your daughter and explore how you can work together.

# AFFIRM HEALTHY RESPONSES TO FEEDBACK

Girls who accept criticism with grace see the forest for the trees. Their mistakes do not define them or their experiences. As one junior put it, "I kind of take it as a compliment that they notice I can do better and that all I have to do is try harder." These girls grasp the positive intentions of the person giving the feedback. One freshman explained that even when her coach yelled at her, "I just try and take it in a positive way, because he's just trying to help rather than put us down." Recognize and honor your daughter when she does it right.

# MAKE IT A PRACTICE

You can increase your daughter's comfort with feedback by asking her to assess her performance regularly. For example, what does she wish she had done differently on the exam? Why does she think she didn't get the part in the play? This is delicate work, so do not try this when she is upset. Accept only reasonable responses; "I played the worst soccer of my life" is an exaggeration. Encourage drama-free assessments of her limits.

The point here is for her to practice *self*-assessment. What you think about her performance is, in this instance, beside the point. Try not to agree or disagree with her statements. Listen or empathize. When you pair this with a question that asks her to say what she liked about her performance, she will learn to practice more balanced self-assessments. Knowing her limits will feel more casual and less catastrophic.

WHEN THE CURSE OF THE GOOD GIRL PERSONA LEAVES NO room for mistakes, failure inevitably turns into an attack on the self. When girls cannot relate to their limits in a balanced way, far more is at stake than whether they learn from their mistakes. Like them or not, our mistakes turn us into who we become; they are a vital part of our authentic selves. When girls cannot deal with failure, they turn away from the real, flawed individuals they are becoming.

The drive to be seen as flawless by others replaces the internal compass that drives a girl's intrinsic sense of what she wants to pursue and why. The need to be right eclipses the adventurous risk-taking that makes the difference between Good and Great.

*Eleven*

# CHECK YOUR GOOD GIRL
# AT THE DOOR

Chapter 5 traced the migration of the Good Girl curse from girls' social lives to their academic and extracurricular pursuits. In this chapter I suggest ways to identify and stave off Good Girl behavior in these areas. When Girl World rules become Real World rules, the belief that conflict damages friendships becomes anxiety about vigorous classroom debate. Pressure to be modest interpersonally stunts girls' ability to own their talents. Finally, the aggression that characterizes girls' social disputes becomes the template for public conflict resolution.

The glass ceiling begins taking shape: Girls start avoiding the healthy risks necessary for ambitious thinking and doing. They stop expressing themselves with confidence and do not learn to settle conflicts in healthy ways. Good Girl habits become the foundation of the skill set girls bring to the table as adult women.

# THE IMPORTANCE
# OF RISK

Girls who worried that strong opinions, classroom debate, or being wrong had relational consequences began to lie low in their classes. They avoided situations where risk was required. As a result, they did not develop the skills to speak up, debate, or take a chance on an idea. Their learning potential was shrinking as they sought out the easy options.

The essence of risk is the unknown. You try something without knowing if you'll get it right. You depart from what is comfortable, and in this way break your own rules. Good Girls, who are expected to follow rules and appear perfect, are taught to make little room for risk. Building your daughter's comfort with risk will therefore mean embracing a balanced approach to failure, and the ability to honor, even celebrate, being wrong.

Playing it safe is a self-reinforcing habit: the more comfortable girls become with taking the easy road, the more terrifying failure will become—and the more they will want to play it safe. Below are some ways to encourage girls to take more healthy risks.

**Interview her teachers and coaches.**

Ask the professionals in your daughter's life some of these questions:

- Are you comfortable with her level of participation?
- Does she seem flexible about making a mistake, or does she have a strong reaction to failure? Does she ever stop participating?
- Does she seem to raise her hand only when she has the right answer? (For a coach: Does she play it safe on the field or does she take risks? Is she willing to push herself to try things she's not naturally good at?)
- Is she willing to take on challenging projects and tasks?

- Does she appear nervous to take a stand or share her opinion? (For a coach: Does she use her voice on the field?)
- Does she ask for help when she needs it?

Use your findings to think together about helping your daughter.

Many teachers deliberately tempt girls to take intellectual risks. A middle-school teacher at an all-girls school prefaces difficult questions with an invitation to be wrong. The question "is going to be so hard to answer, and I don't even know if there's a right answer out there," she tells her students. "What do you think?" She calls this tactic a "net" to show her students that "you can have those butterflies, you can have that uncertainty, and still put something out there." Teachers should speak with students about the usefulness of wrong answers and reward them for healthy risk-taking. Later in the chapter I provide suggestions for coaches.

**Identify specific risks she can take.**

Encourage your daughter to set goals that involve taking risks. Try choosing from two aspects of self-expression: the willingness to be wrong and the willingness to engage in debate.

First, define a goal. What does she want to do differently when it comes to speaking in class? Twelve-year-old Aldina said she wanted to take more chances and speak up, even if she was unsure whether she had the right answer. We wrote her goal at the top of a sheet of paper. To map out how she could achieve her vision, we drew three concentric circles.

The smallest circle was Aldina's *Comfort Zone*, or the behavior she currently found easiest in this area. Aldina said she was most comfortable "raising my hand only when I know I'm right." We wrote that inside the circle.

The middle circle would be Aldina's *Risk Zone*, or an action she could take to bring her closer to her goal that would be stressful but not over-

## GOAL: I WANT TO BE MORE COMFORTABLE HAVING THE WRONG ANSWER IN CLASS

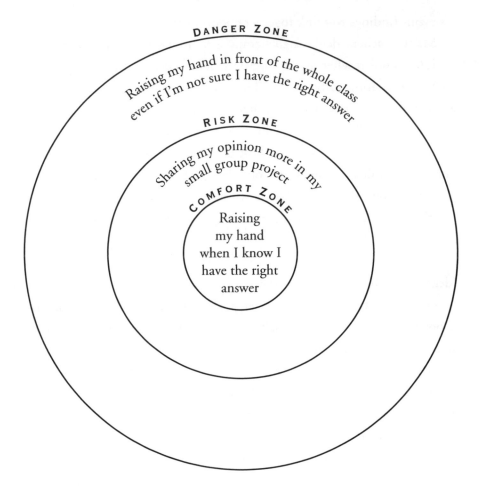

DANGER ZONE

Raising my hand in front of the whole class even if I'm not sure I have the right answer

RISK ZONE

Sharing my opinion more in my small group project

COMFORT ZONE

Raising my hand when I know I have the right answer

whelming. Aldina thought about it. She said, "I could try sharing my opinion more in my small group project."

The outer circle was Aldina's *Danger Zone*, an action that would help her reach her goal but which felt impossible. "Raising my hand in front of the whole class even if I'm not sure I have the right answer," she said breathlessly. "But I'm not doing that, no ways." I reassured her that she didn't have to; she only had to write it down as something that she might do someday and which would bring her closer to the goal. We talked about a specific day she might try to do something in her risk zone.

The zone exercise is a simple, fun way to identify realistic risks with your daughter. By breaking down a big goal into smaller parts, she can differentiate between the truly scary and the maybe-I-could-give-it-a-try. For example, a girl might think, *I hate speaking in class.* By zeroing in on which aspects of speaking up bother her, she can identify circumstances where she would feel comfortable.

As Aldina spent more time in her Risk Zone, what was once foreign and stressful to her became familiar. The Risk Zone began to feel more like a Comfort Zone, and her Danger Zone looked a lot more reasonable.

Other girls working on setting goals for classroom participation have created zone charts.

You can use the zone exercise to think about risk-taking in a range of areas: school, clubs, and sports. The possibilities are limitless! Girls have used it to set goals to take more leadership positions in class projects and become less bossy in group work. They use it to set personal goals to be more outgoing with peers, make more eye contact, and become less concerned with what others think.

**Explore the benefits of risk.**

Risk is the possibility of being wrong, but it's also the chance you might be right. The girls I met who were comfortable with risk grasped the benefits of taking a chance. Girls unafraid to give a wrong answer believed that putting themselves out there projected confidence. As one sophomore saw it, "It's good for your self-esteem to show yourself and to show everyone else, 'Who cares?'" They also saw how staying silent compromised their learning. Play it safe, one freshman said, and "you miss an opportunity."

If your daughter needs more prodding, it will help to discuss the benefits of risk in her life. Return to her three zones and identify the pros and cons of each.

**Comfort Zone:** Raising my hand only when I know I have the right answer.
**Benefit:** I have the right answer.
**Disadvantage:** I don't try things that challenge me. I don't participate as much as I could.

**Risk Zone:** Disagreeing with peers who are my friends.
**Benefit:** I say what I think. I fully engage in my work.
**Disadvantage:** People might not agree with me. I might offend someone.

**Danger Zone:** Disagreeing with someone who is popular.
**Benefit:** I speak my mind.
**Disadvantage:** People might talk about me behind my back because of what I say.

Making the connection between risk and reward will offset anxiety and provide concrete incentives to try new things.

As your daughter maps out her zones, be careful not to weigh in too strongly. Do not minimize or talk her out of her choices. Stay firmly in the realm of gentle questions: Why do you feel this way? What are you worried will happen? What's the worst that could happen? Avoid judgment, remembering that you will each have different definitions of risk. Empathize. Recognize that she is taking a risk just by acknowledging her fears.

Risk-taking girls seem to have a more reasonable self-image. They accept their limits. A sophomore described watching her struggling classmates choose silence over asking a question and being called stupid. She herself didn't mind being wrong. "It's, like, I'm just trying to learn," she told me. She realized that asking meant admitting she didn't know everything, but, she concluded, "I know that's personally better for me." Her self-awareness enabled her to distinguish between what she knew to be true for herself and what others might have wanted and, moreover, to privilege her own needs. Finally, and perhaps most important, girls willing to be wrong had a sense of humor about messing up. If others happened to laugh, they could laugh, too.

Tori, an eighth-grader, saw her ideas and opinions as extensions of herself. By this logic, if her friends made fun of her for her opinions, then they didn't like her for who she was, and she would just find new friends. If her opinion was sound, she told me, "and I know I'm strong about it and I feel comfortable, like, if I feel happy with what it is, then I know that I'm fine with it, no matter what anybody thinks."

**Make a Plan.**

Encourage your daughter to try something in her Risk Zone: Choose a class or extracurricular activity she enjoys. Set a deadline together by which she agrees to take the risk. If she succeeds, celebrate. If she fails, celebrate the importance and meaning of the attempt. What did she learn about herself? How will this experience affect what she does tomorrow? How can mistakes and disappointment push us forward? Why might it be boring to do everything right?

## MEANING WHAT YOU SAY

Self-defeating statements creep like weeds into sentences, obscuring what girls really think and believe. Lost among the "ums," "kind ofs," "likes," and quiet voices are girls' convictions. As Tori said earlier, ideas were extensions of herself. Teaching girls to speak with power is a way to reconnect them with their beliefs, and so with their authentic selves.

Timid voices are hardly owned by girls. Close your eyes at one of my mother-daughter workshops and you might not always be able to tell the speakers apart. Be sure to let your daughter know you're not perfect either. That's how we work at the Girls Leadership Institute: the girls call me out on my tendency to tack "you know?" and "right?" on the ends of my sentences. When we do the work together, we enjoy the experience of mutual empowerment.

Below are strategies for slicing "kind of" and "sort of" off girls' sentences.

**Ask and Observe.**

Tune in to how your daughter speaks when she is expressing an opinion. Keep in mind that she may speak one way in front of you, with whom her interactions are more casual and trusting, and a different way in the classroom, where she's on display and taking more risks. Ask your daughter's teachers and coaches how she expresses herself during class and practice. How is her volume? Does she articulate well? Does she speak with a reasonable amount of confidence? Does she apologize before she speaks? Keep in mind that some girls are simply shy and not able to speak up.

**Break the Script.**

When Lindsay was studying to get her driver's license, she compared herself to another girl and moaned, "My parking stinks!" She did a double take when her mother, Heather, agreed. "Gee, Mom, you could have said, 'Oh, no it doesn't, Lindsay!' " Heather recalled her daughter saying. "And I said, 'But it does!' And she even said it did. She was, like, blown away that I would say that. And I said, 'I was just agreeing with you!'" Heather refused to endorse Lindsay's negative self-talk, which she was using to earn a compliment. The script Lindsay was accustomed to had been broken.

During certain workshops at GLI, we ask girls to blow silly-sounding whistles when girls or adults use self-defeating speech or gestures. Though abrupt, the whistle blasts produce rapid changes in girls. Speech patterns once unconscious become obvious, and girls immediately begin correcting themselves. They also take pleasure in helping each other. At home it might be useful to choose a code word together that accomplishes the same goal as the whistle. I used the word "hair" to alert a girl to her unconscious hair-twisting when she spoke in workshops.

Your vigilance will give your daughter chances to try "like"-free sentences, but don't forget she's still a girl. She is using the quirks of the language to bond with her peers and, in adolescence, set herself apart from adults. Let girls know they need to be fluent in two languages: one is Girl Talk, and the other is the language you speak in the Real World. I try to do this by example: When girls spend downtime with me at GLI, they see that I speak casually. I indulge in "like," "you know," and "whatever." When it's time for me to give a speech or workshop, they know I speak the Real World language. Girls do not need to remove Girl Talk from their vocabulary. They need to learn to switch into the other language when the time and place require it. Success in life demands fluency in both.

However you decide to work with your daughter on this, remember to be gentle. Don't correct her in front of other adults or her friends (unless you're correcting her friends, too, and then brace for the eye-rolling). Never correct her when the stakes are high. Being told that you are doing something wrong, no matter how well intentioned, is never easy. This is an exercise best done together and at home.

### Encourage her to identify her strengths.

Girls lose self-esteem in adolescence because they dissociate from the nuts and bolts of who they are. Communication expert Peggy Klaus writes that knowing your strengths means fully knowing your self, "bringing forward your best parts with authenticity, pride, and enthusiasm." Articulating your strengths can thus be a powerful antidote to the Good Girl curse, instilling a sense of what makes each girl unique. It will also buffer girls' resilience as they face tough challenges. In the job and college applications that demand to know what makes them special, the ability to self-promote will be vital.

Create opportunities for your daughter to practice asserting her strengths. Ask her what she liked about her performance in a game, a recital, a school project, or a test. If she says, "I liked that I made friends," or "I liked that I worked well with others," push her to say something about her skills, like having a good jump shot, or intrinsic qualities, such as being determined.

Encourage her to accept compliments. Too many girls automatically deflect when told they did well, kicking into "No, I'm not," or "You are, too!" Girls should practice saying thank you when they are recognized. This is a small but important lesson in affirming the fruits of hard work and talent.

If you can make these practices a regular part of your family life, your daughter will have a safe place to practice the skills Girl World often punishes. It is normal for her to resist at first. Join her in acknowledging the dangers of speaking highly of yourself among girls. Still, you are not telling her to waltz into school tomorrow and chirp, "Doesn't my butt look amazing?" You are making the point that even if self-promotion amounts to Girl World failure, being able to say what you are good at is a language girls need for Real World success.

**Invite girls to discuss their mixed feelings about success.**

Jealousy is a normal if uncomfortable thread that runs through the fabric of girls' lives. Mixed feelings about female strength are unavoidable in a world still governed by Good Girl rules. Some of it is simply about wanting what others have, and some of it is culturally bred: Good Girl pressure creates impossible expectations of being both flawless and modest in proportions unspecified, setting up invisible tripwires that trigger peers' ire. The girls who punish success act as Good Girl agents, policing peers back into Good Girl modesty. I remember sixteen-year-old Allison, who bemoaned the nastiness of her peers but then said,

> I'll even admit to, like, hearing people speak in class and thinking they're, like, conceited because of the answers that they're giving. And I know it's not right to think, but sometimes the tone they use when they're saying the answer, I just feel like . . . like they think they're better than everyone else. And then I think, *Oh, if I give an answer [like that], people will think the same way about me.*

The Curse of the Good Girl is most virulent when no one talks about it. Explore the tensions between Good Girl pressure, which draws a perimeter around girls' potential, and the authentic desire to succeed on one's own terms. The Good Girl ruse is immediately exposed. Girls begin to understand what is guiding their often unreflective anger toward other girls. If we don't admit it, we can't get past it, and we will continue to silence other women and girls.

# BRING CONFLICT OUT IN THE OPEN

All-female extracurricular groups brim with the potential to change girls' habits of indirect conflict resolution. Athletic teams in particular can become refuges from Good Girl pressure, places where girls can raise their voices and take up space. The powerful tension between athletic and Good Girl expectations is an unexpected opportunity for change. Teams can help girls let go of Good Girl pressure and experiment with a new set of norms.

**Explore the Good Girl/Great Athlete Tension.**
Discuss the friction between Good Girl pressure and the demands of being a Great Athlete. Have the team work together to make a list of the

qualities a typical Good Girl has. Then have the team list the qualities that make a Great Athlete.

Place the lists alongside each other. Ask the players what about being a Great Athlete jibes with being a Good Girl and what's in conflict. You will find that girls' lives on and off the field can seem like two different worlds, with two sets of rules and norms. For example, a Great Athlete on the field is aggressive, confident, bold, and loud. What can such girls get called at school? "Conceited," "bitch," or "lesbian," most likely. Consider how the different worlds send girls mixed messages. Outline the expectations of each world, using the sample below:

| QUALITY | OFF THE FIELD: GOOD GIRL EXPECTATIONS | ON THE FIELD: COACH'S EXPECTATIONS |
|---|---|---|
| Assertiveness | Girls are supposed to be nice, friends with everyone, not get in fights. | Athletes need to communicate, ask for help, tell someone where to be or what to do. |
| Ability to deal with conflict | Girls don't say anything to one another's faces. | Athletes need to get things out in the open and trust each other. |
| Confidence | Girls should be modest, or else people might think you're conceited. | Athletes need to appear strong, skilled, and in control. |

How do these different cultural expectations play out on the team? By exposing the forces that confuse and divide girls, the team can explore strategies for change.

**Create New Rules and Expectations.**

Just as teachers consciously promote risk-taking in the classroom, the best coaches encourage similar departures from Good Girl norms on the field. A male middle-school girls' soccer coach in the Northwest told a public radio show, "I really enjoy teaching girls to be more selfish. They come in, their basic mentality is, 'Let me give the ball up to my teammate.' . . . I want them to be able to control their territory and let them take their life over." He taught his players to embrace a philosophy on the field that went something like this: "I own my area. I will share it with you. We can work as a team, but don't you try to knock me out of my area. Not gonna happen."

Good Girl pressure tells girls to be friends with everyone, which means that when a girl doesn't want a friendship, she has no other version of relationship to consult. A high-school club soccer coach, also male, made it a point to introduce his players to other kinds of relationships. He recalled a player who said she had been indifferent to a teammate's problems because the two girls were not friends. Whether or not she's your friend, he told her, "is not the issue. She's your teammate. This is a different social structure than what you know at school."

This coach worked with another player who assured him she was a vocal leader on the field, yet she was barely audible during games. In her mind, and perhaps by Good Girl standards, she was loud. "I don't think she confronts people, I don't think she deals on a vocal level at all," he told me. "I have to make her understand that saying something in a group setting is not leadership." The coach understood he needed to suggest and support new norms.

To help establish teams as places where Good Girl norms don't apply, coaches should clearly define team expectations, including:

- Giving and receiving peer feedback with respect
- Knowing the difference between being assertive and being aggressive

- Leaving personal conflicts off the field
- Addressing team-related conflicts immediately and directly (even if they originate off the field)

Empower captains to support and enforce the new norms.

**Assess the Conflict-Resolution Behavior of the Group.**

Coaches should ask teams the following questions in a formal meeting or in small groups, ensuring that names are withheld from the discussion.

- When a problem arises between teammates, how are conflicts resolved? Without describing a specific incident, can you walk me, step-by-step, through the events that typically occur?
- Do conflicts on this team go off the field and into school, and vice versa?
- Are there any issues that continually spark conflicts, such as someone's "thinking they're better than me" or "telling me what to do?"
- Without using names, give me some examples of aggression or bullying you have witnessed.
- Do people feel comfortable addressing problems face-to-face? If they do, are you satisfied with how it happens? If they don't, why? What happens instead?
- What's the most important thing I don't know about how girls treat each other on this team?
- If you could change one thing about the way girls interact with each other on this team, what would it be?

Ask how the team's trust, unity, success, and potential are affected by the group's conflict-resolution dynamics.

**Introduce a Conflict-Resolution Protocol.**

In chapter 9, I introduced the Four Steps, a road map for resolving interpersonal conflict. Adopt the Four Steps, or something like them, as the official conflict-resolution protocol for the team. Empower captains to ensure that the steps are being followed, mentor younger teammates, and guide girls away from destructive behavior. Using the Four Steps should be a rule, not an option. Make the protocol an antidote to aggressive behavior and its adoption a team commitment to maintaining a grudge- and drama-free zone. By bringing girls' feelings above the surface, you provide a counterpoint to Good Girl norms and build a more coherent, successful team.

GOOD GIRLS AND GREAT LEADERS DO NOT NECESSARILY EXIST in opposition. The Good Girl proclivity to avoid conflict can influence a leader to put a premium on courtesy and civility. The fear of standing out can evolve into a management style in which the leader allows others to shine. Stopping the migration of Good Girl habits does not mean snuffing out the values that girls cherish. What it does mean is helping girls strike a balance between being other- and self-oriented. Girls look to their mothers for direction.

*Twelve*

# FROM PERFECT MOTHERS
# TO REAL MOTHERS

The mothers held lipsticked glasses of red wine, circled a large sheet of paper, and laughed. They were reading their description of the "Perfect Mother," or who they thought society expected them to be.

"Perfect kids!" one said. "Polite, well-behaved, and amazing students."

"Spotless house!" another chimed in.

"Perfect body. Oh, and sex all the time with her partner," the woman next to her offered, snorting.

"She volunteers," one said.

"Organic food *only.* Cooks every night."

"No yelling. No temper."

"Has a career, but it never, ever interferes with family."

When they were done, I asked the women to read a second list, which they had made the day before: the qualities they hoped to model for their daughters.

"Honesty," one read.

"Assertiveness."

"Not caring about being perfect."

"Saying what you need."

I taped the lists, "Perfect Mother" and "Role-Model Mother," to the wall, side by side. The women's eyes began moving between them, comparing and contrasting. They were seeing, for the first time, how being a culturally acceptable mother can model the opposite of what they wanted to instill in their daughters.

"You know," one woman said, breaking a long silence, "my daughter asked me what my hobbies were the other day, and I couldn't answer."

Ruth, raven-haired and plump, spoke next. "My daughter, out of the blue, said, 'Mom, what are you going to do when we're all gone?' It was like, I can't believe she sees that the kids are my whole life. I don't know, maybe I didn't even see that." Her daughter had been encouraging her to take an exercise class, she added, "but I never make time for it."

In chapter 6, women described a loss of authentic self to mothering that bore a disturbing likeness to the loss experienced by many adolescent girls. The pressure to nurture everyone before herself, excel at tasks both professional and domestic, and produce "perfect" children manifested in behaviors that set a bleak example for girls.

It is difficult to overstate a mother's influence on her daughter. Deborah Tannen writes that mothers serve "as models for daughters of how to talk, and how to use language to negotiate relationships and the world." A 2008 study by the Girl Scouts of America found a "close alliance between mothers' own ambitions and outlook on life with their daughters' aspirations and motivations." In the same study, girls cited mothers as their most important role models. In this section I offer ways for mothers to identify and model the qualities they most want to instill in their daughters.

# REFLECT

Make two lists, one of the qualities you hope to model for your daughter. Label this "Role Model Mother." Next, make a list of what you think society says Perfect Mothers look and act like. Label this "Perfect Mother." The lists below are from a recent workshop I conducted:

## ROLE-MODEL MOTHER

Confidence

Social responsibility

Integrity/honesty

Common sense

Independent thinker

Truthful

Strength

Self-respect

Adventurous/
risk-taker

Assertive

Kind

Sense of humor

Supportive

Inquisitive

Independent

Nurturing

Creativity

Patience

Compassion

Intelligence

Self-forgiveness

Self-worth

Ambition

High standards for
friends

Spirituality

Generosity

Happy

Can ask for what
she needs

Relaxed

Doesn't care about
being perfect

## PERFECT MOTHER

Organized

Consistent

Multitasker
(well!)

Put-together

Cooks dinner

Cleans house

Martha Stewart
(creative,
everything
looks great)

Perfect children (well
behaved, not
disruptive, smart,

no drugs,
respectful)

Community
service

Volunteers for
school

Successful career (but
doesn't interfere
with parenting)

Hot

Perfect partner

Has sex

*Leave It to Beaver*

Patient

Work/life balance

Has it all

No yelling

Organic/local
food only

Organized

Doesn't judge kids

Empowering

Crafty

Well dressed

Perfect body

Active at school

No fast food

Good coach

| Always has right answer | all the chores, makes money, no fighting) | Good hostess Well traveled |
|---|---|---|
| Good wife (no questioning, does | Comforts kids | |

Locate yourself in the Perfect Mother list. How does cultural pressure to be a Perfect Mother affect the kind of person you become at home? How does it affect your parenting? What kind of example might it set for your daughter? Explore the answers by filling out the chart on page 241. Consider how, when, and where you might break the habits you—and she—are better off without. Some examples are below:

**Take an Inventory of Your Selves.**

Do you wear different selves like so many outfits? Are you a different woman at work, at home, and with your spouse?

For example, you may feel relatively indifferent to others' opinions of you on the job but more sensitive about your family's reputation at home. Deborah Tannen writes that mothers try to protect their children by managing the family's impression on the outside world. These women implore their children to evaluate their behavior in terms of what "other people will think." Yet urging a daughter to measure herself against others' perceptions can reinforce the self-consciousness that limits healthy risk-taking in girls.

Consider the qualities or skills you leverage at work that you leave outside the door at night. For instance, some people find setting boundaries easier at work than at home. They may refuse a colleague's invitation to shoot the breeze or take an hourlong lunch when they need a break. At home the story can be completely different. The pressure on mothers to be selfless at home means that too many of their daughters discover their leadership potential only after walking out the front door. What would it mean to have leadership begin at home?

| PERFECT-MOTHER BEHAVIOR AT HOME | WHAT MY DAUGHTER MIGHT LEARN FROM THIS | WHAT I MIGHT DO DIFFERENTLY | BE SPECIFIC: WHEN, WHERE, AND HOW WILL YOU DO IT? |
|---|---|---|---|
| Try to keep people from fighting or being angry in the house. | Anger and conflict are bad. | Make room for anger. | Let my daughter be angry for a half hour longer than I usually do. Try not to shut down fights between my kids but instead redirect them into more respectful conflict. |
| Frantic need to be on time. | To be intolerant of imperfection in others. | Stop acting like being late is catastrophic. | Stop rushing my daughter to dance class and obsessing about calling ahead to say we're late. |
| Compulsive need to straighten up the house constantly. | To be overly concerned with image and how things appear, instead of her own internal state or needs. | Let a mess accumulate for a longer period; delegate some responsibilities to the rest of the family. | Stop fluffing the couch pillows every time someone gets up. Schedule a family meeting to talk about chores. |
| Rarely make time for myself. | Sacrifice her needs for others. | Do more for myself. | Say no the next time the school asks me to do something. Take an exercise class. |

**Assess Your Response to Your Daughter's Anger.**

As I showed in chapter 6, many mothers said their daughters' anger made them anxious or afraid. These women strained to resolve conflicts before their daughters were ready, or they avoided them entirely.

In every mother-daughter conflict, there are two levels of learning: On the first, mother and daughter hash out an actual issue being contested— say, what time a curfew should be. On the second, the daughter learns a lesson from her mother about how to have a conflict with an intimate.

Consider your approach to conflict with your daughter and the messages you may communicate about conflict and anger. Whether you leave your angry daughter alone, respond to her in kind, or stand anxiously at her locked door pleading with her to come out, reflect on the following questions: What do you do when you have a conflict with your daughter? What emotions and thoughts do you experience when she is angry with you? What, if anything, do you fear? Are these thoughts and fears rational? How do they influence your response?

Contemplate the "big picture": What messages does your overall behavior in conflict with your daughter teach her about conflict, emotions, and relationship? What do you explicitly tell your daughter about her anger or behavior in conflict? I met one girl whose mother responded to her anger by warning her that "no one will want to live with you when you grow up if you act like this." She learned from her mother that her anger was toxic to relationship.

Is your response to conflict with your daughter similar to how you handle conflict in your other relationships? The women I interviewed in chapter 6 described reacting to conflict with their daughters the way they reacted to problems with friends. A Good Girl still lived inside these women, fearing that conflict would terminate her relationships. By allowing the Good Girl to manipulate their response to conflict, the mothers were transmitting destructive messages directly to their daughters.

Deborah Tannen observes that mothers interpret being different from their daughters as being distant from them. Keep in mind that your daughter is trying out versions of conflict and anger as a way of figuring out who she is, not unlike the way she might try a new look or sport. How you greet this version of your daughter will play an important role in determining her comfort level with these new experiences.

# PLAN

To deepen your vision for your daughter, write her a letter (you don't have to send it) and explore these questions:

- What do you wish you had known when you were her age? Think about the girl you used to be and the woman you are today. Focus on what you have learned about relationships, conflict, and self-confidence.
- What does being yourself mean to you?
- What did the female role models of your childhood teach you? If you did not have any, what do you wish you might have learned from a caring adult woman?

You have learned many lessons in your life. By defining them for yourself, you can begin thinking about how to convey practical wisdom to your daughter, in both what you say and how you act.

**Set Parenting Goals.**

When you imagine your daughter in ten years, who do you see? You have probably thought about the kind of character you hope she'll have: you want her to be kind, respectful, responsible, and so on. Now focus your vision on the specific competencies she will need to overcome the Curse of the Good Girl. For example, you may want your daughter to be independent, but what does that look like, practically speaking, in everyday life? Does it mean refusing to bring a forgotten uniform to school so she has to figure out what to do on her own? How will you make that vision a reality?

I've explored several skills in this book: the ability to identify, express, and own negative emotions; to accept negative feedback; to admit mistakes; to express an idea that might be "wrong"; to state opinions with confidence; to identify and celebrate strengths; to approach interpersonal and extracurricular conflicts directly; to allow for conflict within a relationship; to ask instead of assume, and so on. Which will your daughter need to learn in order to reach her full potential?

Don't hesitate to ask a trusted coach, teacher, counselor, or relative for help. The adults in your daughter's life almost certainly observe parts of her that may yet elude you; you may not know, for instance, that your daughter has trouble stating her opinions with confidence in a classroom.

Take your goals and make a plan. What will your daughter need to learn these skills? Whom will you consult for advice? Which resources will you leverage in your community? A Girl Scout troop may give her an opportunity to lead a group. A sports team could provide a vehicle for talking about her strengths. Summer camp could be the place where she will make friendships that help her become more direct in relationship.

Be proactive, but don't go overboard: it's probably a good idea to keep your teaching goals to yourself. Your daughter might recoil if she thinks her mother is initiating a major self-improvement program. As always, keep your expectations reasonable. What falls short is still an effort; the attempt can be as integral as the accomplishment.

# DO

Be the change you want to see in your daughter.

**Try to Tell the Truth Every Day.**

Take an inventory of your day and map out the moments you can communicate with strength in front of your daughter. Is it in the car-pool lane? A restaurant? Send back the french fries the way my mom did, or say you're sorry, you can't drive the late-night car-pool shift because you're too tired. When someone asks how you are feeling, answer as honestly as you can. Do this all respectfully, remembering that you are teaching your daughter a language of truth-telling.

Be prepared for a little mayhem. Most girls don't abide this easily. When my mother asserted herself, it drove me crazy. But the example I needed—and that your daughter needs—is often the one that indeed makes her most uncomfortable. That's how you know you've hit the spot.

**Put a Premium on Authenticity.**

Celebrate the rougher edges of life: honor mistakes—yours, hers, and your family's—and try to handle them with humor. Mary, from chapter 6, seemed bent on having Patricia be a perfect little daughter, a Mini-Me whose every blemish pained her mother. Tannen writes, "If the measure of a mother's success is the perfection observable in her children, then the children bear a burden equal to her own: Whenever they are less than perfect, they are letting their mothers down." Mary's daughter certainly felt, if unconsciously, how much she disappointed her mother. In a culture that's telling girls to aspire to flawlessness, your embrace of mistakes, limits, and failure will be priceless.

**Be a Little "Full of Yourself."**

Curb self-deprecating comments about your own body and eating habits, even the throwaway ones like, "I was good today because I didn't have dessert." Say thank you when you receive a compliment or an apology. Avoid putting yourself down in front of your daughter.

**Develop Her Intrinsic Self-Worth.**

Put aside her accomplishments, physical appearance, or social status. Say something positive about your daughter's character as often as you can. Affirm the person she is instead of what she does, who she likes, or what others think.

Finally, teach her Three Rules of Relationship.

1. **Not everyone is going to like you.** Your daughter does not need to be friends with everyone, but she does need to respect everyone. And just as she may not like everyone, not everyone will like her. That's okay, too; the measure of her worth is not her relationships but who she is. When a girl meets a new person, she often automatically strives to be likable, even before she has decided whether or not she likes the new person herself. Tell your daughter to switch the order: size up the person before you start worrying about what she thinks of you.

   Relationships nourish us, but they cannot be the only source of our fulfillment. We are less likely to seek others' approval when we know who we are and what we want; developing a passion, whether through work, a hobby, a religion, or a sport, is key to accessing this knowledge.

2. **Friendship is one of many possible relationships in life.** Good Girl pressure to be friends with everyone can sabotage personal and professional pursuits. Girls need to know that being a friend is only one version of relationship. There are many others they will encounter: teacher, coach, subordinate, boss, spouse, acquaintance. If your daughter applies the rules of friendship everywhere, her expectations will be skewed and she will likely be disappointed and hurt. She may also compromise her authority.

3. **When truth and friendship cannot coexist, get rid of the friendship.** If you cannot safely be honest with another person, you should not be in the relationship. A friendship that lives without

truth is an empty husk, an automatic indication that the relationship must be repaired or discarded.

Be realistic about the costs of female strength. No amount of modeling or teaching will change our reality: females who openly talk about their strengths, speak up, and tell the truth are often punished for it. They may be called "bitch," "conceited," or worse. Talk with your daughter about the costs of truth-telling and the difference between what may be "normal" at a particular moment and what is "right." Cite times in history when it was "normal" to segregate people, but "right" not to; when the institution of marriage made domestic violence "normal," even though it wasn't "right." The same applies to displays of female strength. It may be normal to punish women and girls, but it certainly isn't right.

At stake is nothing less than your daughter's integrity. The journey will be filled with battles large and small. They are not hers alone to face. Girls are always watching. What are they learning? Make yourself a counterpoint to Good Girl pressure, and your example will shelter your daughter through the storm.

# The Greater Voice
# of Myself

There is little beyond the reach of today's American girl, for whom
equality is the freedom to create a life of her own design. Girls have
won the right to walk through any door they choose and shake the hand
of whoever is standing behind it.

Yet too many girls walk through doors only to offer limp handshakes,
avoid eye contact, or giggle during an introduction. Their laughter is
anxious: they are uncomfortable with the expected display of personal
strength. Distracted, they worry about what others might be thinking.
They are unable to be themselves.

At twenty-three, Zoe had a top college degree and a black belt in karate.
She was an elite, nationally recognized college basketball player. When I
hired her to work at the Girls Leadership Institute in 2008, she was between jobs and figuring out her future.

She was a dream hire. Her confidence was preternatural, and even the
shyest girls were drawn to her. They chose her, over and over: to play basketball, to tell her things they had never said to anyone. They just wanted
to be near her.

Tall and quiet, Zoe loved the work of empowering girls, but she said little about herself. A month after camp ended, I got an e-mail. After playing pickup with some guys in Manhattan, she started thinking about her basketball career.

"I've been realizing," she wrote, "how much I underachieved." She could have been an All-American, she said, but she held herself back on her college team. "I didn't want to upset teammates, wanted teammates to like me, didn't want to ruffle feathers. I think there was other stuff, too, not wanting to be what I thought was selfish, which was really just ambitious." She knew how good she was, but she held herself back.

The need to focus on how you seem to others, rather than who you are, is the Curse of the Good Girl in action. The curse persists despite the many accomplishments of the movement for gender equality. It constricts the full bloom of personhood in girls, telling them that only so much of who they are will be accepted: the girl who feels only Good feelings, who does everything flawlessly and without error, who unfailingly puts others before herself.

Despite every door that has opened, girls continue to grapple with confusing, conflicting messages about personal authority: be successful but say nothing about it, or about yourself; be strong but don't make anyone angry; and be confident, as one girl told me, but do it "quietly."

Taught to value niceness over honesty, perfection over growth, and modesty over authentic self-expression, girls are locked into a battle with a version of themselves they can never attain. Their internal resources are drained by the energy and ruthless self-evaluation required to live up to this impossible set of personal standards.

In fact, it will not be enough to open doors for girls. It is the act of crossing the threshold and taking up space that now requires our attention. In the twenty-first century, freedom comes with a catch: despite being told they can *do* what they want, the most privileged girls still lack permission to *be* who they are.

The final frontier of girls' empowerment is therefore the most personal.

Our focus must change from the glass ceiling of an industry, like business, to the individual glass ceilings that the curse erects in the souls of millions of girls.

This book has been my attempt to map this internal frontier. It offers an inventory of skills girls need to assert their Real Girl selves and break the Curse of the Good Girl. More work is needed. We must establish new priorities for girls' education and create a catalog of Real Girl skills that can be formally taught and evaluated. In a world that values Real Girls, teachers will put a premium on intellectual risk-taking and reward classroom debate. Coaches will incorporate giving and getting feedback into team culture. Families will create spaces for girls where a full range of feelings are valued and expressed, and where failure is embraced as an opportunity. Relationship management will be embraced as a vital life skill, and the challenges and obligations of relationship will be openly discussed.

The curse may long defy our efforts. Girls live in a world where Real Girl behavior earns them labels like "mean" or "conceited." They watch the curse follow women into adulthood, where the powerful are labeled "bitches." The culture will surely continue to undermine female strength. For this reason the most important work we can do is by example. As more adult women assert their Real Girl selves, they will empower their daughters to ignore the Good Girl rules and live by their own. Fathers who value Real Girl behavior in their spouses and daughters will give girls critical permission to embrace authenticity.

In June 2008, I watched Hillary Clinton concede her candidacy for president. "Although we weren't able to shatter the highest, hardest glass ceiling," she told a cheering crowd of her supporters, "thanks to you, it's got about eighteen million cracks in it," she said, referring to her popular vote count.

Indeed, in state after state, 18 million people threw the Good Girl rules out the window. They chose to value Real Girl grit over Good Girl artifice. Each voter decided it was more important for a woman to lead than to be modest, nice, or self-effacing. Her candidacy revealed to girls that there is a world of higher achievement and fulfillment for those able to break the curse.

There is also a precious, spiritual gift. In a commencement address at Stanford University, Oprah Winfrey described breaking her own Good Girl curse. Early in her career, a supervisor suggested that she change her name to the more saccharine "Suzie." She thought about it. It was a Good Girl version of herself, and she knew it. "Hi, Suzie," she recalled. "Very friendly. You can't be angry with Suzie." She declined. "It didn't feel right," she explained. Soon after, as a news anchor, she tried parroting the polished reading of Barbara Walters. Then, too, something inside her resisted.

It was, she told the graduates, the "greater voice of myself"—what she authentically felt and thought—that steered her through the difficult decisions of her life. This is the voice we want every girl to hear, loud and clear. It is the voice of the deepest part of ourselves: what makes us passionate, what we hunger for, and what we desire. It is, as the feminist theorist and poet Audre Lorde would say, "the *yes* within ourselves." The voice will allow girls to live truthfully and with integrity. It is the antidote to the Good Girl curse.

On the last day of camp in 2008, Janay, an African-American high-school freshman, ran back breathlessly through airport security to hand a staff member a note for me. "I didn't really get to say what I wanted to say to you," she wrote. "Before I came here, I didn't know who I was anymore. And now I feel I know myself better than anyone in the world. . . . [Before GLI] I would always criticize myself, put myself down, and ask almost everyone, 'How do I look?' And I realize that won't ever help me. I need to know these things for myself." She continued, "I'm going to be the person I WANT to be . . . not for whoever wants me to change." She acknowledged my help in this journey, but, she concluded, "The reason is . . . somewhere deep inside, I wanted change for me, put my mind to it, and accomplished it."

Janay had discovered something it took me many years to learn: The greater voice of myself cannot be given as a gift. It cannot be learned or taught. It lives inside every girl. Janay had found it, and so had Zoe. It does not always emerge in a blast or a dramatic moment. More commonly it comes in flashes, as when a middle-school girl drops her "cool" front and quacks like a duck, just because she feels like it, or a high-school girl decides to run in the school elections, even if she's afraid to lose. Our task is to help girls find the voice that is already there and to create spaces where they can safely access it. We can do it every day, in the tiniest of moments, for them and by example.

The most precious gift we can give girls is the liberty not only to listen to the greater voice of themselves but to act on it. This is the simplest kind of freedom and the most sacred sort of empowerment.

# APPENDIX

. . . . . . . . . . . . . . . . . . . . . . . . . . . . . . . . . . . . . . . .

## GUIDING ANSWERS TO PART II EXERCISES

## CHAPTER 7

### IDENTIFYING INSIDE FEELINGS:

JESSICA: Brit, can we talk for a second?
Jessica's Inside Feeling: *nervous, anxious*

BRITNEY: Uh, sure. . . .
Britney's Inside Feeling: *nervous, anxious*

JESSICA: So you know how Stacy and I have been managing the basketball team this year?
Jessica's Inside Feeling: *nervous, anxious, guilty*

BRITNEY: Of course I do. What about it?
Britney's Inside Feeling: *scared, nervous, anxious*

JESSICA: Well, nothing. I mean, it's just that . . . I . . . I think I might go on vacation with her family this year.
Jessica's Inside Feeling: *guilty, anxious*

BRITNEY: Oh . . . really?
Britney's Inside Feeling: *shocked, hurt, sad, disappointed*

JESSICA: Yeah. They have this amazing vacation house and a boat.
Jessica's Inside Feeling: *excited, guilty*

BRITNEY: Oh . . . Okay . . . but you've always gone away with my family for New Year's since third grade.
Britney's Inside Feeling: *betrayed*

JESSICA: Well, I know! I know. But your grandma is going with you guys this year. Right?
Jessica's Inside Feeling: *nervous*

BRITNEY: I guess. . . .
Britney's Inside Feeling: *hurt, embarrassed*

JESSICA: So, like, I really wanted to check with you before I got tickets to go with Stacy. I mean, I know you didn't buy tickets yet, and I figured you'd be totally cool with it, but I just wanted to double-check, right?
Jessica's Inside Feeling: *anxious*

BRITNEY: Uh . . . yeah.
Britney's Inside Feeling: *sad, hurt, betrayed*

JESSICA: Cool! Because my parents are talking with Stacy's parents tonight, and . . . well, I just wanted to make sure you were cool with everything.

Jessica's Inside Feeling: *guilty*

BRITNEY: Sure.

Britney's Inside Feeling: *betrayed*

JESSICA: Okay. I gotta go. Bye, babe!

Jessica's Inside Feeling: *relieved*

## TURNING YOU STATEMENTS INTO I STATEMENTS:

| EXAMPLE | You've been ignoring me lately. | I felt **hurt** when you **didn't save a seat for me yesterday at lunch.** |
| --- | --- | --- |
| **Something a parent might say to a daughter** | You never clean up your room. | I feel disappointed when you do not clean up your room, and I have asked you three times this week. |
| **Something a daughter might say to a parent** | You are the strictest parent out of all the parents I know. | I felt embarrassed when I was not allowed to go to an R-rated movie this weekend and most of my friends were. |

| Something a friend might say to you | Why are you always asking me to tell you secrets about other people? | I feel uncomfortable when you ask me to talk about things Sophie asked me to keep between us. You asked me once at the dance and then again last night. |
|---|---|---|
| Something you might say to a friend | You never ask me what I want to do. | I feel put down when you don't ask me what I want to do when we hang out. The last three times we've gotten together, we picked the movie you wanted to watch. |

# CHAPTER 8

## LEARNING TO IDENTIFY ASSUMPTIONS:

1. She told me she had no plans this morning, but I just heard she was going to the movies with my friends. *I guess she didn't want me there.*

EMOTION(s): hurt, angry
THOUGHT(s): I guess she doesn't think I'm cool enough to go.
ACTION(s): Gossip about her. Go to my room and be by myself.

2. We were just having this huge conversation online and she signed off. *I must have said something to offend her.*

EMOTION(s): Nervous, scared
THOUGHT(s): What did I do? Why is she mad at me?
ACTION(s): Talk to another friend and see if she knows what I did. Be cold to her the next time I see her at school.


3. *Those girls are talking about me.* They keep looking at me while they're talking.

EMOTION(s): Angry, annoyed, anxious
THOUGHT(s): What are they saying?
ACTION(s): Talk about them to my friends and find out if they are mad at me.


4. *Mrs. Sales doesn't like me.* She says I'm not working up to my potential.

EMOTION(s): Sad, frustrated
THOUGHT(s): Forget it. I hate this class.
ACTION(s): Stop participating.


5. Tess is talking to Mike, the guy I have a crush on. *She's trying to take him away from me.*

EMOTION(s): Angry
THOUGHT(s): She has no right to do that. I hate her.
ACTION(s): Stop speaking to her. Talk about her to my friends.

# CHAPTER 9

## IDENTIFYING CONFLICT CONTRIBUTION:

### Contribution

KENDRA'S CONTRIBUTION: She held Jared's hand.

ELISE'S CONTRIBUTION: She left in the middle of the movie and gave Kendra the silent treatment.

LAUREN'S CONTRIBUTION: She forgot to set her alarm and yelled at her father.

JOHN'S CONTRIBUTION: He didn't wake Lauren up. He also told her she was overreacting.

NICOLE'S CONTRIBUTION: She gave Danielle the silent treatment and made Danielle find another way to get to her friend's house.

DANIELLE'S CONTRIBUTION: She was impolite to her mother's colleague.

WHITNEY'S CONTRIBUTION: She signed off of IM after telling Rachel she was upset, essentially walking away in the middle of the conversation.

RACHEL'S CONTRIBUTION: She tried to turn Sharynnn333 against Whitney.

## FINDING THE FOUR STEPS OF HEALTHY CONFLICT:

### Four Steps for Rebecca

AFFIRM THE RELATIONSHIP: Jewel, our friendship is really important to me, . . .

I Statement: I feel sad that we don't hang out as much as we used to. We used to have lunch at least once a week, and we don't do that anymore.

Contribution: I realize I shouldn't have intruded on your lunch with Annaluz.

How Can We Solve This Together: I can give you and Annaluz more private time. Can you and I have lunch one day this week?

# CHAPTER 10

## Recognizing Your Crazy Freak-Out Voice:

1. *Dad said I needed to come home before midnight. He doesn't trust me. I can take care of myself.*

Crazy Freak-Out Voice: *He doesn't trust me.*
Why: *This is mind-reading. You cannot conclude that your father doesn't trust you because of one thing he asks you do.*

2. *I got a ninety-two on the test. Danielle got a ninety-three, and we had the exact same answers. I don't know even know why I bother. Ms. Nakra totally wants me to fail.*

Crazy Freak-Out Voice: *Ms. Nakra totally wants me to fail.*
Why: *This is mind-reading. You don't know what Ms. Nakra thinks.*

3. *I'm an idiot. The yearbook editor said I forgot to write the names of the people on the backs of my photographs. Now I can't remember who they are.*

CRAZY FREAK-OUT VOICE: *I'm an idiot.*
WHY: *This is labeling. Making one mistake does not define who you are as a person.*

4. *I forgot to ask the car pool to stop at the store on the way home so I could get my mom an ingredient she needed for her dinner party. The party is going to be ruined.*

CRAZY FREAK-OUT VOICE: *The party is going to be ruined.*
WHY: *This is fortune-telling. You don't know how the dinner party will go, and one missing ingredient will probably not ruin a dinner.*

5. *My friend just told me I talk about myself too much and that she feels like she can't really talk to me when she has a problem. I am a horrible friend.*

CRAZY FREAK-OUT VOICE: *I am a horrible friend.*
WHY: *This is labeling. One thing you do wrong does not determine the kind of friend you are or aren't. There are lots of aspects to friendship.*

# ACKNOWLEDGMENTS

Many years ago, Simone Marean took the workshop ideas that I was scribbling down on napkins and turned me into a teacher. Together, we created the program from which most of this book emerged. She is my partner and my friend. This work would not be possible without her persistence, wisdom, and support.

It is no small honor to be edited by Ann Godoff, a true Real Girl if there ever was one, whose inspired vision lifted this book. Lindsay Whalen's unwavering devotion can be found in every page. She has been a steady, dear partner in this venture, and I am privileged to have a young woman of such giant intellect in my corner.

I would like to thank the following people for their help with this project: Lyn Mikel Brown, Kim Kaminski, Courtney Martin, Robin Stern, and the administrators and counselors who hosted me at their schools. I am grateful to the GLI families who have entrusted me with their daughters every summer.

I also wish to thank my superhero agent, Gail Ross, and Howard Yoon; my editor, Jane Isay, for her unmatched mix of moral support, friendship, and sparkling insight; and my crack, kickass interns, Blaine Edens and Lilly Jay, for their courage, truth telling, and smarts.

# ACKNOWLEDGMENTS

Thank you to KR for helping me over the hill in Prospect Park and through every challenge. The extraordinary Ann Weinstein: we did it! My family: Claire and Luiz Simmons; Tony Kirley; Frances, Bill, Sergei, and Ziggy Goldstein; and Lia Simmons. To Bernard Simmons, my loving friend, guardian, and press secretary: I am the luckiest granddaughter in the world.

My guides, my rocks: Julie Barer, Maggie Bittel, Luke Cusack, Barry Daggett, Denis Guerin, Ellen Karsh, Emma Kress, Cathie Levine, Josh Moses, Heather Muchow, and Lissa Skitolsky. My breakfast partner of twenty-plus years, Daniella Topol: this writer's got no words. My beautiful muse, Yvette Esprey. And last but not least, Rosie the dog, my unquantifiable source of peace, for the park walks and reality checks.

# NOTES

· · · · · · · · · · · · · · · · · · · · · · · · · · · · · · · · · · ·

## INTRODUCTION:
## THE CURSE OF THE GOOD GIRL

1. J. Schoenberg, K. Salmond and P. Fleshman, "Change It Up! What Girls Say About Redefining Leadership" (New York: Girl Scouts of the USA, 2008).
2. "The Supergirl Dilemma: Girls Grapple with the Mounting Pressure of Expectations." (New York: Girls, Inc., 2006).
3. Roni Cohen Sandler, *Stressed-out Girls: Helping Them Thrive in the Age of Pressure* (New York: Penguin, 2006).
4. Miss Hall's School for Girls, "Girls & the Next Generation of Leadership: Translating High School Aspirations into Formal Leadership in Adulthood. Report on a National Survey of Personal Authority and Leadership in Teens." (Pittsfield, MA: 2007).
5. Ibid., p. 12.

## CHAPTER 1: THE MYTH OF GIRLS'
## EMOTIONAL INTELLIGENCE

1. Researchers have gone to great lengths to celebrate the enlightened emotional natures of females. Dr. Louann Brizendine's 2006 bestseller *The Female Brain* claims that if you

mapped the areas for emotions in the brains of men and women, "in the man's brain, the connecting routes between areas would be country roads; in the women's brain, they'd be superhighways." Women use both sides of the brain to process emotions, she writes, while men use only one side, and the "hub" of emotion and memory formation is larger in the female brain. Others have reported that by age two, girls have wider emotional vocabularies than boys do. Girls speak two to three times more words than boys do, and faster—250 words per minute for girls and 125 words per minute for boys. Parents use more emotion words and display more emotion with their daughters.

2. Emotional intelligence enjoys multiple definitions and can apply to a wide range of skills and competencies. In this text the term is used specifically to refer to a girl's ability to identify, express, and accept her emotional experience.

3. Some researchers and coaches refer to three other areas of EI: Self-Management, Social Awareness, and Relationship Management. For a complete discussion, see Daniel Goleman, *Emotional Intelligence* (New York: Bantam, 1995).

4. Elizabeth Debold et al., "Cultivating Hardiness Zones for Adolescent Girls: A Reconceptualization of Resilience in Relationships with Caring Adults," in *Beyond Appearance: A New Look at Adolescent Girls,* eds. N. Johnson, M. Roberts, and J. Worell (Washington, D.C.: American Psychological Association, 1999).

5. Lyn Mikel Brown and Carol Gilligan report hearing girls frequently say, "I don't know" in *Meeting at the Crossroads: Women's Psychology and Girls' Development* (New York: Ballantine, 1992). Tracing this recurring phrase from childhood into early adolescence led Brown and Gilligan to discover girls' dissociation from their strongest thoughts and feelings, a response to what they called "the tyranny of the nice and kind." This dissociation led the girls in their study to take their authentic voices out of relationship.

6. Brown and Gilligan also document girls' attempts to have perfect feelings.

7. Despite the increasingly fashionable use of brain imaging to interpret gendered behavior, girls learn how to channel their escalating emotions from media and a market that define girls as deeply invested in "drama, drama, drama." While a change in hormones or biology may be predetermined, its expression is not.

8. Miss Hall's School for Girls, "Girls & the Next Generation of Leadership: Translating High School Aspirations into Formal Leadership in Adulthood. Report on a National Survey of Personal Authority and Leadership in Teens" (Pittsfield, MA: 2007).


# CHAPTER 3: THE GOOD FIGHT: GIRLS IN CONFRONTATION

1. T. J. Ferguson, et al., "Guilt, Shame and Symptoms in Children," *Developmental Psychology* 35 (1999): 347–57.

2. Judith Jordan, "Relational Resilience in Girls," in *Handbook of Resilience in Children: Issues in Clinical Psychology*, eds. Sam Goldstein and Robert Brooks (New York: Springer, 2005).

## CHAPTER 4: ALL OR NOTHING: GIRLS AND FEEDBACK

1. C. S. Dweck and N. Reppucci, "Learned Helplessness and Reinforcement Responsibility in Children," *Journal of Personality and Social Psychology* 25 (1973): 109–16.

## CHAPTER 5: GIRL MEETS WORLD: BREAKING THE GOOD GIRL GLASS CEILING

1. Gail Evans, *Play Like a Man, Win Like a Woman: What Men Know About Success That Women Need to Learn* (New York: Broadway, 2000).

## CHAPTER 6: MY DAUGHTER, MYSELF

1. Susan J. Douglas and Meredith W. Michaels, *The Mommy Myth: The Idealization of Motherhood and How It Has Undermined Women* (New York: Simon & Schuster, 2004).
2. Deborah Tannen, *You're Wearing That? Understanding Mothers and Daughters in Conversation* (New York: Ballantine, 2006).

## CHAPTER 7: I FEEL, THEREFORE I AM: BUILDING EMOTIONAL INTELLIGENCE

1. Marsha Linehan, *Skills Training Manual for Treating Borderline Personality Disorder* (New York: Guilford Press, 1993).
2. I learned this exercise at a "Difficult Conversations" seminar at Harvard Law School in June 2005.

## CHAPTER 10: FACING CRITICISM
## WITH CLEAR HEADS

1. Martin Seligman, *The Optimistic Child: A Proven Program to Safeguard Children Against Depression and Build Lifelong Resilience* (New York: HarperCollins, 1995).
2. Dennis Greenberger and Christine Padesky (New York: Guilford Press, 1995).

# INDEX

· · · · · · · · · · · · · · · · · · · · · · · · · · · · · · · ·

mothers *(continued)*
  pressures on, 109, 240
  real, 237–47
  reflection by, 238–43
  resources for help for, 244
  as role models, 109, 120, 123–24, 133–34,
    168, 176, 187, 209, 235, 237–47
  role models for, 243
  role of, 127, 235
  and school for emotional learning, 131–32
  self-reflection of, 215–16
  split personas of, 112–13, 114
  and steps of healthy conflict, 192–94
  and strategies for becoming a Real Girl, 127
  wake-up calls for, 121–23
  in workplace, 112–13, 114–15, 120, 240
  *See also specific topic*
Myths About Emotions (Linehan), 138–42

needs, ranking of primary life, 51
negative cognitive sets, 45–46
"never," 153
"new momism," 111–12
"no offense," 63–65, 173–76
No-Joke Zone (NJZ), 174–75
normal, what is, 247
"not a big deal," 19–24

Ophelia phenomenon, 10, 104

Padesky, Christine, 207
parenting, 15, 243–44
parents
  aggression by, 214
  cautions for, 215–16
  and coaches, 86, 88, 90, 214–15, 218
  and emotional intelligence, 25–27, 131–33
  and feedback/criticism, 85–90, 214–16
  as models, 87
  pressures on girls by, 85–90
  self-knowledge of, 216–17
  and strategies for becoming a Real Girl, 128
  and teachers, 85–90, 214–15, 218
participation, in school, 96–98
Patton, Bruce, 176–77
peer culture, 11, 50, 53, 54, 62
peers
  and conflict/confrontation, 62, 63, 73, 195–97
  and criticism, 78, 209
  and emotional intelligence, 134
  and feedback, 78
  and Good Girl behavior in Real World, 230–31

and hints, 167
nastiness of, 231
and steps of healthy conflict, 194–95
Perfect Mothers, characteristics of, 237–43
perfection
  and emotional intelligence, 26–27
  *See also* Good Girl: characteristics of
personality, 5, 9, 60
plan, and Perfect and Real Mothers, 243–44
pleasers, 2, 128, 134
power, 71, 72, 95, 114–15. *See also* control
practice, and steps to healthy conflict, 190–94
prior behavior, and confrontation, 62–63
professional women, 9, 103, 107–8, 205
"pushing," 152–53, 193–94, 230
put-downs, 101–2, 157, 245, 252

race, 11, 29
Real Girl, 10, 124, 127–30, 251
Real Mother, 237–47
Real World, Good Girl behavior in, 221–35
reality shows, influence of, 29
reflection, by mothers, 238–43
relationships
  affirmation of, 188, 191, 192, 194
  and characteristics of Real Girls, 10
  and communication rituals, 35–52
  conflict as end of, 91–92, 93–96, 115, 242
  and emotional intelligence, 15–16, 18, 19–27,
    28–34
  fear of losing, 93, 94, 98
  as getting back to normal, 186
  girls' attitudes about, 8
  and impact of Curse of the Good Girl, 6, 7
  importance of, 93
  and ranking of primary life needs, 51
  Three Rules of, 246–47
  *See also* conflict/confrontation; friendships;
    *specific topic*
reputation, 54–55, 62, 67, 108, 184, 186, 240
resilience, 196, 214–15, 230
respect
  and building emotional intelligence, 145
  and confrontation, 65
  and criticism, 209
  for emotions, 139
  and Good Girl behavior in Real World, 233
  and "just kidding" and "no offense," 176
  and NJZ, 175
  and rules of relationship, 246
  for teachers/educators, 86
  and truth, 175, 176

responsibility
  and apologies, 187
  avoidance of, 81, 173
  and confrontation, 54, 56, 65
  and denial, 217
  and feedback/criticism, 85, 217
  of friendship, 167–68
  for mistakes, 53
  ownership and personal, 85
  and owning up to conflict, 177
  and truth, 173, 177, 181, 187
résumés, inner, 10
right, what is, 247
risk
  avoidance of, 222
  benefits of, 225–27
  and characteristics of "Bad Girls," 4
  and characteristics of Good Girls, 2
  and confrontation, 56
  and criticism, 219
  and feedback, 76, 79
  girls' attitudes about, 8
  and glass ceiling, 97, 104
  and goals, 223–25
  and Good Girl behavior in Real World, 221, 222–27, 228, 233
  identification of, 223–25
  and impact of Curse of the Good Girl, 6
  and Perfect and Real Mothers, 240
  and winning and losing conflict, 196
role playing, 157–58, 194
"Rules of Engagement" (GLI), 169–71

saving face, 62–63, 186
school
  conflict in, 91–92
  and glass ceiling, 91–92, 93, 96–98, 108
  See also classroom; teachers
self
  acceptance of, 6, 173
  affirmation of, 18
  assessment of, 218–19
  assumptions about, 199
  blaming of, 21, 46, 48, 69, 77, 119, 120, 177, 216
  changing perspective about, 199
  and characteristics of Real Girls, 10
  and confrontation, 55, 56, 58, 60–61, 69, 72, 73
  criticism of, 83–84, 217, 252
  and culture, 1, 3

  and emotional intelligence, 27, 34
  failure as attack on, 219
  and feedback, 82, 83–84, 85, 89, 90
  freedom of, 56
  and glass ceiling, 104
  and impact of Curse of the Good Girl, 5–6
  inventory of, 240
  judgment of, 140
  and mother-daughter relationships, 122, 123–24
  obsessing over, 58
  and overreacting to conflict, 173
  of Perfect and Real Mothers, 238, 240
  punishment of, 33, 200–201
  splintering of, 104
  and standards for selfhood, 6
  and strategies for becoming a Real Girl, 127
  voice of, 249–53
  See also authenticity
self-awareness, 16, 85, 124, 131–32, 133, 152, 188, 196, 227
self-censorship, 93
self-concept, 10, 58, 60, 72, 84, 122, 226
self-consciousness, 37, 39, 240
self-defeating statements/gestures, 92, 99, 100, 227–31
self-destruction, 16, 40–41
self-discovery, 129
self-esteem, 10, 37, 46, 56, 69, 81, 87, 225, 229
self-expression, stifling of, 91–92
self-help books, 9
self-injury, 33, 34
self-knowledge, of parents, 216–17
self-reflection, 52, 129, 215–16
self-talk, negative, 228
self-worth, 172, 246–47
Seligman, Martin, 87
shame, 24–27, 56–59, 73, 82, 141, 148, 200, 217
"she/he hates me," 79–81, 202–5, 211
siblings, 115
Sjostrom, Lisa, 165
"Smart Voice," 212–14
socioeconomic status, 11, 29, 89
"sort of," 227–31
speaking, indirect, 98–104
specialness, 85–90
Stern, Robin, 135–36
Stone, Douglas, 176–77
strengths, 91, 92, 101–4, 229–30, 244, 247
stress, 5, 6, 21, 59, 61, 76